photo by Ed Swinden

Chris Searle was born in Romford, England, in 1944. He has been a teacher all his working life, in schools and universities in east London and Sheffield in the UK, in Canada, Tobago, Mozambique and Grenada, and at present at the University of Manchester.

He has written or edited some fifty books on subjects as diverse as education, poetry, language and cricket, among them *The Forsaken Lover* (which won the Martin Luther King Award in 1973), *Classrooms of Resistance, The World in a Classroom, We're Building the New School!, Words Unchained: Language and Revolution in Grenada* and *Pitch of Life*. His most recent collection of poetry is *Lightning of Your Eyes*. He writes a weekly jazz column for the social-ist daily newspaper, the *Morning Star*.

FORWARD GROOVE

Jazz and the real world from Louis Armstrong to Gilad Atzmon

Chris Searle

northway
publications

Published in 2008

Northway Publications
39 Tytherton Road, London N19 4PZ, UK.
www.northwaybooks.com

The publishers acknowledge with thanks the kind permission of copyright holders to reprint quotations used in this book. Permissions have been sought in all cases where the identity of copyright holders is known.

A CIP record for this book is available from the British Library.

ISBN 978 09550908 7 5

Printed and bound in Great Britain by Cromwell Press Ltd, Trowbridge, Wiltshire.

contents

acknowledgments

I would like to record my thanks to the following people, some no longer living, who have helped and educated me in a lifetime's love of jazz: Brian and Claude Spurin, Graham Colombé, Mel Robinson, Bruce Turner, Michael Garrick, Gilad Atzmon, John Kendall of Dobell's secondhand jazz record shop, Mark and Alan in Honest Jon's of Ladbroke Grove, John Stevens and Trevor Watts, Ronnie Scott and Peter Wallis. I also wish to thank Joe and Alan of Rare and Racy, that wonderful emporium in Sheffield, and Francisca Fuentes for her excellent wordprocessing. Finally, my thanks and deep respect go to Ann and Roger Cotterrell, for their publishing skills and huge commitment to the music they love.

introduction

A lifelong love of jazz goes back to early teenage years in suburban London, where its eastern sprawl meets Essex. I found two friends who loved the music from different ends of the jazz spectrum. Looking back, I suppose one was a revivalist. He played me his Kid Ory and George Lewis 78s, but the record he was most proud of, and which had a big effect on me then, was 'Pinetop's Blues', played by the boogie-woogie pianist, Pinetop Smith. It started everything for me, and I began to save up every penny to buy my first LPs of King Oliver and Jelly Roll Morton. I still have them today. Then my other friend, Bill, who pooh-poohed my first friend's more raw tastes (jazz lovers were often very priggish and not the least eclectic in those 1950s and early 1960s days), proudly played me his EPs of Charlie Parker, the postwar recordings of Lester Young and the thunderous hardbop drumming of Art Blakey. This was 'real' jazz, he said.

Then, when I was sixteen, another friend's father opened up a jazz club in the large side room of the Elm Park Hotel, on the fringes of Dagenham and Hornchurch. Since I was the tallest and heaviest of his friends (seventeen and a half stone was my one-time adolescent apex), he suggested I become doorman, bouncer, and cloakroom attendant all in one. I didn't earn any money, but free entrance to the St Louis Jazz Club every Friday and Sunday night was joy to be alive for me.

St Louis Nights . . . In Elm Park

This was 1960 and the heart of the 'trad fad'. Twice weekly I listened to Kenny Ball and his searing Ilford dixieland sound, or Dick Charlesworth and his City Gents, Cy Laurie's Jazz Band, Bob Wallis and his Storyville Jazzband, the bands of Mickey Ashman, Graham Stewart, Alan Elsdon and the thirties' veteran, Nat Gonella. But the band I really loved seemed to fly a flag of authenticity and have a special integrity every time it played at the St. Louis. And that was the Ken Colyer band. I have often asked myself when reviewing the host of his 'discovered' live sessions or reissued vinyl classics, now out on CD, why was his sound so different from the rest, and so unique? Most admirers said it was obvious – he had been there!

As a young jazzman seeking the roots of his beloved music, he had worked his maritime passage as a merchant seaman via Cape Town, Port Sudan, Zanzibar, Auckland, the Pitcairn Islands and Panama to the Crescent City, jumped ship and stayed with and played with the great veteran jazzmen. And this Norfolk man from Great Yarmouth was among the first white players to do this. The New Orleans jazzmen who invented and still played this unique and beautiful sound, we learned, were not allowed in the front entrance of the hotels in their home city, they had to use the service lifts and the waiters' lavatories and they still played to segregated audiences. Colyer had lived with them and recorded on a portable tape recorder in their front rooms, putting the microphone in the kitchen – according to the sleevenotes on the Vogue EP, *Ken Colyer in New Orleans*, which I snatched up for twelve shillings and sevenpence from the Co-op store in Romford, Essex, when I saw it – including very basic waxings of 'Gravier Street Blues', 'Frankie and Johnny', 'That's a Plenty' and 'Winter Wonderland'.

Colyer was without doubt my first living jazz hero. I heard just about his first 1960 session at the St Louis with the seventeen-year-old clarinettist Sammy Rimington – a few months older than me at the time – who had come into the band to replace Ian Wheeler, who had duetted marvellously with the New Orleans clarinet man George Lewis when he played with the Colyer band on his visits to England in 1957 and 1959. My identification with Rimington was total; I wanted him to succeed with all my teenage heart. Colyer was the most unmercenary of jazzmen, but there were also rumours of his radicalism – his forming of a marching band to play on the Aldermaston 'ban the bomb' marches. So whenever I heard him playing 'Maryland', I heard 'The Red Flag'. Later, when I knew more and he played 'Streets of the City', I heard the American Lincoln Brigade Spanish Civil War Song, 'There's a Valley in Spain Called Jarama . . . ' and when Colyer and Lewis played 'Red Wing' together on the 1959 *Live in Germany* album, I heard Joe Hill's lyrics behind the choruses:

> Will you still be slaves
> And work for wages?
> It is outrageous,
> Has been for ages
> For the world by right
> Belongs to toilers
> Not to the spoilers
> Of liberty!

Blue Monk in Stepney

These stories stayed with me, and although I loved the white Englishmen who played jazz, and wished I could be like them, it was always a black music to me. I loved Colyer because he loved and respected George Lewis and the New Orleans veterans – and this was so clear in the music that he played. He was borrowing the music of the Crescent City, acknowledging it, playing it in his band's own very English way, and then handing it back to its true owners. I liked that. I loved the altoist Bruce Turner, whom I got to know later when he played free for a *Jazz Against Racism* event which I organised, because he always remembered where the music that he played so brilliantly and with so much feeling came from – without humility, but with understanding and love, and a creative sound of emulation. For the *Jazz Against Racism* performance, Bruce brought a trio of the finest British jazz musicians with him: the golden pianist Michael Garrick who had led a brilliant quintet in the sixties with Jamaican altoist Joe Harriott and Vincentian trumpeter Shake Keane, the arch-bassist Dave Green and the dynamic drummer Alan Jackson. Bruce told me that there were two kinds of jazz musician. There were those who played the music out of love and respect for its inventors, the poor and mostly black people for whom it was their heartsong and the story of their lives, and those who saw it as little more than a series of sonic artefacts, disconnected from ordinary people and their struggles. Bruce made me think of Archie Shepp's words – that jazz was a black music lent to the world – but that the world had better respect it and the people who invented and continue to invent it. I loved to watch and listen to Lol Coxhill when I found him playing for his living on Waterloo Bridge, blowing his soprano sax with so much inventiveness and power, even there, with such transient listeners. When I emigrated to Canada in the mid-sixties, the first US city I was determined to visit was New Orleans, and as I sat listening to the miraculous clarinet of Louis Cottrell, the rumbling blues piano of Fatman Williams, the growling slides of Frog Henry, the dancing trumpet of Ernie Cagnolatti and Baby Dodds revisited in the hot drumming of Louis Barbarin, I understood whence jazz had come, and how far it had travelled to reach Elm Park, Essex, too.

Back in east London as a teacher in the early seventies, I met the astonishing drummer John Stevens and his friend, the ebullient altoist Trevor Watts. Invited by a progressive music teacher, they came to teach jazz workshops at school – a forbidding Anglican drill-hall where the wonderful children of east London were offered so little. John and Trevor – both leaders of the British free jazz movement, had them tapping and blowing 'Blue Monk': the children loved the music and, even more so, the musicians that made it happen. I was teaching poetry in a nearby classroom and heard the choruses directly. It was a beautiful, pristine sound that would have enthused Monk himself, at the time ailing in silence, homebound and secluded in his New York flat. But some teachers complained to the Head about the 'noise', that it was a disturbance, and that was that; they had to stop and they had to go. But these two formidable jazzmen opened up another world of jazz to me. I followed them to their Friday night sessions at the Plough pub in Stockwell, south London, where John had a regular weekly duo with Stan Tracey the nonpareil of British jazz pianists, and sometimes that became a trio with the South African bassist, Harry Miller. Their guests were British jazz legends like the Barbados-born trumpeter Harry Beckett or the wailing altoist, Mike Osborne. When Ornette Coleman's original trumpeter Bobby Bradford came to England, he stayed with John, who brought him to one of our poetry sessions at the Half Moon Theatre, a converted Victorian synagogue in Stepney, and I found myself shouting out my attempts at socialist poetry accompanied by the huge sound of John's drums, with Trevor and Bobby, plus my two friends Mel and Graham on, alternatively, piano, trombone, clarinet and tenor, and me on military bass drum. Free jazz indeed!

And if I had harboured any doubts about the power of jazz as a political music, potent and real, they would have been dispelled for me that night in the old synagogue, now demolished, in Alie Street. I belted out a version of 'St. James Infirmary', re-named 'St. Katherine's Dockyard' after the property speculation in progress at the nearby St. Katherine's Docks, where the Victorian grandeur was being transformed into the World Trade Centre and the multi-million Tower Hotel for the visiting rich, while local East Enders were being evicted and shunted away in the rush for property profits. The construction multi-national Taylor Woodrow had the lucrative building contract, and were already transforming the east London landscape. So,

> I went down to St. Katherine's Dockyard
> Saw Taylor Woodrow there
> All dressed in his corporate dollars,
> So rich, so cold, so bare.

Behind me, Bobby and Trevor wailed blues passages and John's drums pounded jazz indignation. Then we did 'David Oluwale', dedicated to the life and death of the homeless Nigerian who was repeatedly assaulted by two Leeds policemen and died as he tried to find shelter along the city's riverside in April 1969:

> All along the River Aire
> They chased you in their hate,
> They screamed out 'UGGIE, UGGIE!'
> With the power of the state.
> They threw you into doorways,
> They kicked you in the balls,
> They smashed your head till you were dazed,
> From your mouth blood drools.
> They hounded you for twenty years,
> They saw that you were black,
> When you were lame they gave you tears
> They kept you on the rack.
> > David Oluwale
> > Your blackness soon will rise,
> > David Oluwale
> > Your drums will pound the skies.

And John's drums made a storm of jazz thunder, with Bobby and Trevor weaving inside each other's searing notes beside him. I had never been so close and involved with such musical power and artistry before, and any genesis that this book has, was born and stirred in those moments. And John told me about his heroes – the South African jazzmen he had befriended and with whom he played – Louis Moholo, Dudu Pukwana, Johnny Dyani and his own British drums idol, Phil Seamen. His identification with working class people was total – he and Trevor had both learned their instruments in the ranks of the RAF and were turning bugles into peace horns. They lived with the music as if it were, as it was, the sheer breath of life.

So why tell all this? Simply, it is why this book was written. For me, jazz has always told stories of the real world, the world of ordinary people – and the world of excellence in the heart and brain of the ordinary. I am not a musician in any sense. I cannot understand music technically or schematically: I have had neither training nor education in music. Yet I feel that I understand the narrative and the million stories that jazz tells. I have always loved the music from 'Pinetop Blues' onwards, and I love it even more now, in my sixties, than I did as a teenager, when I first heard the glory of the Duke Ellington Orchestra playing the Shakespeare Suite – *Such Sweet Thunder* – at the Leeds Grand Theatre in 1963, in my first year of university. Without really understanding the grounds of their greatness, I sat, my ears mesmerised by Johnny Hodges, Cootie Williams, Paul Gonsalves, Lawrence Brown, Harry Carney, 'Cat' Anderson, Jimmy Hamilton and the Duke himself. I couldn't believe what I was hearing. I was a student of English Literature and I was hearing the great poet and playwright, the very one that I was studying and anatomising in my classes – alive in jazz, his stories streaming out in solo and ensemble and living in the real world of the Yorkshire streets outside. When I heard Gonsalves and Hodges play their saxophone parts as Romeo and Juliet in 'The Star-Crossed Lovers', I was transported for life, kidnapped by jazz.

In my fifties, I set aside my complexes and ignorance about music, and started to write a weekly jazz column for Britain's only socialist daily newspaper, for which I was a regular contributor, the *Morning Star*. I covered concerts, recordings, books on the music and regular appearances at club venues like Ronnie Scott's, the Jazz Café and Pizza Express and, as I heard, listened and read more and more, it became clear to me that jazz and life, no matter how much some critics had tried, could never be separated: that listening to jazz and reading history are one, and that hearing the present is sometimes as much about hearing the future as recapturing the past. Having taught in southern Africa (in revolutionary Mozambique in the mid-seventies), it soon became clear to me that the role of jazz in the US struggle for Civil Rights of the earlier decade was being mirrored in the musical activity within the anti-Apartheid struggle in South Africa. Jazz had many political stories to tell, and the more I listened, the more I heard them.

Texts of the Real World

In this account I study jazz recordings more or less as I would study poems, short stories or other 'texts' in literature – as emotive, accomplished and beautiful statements of raw meaning linked to their times, their history and their connection to the real world and its events. When I argue that they are 'epochal', this is what I mean. I read them, as I would a poem or a story. When they are connected, as parts of a suite, a thematic album or to longer pieces, I read them as I might read a novel. These 'texts' that I have selected are not necessarily the 'best' of jazz – that has not been my purpose, but they are all keys to understanding eras, or critical social and political events. Within these pages I frequently refer to 'the power of titles' as being of significance for jazz musicians and their listeners. Why, for example, did Duke Ellington call his 1929 piece 'Wall Street Wail' when he could have called it many other things? But he wanted to draw attention to the New York stock market crisis. He foresaw the effect it would have on the ordinary people (not only the privileged and white paying customers of the Cotton Club) of Harlem and in other parts of America who bought his records. Why did Dizzy Gillespie call his wonderfully joyous and mercurial trumpet piece of 1976 'Frelimo'? He wanted the power of its title to resonate around the world of jazz that there was a new nation in Africa called Mozambique, which had been struggled for and created over a backward European colonialism by its liberation movement, the Frente de Libertacâo de Moçambique (FRELIMO). Why did the tenorist Ike Quebec call his 1962 piece 'Congo Lament', so closely after the death of the Congo's first Prime Minister, Patrice Lumumba, murdered with the full cognizance of Belgian and US imperial interests? It goes on. Often jazz musicians think of a title, then write the music: more often the music comes first and the title frequently becomes emblematic. And there are many ambiguities and misreadings around titles – something I may sometimes have been guilty of in this book.

Eighteen months after the Civil Rights activist Rosa Parks refused to give up her seat to a white man on a bus in Montgomery, Alabama, on 15 December 1955, thus sparking the city's bus boycott and the first mass action of the Civil Rights Movement, the trumpeter Clark Terry titled and recorded a tune on an album for Prestige: 'Ode to a Bus Seat'. It is a marvellous romping piece, featuring one of Miles Davis' great rhythm sections of pianist Wynton Kelly, bassist Paul Chambers and the explosive Philly Joe Jones on drums, supporting the incredibly fast tenor saxophone of Johnny Griffin and Terry's unstoppable flickering trumpet. Jamaican Kelly contributes a rocking solo before the theme reprises and Philly Joe's drums and a last horn break come crashing to a finale.

Many (most of them white, for such was the hue of most jazz critics of the time) jazz commentators refused to see the connection between Terry's band's excitation of sound and Rosa's conscious defiance, and quoted the brassman emphatically denying that the title was anything to do with Rosa Parks, saying that it referred to long overnight and daytime bus journeys from gig to gig that was the lot of professional jazz musicians of the day. Yet does coincidence run so thematically, so powerfully? Even if the two events were not formally linked, the confidence and new sense of burgeoning freedom that span off the Civil Rights endeavours and successes being achieved in the South, the ex-home of the families of most of the Northern cities' black population, could be heard clearly and powerfully in the notes that the leader Terry (from St Louis), Griffin (from Chicago), Chambers (from Pittsburgh) and Jones (from Philadelphia) played.

By 1963 the Civil Rights struggle was at its apex. Key activist Medgar Evers was murdered in Jackson, Mississippi; the campaigning was relentless in Birmingham, Alabama, and thousands marched to Washington from many points in the USA. 'Freedom Blues', from Terry's album *Tread Ye Lightly*, was dedicated to all those in the heat of this struggle, its unambiguous and open support of all those 'fighting for freedom and equality' made clear and open in the album's sleevenotes. A stop-time march punctuated by Buddy Lucas' harmonica and a succession of fervent solo choruses by Terry, tenorist Seldon Powell and pianist Ray Bryant, 'Freedom Blues' showed that jazz and the real world were manifesting their oneness.

Even further back, in 1940, a few months before Duke Ellington was to deliver his open, uncoded statement and affirmation of black freedom in *Jump for Joy*, he recorded an intriguingly ambivalent song called 'At a Dixie Roadside Diner', with the lyrics – the work of songwriters Leslie and Burke – sung engagingly by Ivie Anderson. I have often wondered about this recording and the Duke's intentions. Such diners 'in the heart of Caroline' and other Southern states were dangerous places for black people and, of course, often notorious centres of uncompromising racism. Many black musicians have told and written how they were forbidden to eat with their white bandmates, and how for their safety's sake they would stay put in their car or coach while white musicians ate their full and then returned carrying a meal for them. And yet this song is a story sung by a black woman about a white man 'whose blue eyes blazed in mine / Like a big electric sign', how they were 'stealing kisses in the dark' of the diners' car park and conducting an explicit inter-racial love affair, dancing rumbas to the music played on a 'slot machine'. All this in the strictly segregated, Jim Crow South.

Ellington begins the track with an introductory piano chorus, including some satirical-sounding quotations from 'Swanee River'. Trumpeter Cootie Williams takes over, playing the melody straight, Barney Bigard's clarinet enters with a spoof Latin-tinged interval, Anderson sings, followed by a stomping Harry Carney baritone solo with some brass riffing behind him. With his extraordinary cultural sophistication, many levels of meaning and mindfulness, and exercising one of the great musical imaginations of the twentieth century, what was Ellington expressing in this performance? For me, behind the trite words and musical ironies is a portrait of a racist society expressed with double-edged artistry and a consciousness attuned and coded to the real world of his listeners' daily experiences and understanding.

Maenya and Mingus

We need to remember that racial pride and protest against racism were not always easy options for jazz musicians, whose livelihoods were extremely risky and capricious, who mostly lived in the lower reaches of the societies where they made their music, and who suffered racism and racial exclusion on a daily basis, even within the professional circles of this music which was truly their invention. Read the life of the astonishing trumpeter Roy Eldridge, for example, who was regularly excluded from the hotels of his white bandmates while on nationwide tours in 1944–45 with the Artie Shaw orchestra – even when his name, as the star soloist, shone in lights over the theatres where they played. Or read too of the privations suffered by the greatest of Caribbean horns, the altoist Joe Harriott of Kingston, Jamaica, as he sought effective treatment in the 'Mother Country' for the cancer that killed him in 1973.

So it is not surprising that mixed into the titles that jazz musicians chose for their music there are double-entendres, codings, hidden implications, puns and neologisms. And one in particular that tells a story is a tune called 'Maenya', written by the Jamaican trumpeter Dizzy Reece and recorded by the Victor Feldman Big Band in September 1955, reissued on the Feldman Jasmine album, *Departure Dates*. Of course, the arrival of the converted troop-carrier, the *Empire Windrush* at Tilbury Docks on June 21 1948, full of hopeful migrants from the 'British' West Indies, marked the onset of a mass movement of black peoples, south to north, in every way as dramatic as that from the southern states of the USA to its northern cities in the first half of the twentieth century. As a part of this mass exodus of peoples, some brilliant jazz musicians were to leave the Caribbean. From Reece to Wilton 'Bogey' Gaynair, from Joe Harriott to Shake Keane and Harry Beckett, they arrived with their horns of gold. Others had come before them in the thirties, creating a vibrant tradition of black British swing – Ken 'Snakehips' Johnson, Leslie 'Jiver' Hutchinson, Bertie King, Dave Wilkins and Cyril Blake. But the arrivant *Windrush* generation of black Caribbean jazzmen became the virtuosi of the new British bop and post-bop scene and were among its prime movers, in every way as creatively potent in the smoky post-war jazz venues of London, as the musicians of New Orleans and the South had been in the speakeasies and clubs of Chicago in the twenties.

Reece's 'Maenya' has an Africanist theme, not unusual from a prolific African-Caribbean jazzman. But when you study the name and its time, it seems to be bearing a more specific story. 1955 was the height of the 'emergency' in Kenya. In England it was everywhere: in the newspapers, on the radio and on the emergent television. The Kenyan resistance movement, the Kenyan African Union, had recruited thousands of militants, both in the slum areas of Nairobi and among the Kikuyu people of the rural areas. At the height of the resistance, the number of freedom forces in the forests around Mount Kenya was estimated at thirty thousand. Many rumours were set down in the British press about the horrors of the so-called 'Mau-Mau', but those who took part in the national resistance never called themselves that name.

In 1953 Dedan Kimathi, the resistance leader, wrote a letter from his headquarters in the Aberdare mountains to the Nairobi newspaper *Habari za Dunia* declaring that only the poor were the Mau-Mau. He also said: 'I do not lead rebels but I lead Africans who want their self-government and land. I lead them because God never created any nation to be ruled by another nation forever.' So what about 'Maenya' in this 1955 context? Reece's title is certainly more than a clue, and his powerful melody with the vibrant conga rhythms, Seamen's thunderous drumming and the succession of high-tempo solos from Feldman's vibes and some of the finest British horns of the era – tenorists Ronnie Scott and Tubby Hayes, altoist Derek Humble, trumpeters Reece and Jimmy Deuchar, combine with the vibrant ensemble sound and Reece's final coda to create as fine and as throbbing a masterpiece of British big band jazz as you will find. But was it about the anti-imperialist resistance in Kenya? Who knows, but I think it was.

And finally, what about Charles Mingus' recording of 'Haitian Fight Song' from his album of 1957, *The Clown*? The year was a key year for the Civil Rights movement – the success of the Montgomery Bus Boycott had led on to the birth of the Southern Christian Leadership Conference and the devising of a full programme for black emancipation in the Southern states. In the sleevenotes to *The Clown*, Mingus states:

> 'Haitian Fight Song', to begin with, could just as well be called 'Afro-American Fight Song' . . . I can't play it right unless I'm thinking about prejudice and hate and persecution and how unfair it is. There's sadness and cries in it, but also determination. And it usually ends with my feeling: 'I told them! I hope somebody heard me.'

There's no mention of Toussaint L'Ouverture and the 1791 Haitian Revolution, when, inspired by the ideals of the French Revolution in 1789 and resisting their hideous oppression, the slaves of San Domingo rose in the most successful and inspired revolt against French colonialism, the Spanish and the British invaders to create the first black republic outside of Africa. The Haitian victory signalled the end, three years later, of the British and American slave trades.

What inspiration for the burgeoning Civil Rights movement was 'Haitian Fight Song'! But had Mingus studied the Haitian Revolution, how much did he know? Had he read the story of Toussaint in C. L. R. James' *The Black Jacobins*? These are questions we can't ask of him; we can only listen to his astonishing bass solo at the start of the performance, hearing him thudding and pounding out the truth of history, then hear Jimmy Knepper's growling trombone choruses, Wade Legge's musing piano and Shafi Hadi's serpentine alto solo as the pace suddenly quickens and he begins to spit out his notes. Mingus comes back with his huge sound, his musical generalship like a

Toussaint of jazz as he plucks out the theme again against Dannie Richmond's tambourines and, as the ensemble riffs build up again beyond a crescendo they gradually slow down, until silence comes almost as a relief.

Jazz and Syncretism

What has been the basis of selection of the jazz 'texts' described in this account, for the eighty years of the recorded history of the music shows thousands of brilliant jazz performances that could have been chosen. So why have I picked out those particular waxed jazz moments that follow? Mainly because they sometimes very obviously, and other times less obviously, allude to a real and specific situation in social or political history that shows how the music can never be divided from its circumstances, and the real world which produced it. And the musicians involved achieve this with an undoubted musical artistry and imagination, as well as a consciousness of the events around them, which they may have expressed not only in their notes, but also their lyrics, through their titles, or in the commentaries that they may have spoken or written about their music.

Finally, I try to give special importance to a unique feature of jazz: its sense of syncretism – begun in New Orleans when so many apparently different musical discourses fused: African, French, Spanish, Caribbean, Christian, indigenous, maritime, riverine – to create a music so hybrid as to defy precedent. Thus arrived jazz as the reconciliation of scattered cultures and diasporan sounds and instruments, the unity of sound and lyric, new demographies and new musical amalgams, fresh realisations of dynamic new alliances – cultural, musical and political, new metaphors of sound forged with old instruments. The world was made again in music with the sound of the unexpected, with the embrace of the diverse – all have been essential to the syncretic power of jazz throughout its history in many places in and out of the Americas. Here's an example among thousands, now spinning on my turntable. It is November 26 1972, three weeks before what became known as the Christmas bombing of Vietnam, when US B52 and F111 bombers flew some 1700 sorties. By 29 December one hundred thousand bombs had been dropped, causing 1318 deaths in Hanoi alone, many of them children. In a New York studio a group of jazz musicians led by an Armenian-American drummer, Paul Motian, a white American bassist, Charlie Haden, a woman flautist Becky Friend and an African-American violinist, Leroy Jenkins, record 'Inspiration from a Vietnamese Lullaby', their music moved and energised by the suffering and struggle of faraway children and the mothers being slaughtered by American airmen. It became part of an album, *Conception Vessel*, issued by ECM, a Munich-based label. This I have learned through fifty years of listening: syncretism and the struggle for peace are two of the essences of jazz.

Nowhere more so than in the musical life of the Israeli alto and soprano saxophonist Gilad Atzmon. 'I was brought up to be an oppressor,' he declares in the sleevenotes of his 2001 album *Nostalgico*. 'A role which didn't suit me and which I couldn't accept.' Atzmon was born in Israel, and grew up in Jerusalem, surrounded by Arab musical influences. 'The Palestinians are completely right – it is their land. The Jews in Israel have abused their kindness for fifty years,' he told me. 'They ask for forgiveness from God, when really they should be asking for forgiveness from the Palestinians.' In 1994 he arrived in England to study philosophy at the University of Essex.

By 1998 jazz was Atzmon's livelihood, and rock and roll too as a member of Ian Dury's Blockheads and, like another brilliant exile, the South African Abdullah Ibrahim, he began recording for the German label ENJA, playing jazz of an astonishing hybridity in his first album for them, *The Orient House*

Ensemble. On it there is an Algerian-style version of Wayne Shorter's 'Footprints', a witty waxing of Ellington's 'In a Sentimental Mood', redrawn as a dedication to the 'cows of Britain' and re-titled 'In a Semi-Mental Moo-ed'. His quartet, the Orient House Ensemble, remembers the building (later seized and occupied by the Israeli army), which was designated as the official home of the Palestinian Authority in Jerusalem, and is composed of two Israelis: himself and drummer Asaf Sirkis, who plays the bandit – an Arab side drum – as well as a conventional kit, and two young Englishmen (pianist Frank Harrison and bassist Oli Hayhurst). On this first ENJA album, the most moving and passionate performance is that of Atzmon's own 'Balladi'. The name is Arabic for soil, and its composer says: 'I wrote it in empathy with the Palestinian people in my determined wish that they will regain their land – the land which belongs to their children.' Listening to Atzmon's choruses of righteous anger and love, I remembered lines from the poetry of the Palestinian laureate Mahmoud Darwish in his poem 'Homeland':

> This land is the skin on my bones
> And my heart
> Flies above its grasses like a bee.

This is the extent of the long journey of jazz, from New Orleans to Palestine, and then forced into exile – into a world, as Atzmon says of *Nostalgico*: 'of unfulfilled dreams and fragmented melodies'. Within this album Ellington's melodies grow again, this time along the margins of Asia Minor, as Atzmon's rendition of 'I've Got It Bad and That Ain't Good' (originally a part of Ellington's 1941 musical, *Jump for Joy*, and a tune which became associated with defiant anti-racist resistance, as will be shown in Chapter 2) recalls Duke to the shores of Palestine, and to Israel itself, called by Atzmon in his sleevenotes, that 'small, colonial, nationalistic province in the eastern corner of the Mediterranean Sea'. There is also an echoing reinvention of Sidney Bechet's 'Petite Fleur'.

Then, in 2005, Atzmon dedicates his album *Musik/Re-arranging the 20^(th) Century* with this pregnant sentence: 'Sooner rather than later musik will free itself and so will the Palestinian people.' *Musik*: even the word is a hybrid; emblematic of Atzmon's art, and his wit, beauty, virtuosity. He weaves poetry into the album, the words of a veteran jazz-rocker, Robert Wyatt, and a true fusion of music and language from a host of different peoples and tongues – astonishing and revolutionary musical alliances of the Arab and the Jew, the Greek and the German, the Italian and the English, to name but a few. And such hybridity is to set aside and replace the betrayals of the last century. 'A market value was attached to every bar,' he avers. 'Music became furniture, a matter of style, a mass global product, an extension of Levi jeans or a secondary product to Coca-Cola.' Not so Atzmon's music. He calls his bandmates 'the soldiers of liberated beauty' – perhaps Ellington might have called the loyal members of his orchestra the same, and 'musik is music when it is stripped of its market value.' The simple, naked melody of his track 'Music' exemplifies this unmercenary sound, but it is in the performance of the wartime popular song, 'Lili Marleen', that folklore becomes jazz and hope becomes music. As Atzmon's horn howls out the barely discernible melody, at first unaccompanied and then no longer alone, the agony and struggle of a generation at war in the dawn in a new century becomes everyone's life and everyone's beauty.

The future of jazz is embedded within its internationalism. Its migratory powers, personified by Atzmon and many others have taken its blue and joyous notes across the world, and they have frequently – as the jazz 'texts' of this book will show, been welded to a message of peace, justice and political freedom. In the sleevenotes of Atzmon's finest and most audacious album called simply *Exile* (2003), he writes:

> in the album we try to tell the story of Palestine, a beautiful and historically ecumenical land that was suddenly stormed by radical Zionist zealots. It is an image of harmony shattered by bloodshed and destruction . . . This album is a call for attention to Palestinian suffering. It is a prayer for the world to acknowledge the Palestinian essential right of return.

A true cause of jazz, and one that is at the heart of every note that Atzmon and his musical friends create – is their birthplace, the land of Palestine. For *Exile* is a passionately realised and beautifully crafted work of art and aspiration. It begins with Reem Kelani's shattering vocal of Monzer El Dajani's lyrics, proclaiming that those who ascend into Heaven have 'their rock' on Palestinian earth. She sings above bowed bass, accordion and a fusion of eastern Mediterranean sounds:

> No matter how long it takes me
> My children and I
> And my children's children,
> We're going back to our homeland.

And taking the same road is Atzmon's mysterious soprano reed and Sirkis' dancing drums in 'Al-Quds', with Kelani singing the Arabic words of Darwish:

> My night has been long
> Stretched over garden walls,
> But I have not lost the way.

Atzmon's white hot irony is explicit in his composition 'Jenin', a story of Zionist hatred and murder, its tune inspired by a Jewish ballad telling the tale of a city destroyed in a pogrom: 'The decision to make use of Jewish and Israeli tunes was very deliberate,' writes Atzmon. 'Jewish history is an end-less story of persecution, agony and anguish,' mirroring that of Palestinian neighbours. In 'Jenin', Atzmon's saxophone voice is full of mourning and Yaron Stavi's bass booms like a forest of consciousness. 'Ouz' seems like a dance of joy, until you realise it is a dance of Israeli occupation and expulsion. Then the elation takes on a sudden brutal edge, as Harrison's piano chorus seems to tell two stories – and the power of Atzmon's saxophone makes you think that perhaps a whole martial reed section is playing.

Exile is a signal album, and one which I believe truly looks into the ear of jazz. Its musicians are inventing new syncretic cultures actually as they carve out their sounds, mocking the separatist chauvinisms that beset their part of the world. It is a shout of jazz unity, of an integral music that creates a way of hearing, seeing and living in the world, that is truly worthy of that 'ecumenical' land for which they hope and strive.

Refuge

'If you read the titles of the tracks of my new album, *Refuge*, one after the other, they make a poem', Atzmon told me in October 2007 as we walked up Ecclesall Road in Sheffield before a gig. So I did, and here they are:

> Autumn in Baghdad
> Spring in New York
> In The Small Hours
> The Burning Bush
> Her Smile
> Her Tears
> My Refuge
> Just Another Prayer for Peace

'That is what the record is about. I don't care if we talk about divisions or categories of musical styles, whether it's

Jazz, World Music, Soul or whatever. If there's anything we can produce as artists, it's beauty. And since our elected politicians are producing nothing else but ugliness, in particular for the people of Palestine and Iraq, we artists must produce beauty.'

'Sometimes I think that *Refuge* is a story, a humanist story of a journey from Iran to Venezuela. I travel all over the world. In Europe, all across the EU, I see and feel alienated countries and their peoples who have lost contact with themselves, cold and with so much that is inhumane. But when I go to places like Istanbul or Argentina for example, I can feel the humanity much more.'

'I was born in Israel. Now, three of the members of the Orient House Ensemble are from Israel. So I know deep inside me that the Hebraic identity is the most radical version of the idea of Jewish supremacy which is a curse for Palestine, a curse for Jews and a curse for the world. It is a major destructive force. That is the beast still inside me, the beast that every day I try to turn into beauty through my music. For an Israeli to humanise himself, he must de-Zionise himself. In this way, self-hating can become a very productive power. It's the same sense of self-hating that I find too in Jews who have given the most to humanity, like Christ, Spinoza or Marx. They bravely confronted their beasts, and in doing so they made sense to many millions.'

These words were some sharp preface to a performance in a South Yorkshire jazz club, with most of the tunes coming from *Refuge*. Before I heard them again live, I read what Atzmon had written in his sleevenotes. He remembers that when he founded the Orient House Ensemble in 2000, he believed that music could be a 'message of peace', but now, 'eight years later, I must admit that I may have got it wrong. This is our fifth album. We have performed hundreds of concerts around the world and somehow peace is nowhere near. Every day a new conflict comes to life. Once a week a newly-born fear is shaped into a sinister agenda wrapped in an image of Western goodness. As far as my homeland is concerned, peace has never looked so far away.'

Atzmon now says that music is not the messenger, it has become the message as well as a refuge. And it has given him new hope. He told me a story close to his life: 'The morning after I played at the concert for Medical Aid for Palestine, I went to an assembly at my son's school in north London. The school is lucky because it has a wonderful music teacher, a man who loves jazz and the children love him. He's a fine musician too and he gets the children playing beautiful things. This morning he had 700 of them singing along with Louis Armstrong on 'What a Wonderful World'. And as the record ended, they were all singing, and they just carried on, without Louis. Well, my son is very young and so are his schoolmates. They didn't know about Bush and Blair, and it made me think, perhaps it is a wonderful world like Louis sang, if we can only defeat and go beyond the politicians' sinister agenda. I felt this optimism, listening to Louis and all those children. I felt the future, it affected me a huge amount – and now I play 'What a Wonderful World' to end all my performances.'

As soon as you listen to the album's opener, 'Autumn in Baghdad', you can hear how Atzmon's saxophone voice has changed during a decade. His sound is much fuller, much more sodden with experience, much more enfolding, and as he plays you can almost hear his words, so vocalistic is his timbre. Sometimes I thought that I was hearing the horns of Rahsaan Roland Kirk, or Yusef Lateef, or in particular the late Native American, Jim Pepper. The tune has an Ellingtonian beauty and simplicity, a pure melody beginning from a sound close to exhausted quiescence with pianist Frank Harrison's lone piano preceding a crying Atzmon alto, the sound searching, questing, wandering, sorrowing, growing towards a crescendo of empathy. 'When I first came to London,' Atzmon told me, 'I met some Iraqis. They had wonderful things to say about Baghdad.

Look at the wreckage now. What have we done? We elected the leaders who did this.'

That 'Spring in New York' should be juxtaposed to the late year in Iraq's mauled capital is a sonic irony in itself. Yet the repeated soprano riff, the electronica, the discord and assumed assurance all betray a sound of the insecure, the attitudinised and the vulnerable, the persona of power stuffed with emptiness. It is only in 'In the Small Hours' that there is time and space enough to reflect and contemplate, with the troubled sounds of Atzmon's alto and Harrison's tapped-out Fender-Rhodes chorus before Asaf Sirkis' grilling drums, that the enormity and price of the sorrow can be reckoned.

I asked Atzmon whether 'The Burning Bush' was a reflection of the US President. 'It is,' he said. 'He represents a major destructive force in the world, with few brothers or sisters like him in history. And beyond all the destruction and lost lives, Bush and Blair have committed it all on our behalf. They are our elected leaders. They have turned us too into criminals.' And the wailing, tormented notes spear towards Palestinian and Iraqi skies with distant, chanting voices and a gradual acceleration of sounds, as the victims of imperial violence deal with their compounding pain and rage in a world which, in Atzmon's words, 'is becoming more and more hostile'. As the track ends, Sirkis' drums are like mountain peaks, spectators to human agonies which grow and crescendo, then fade into pained continuity.

After such cataclysmic sounds, 'Her Smile', starting as an Atzmon/Harrison duet, radiates a sudden harmony, with the soprano horn picking out paths of ecumenical beauty over Yaron Stavi's bowed bass. 'Her Tears' must follow, as they do, with Stavi's bow still brushing his deep strings with lamentation. As Atzmon writes: 'Submerged in tears, one comes to realise oneself, a music prevails,' and 'Her Tears' are transformed into a Levantine blues, a deep song of real life, pain and enduring survival. While at the centre of 'My

Refuge' is a horn cadence, a falling on an immense scale, before the music ascends to a joyous, almost Latin American carnavallic conviction with the infusion of Paul Jayasinya's singing trumpet.

'Just Another Prayer for Peace' is the album's final track, prompted by Sirkis' subliminally ironic martial drums, provoking thoughts of US soldiers in Baghdad, British marines in Basra and Israeli troops and armed settlers across the West Bank, as Atzmon's horn sings as a voice of human resistance steeped in invasion and the pain of foreign trespass. The naked lucidity of his sound and that of Harrison's picked-out, crystalline notes become a unified human song to other humans to promote the blessings of peace and freedom for lands that are occupied, shattered and starved – in Palestine, in Iraq, anywhere and anytime.

I asked Atzmon about his hopes for a liberated Palestine, and how the ecumenical vision of his own music, taking from Hebraic, Arabic and Turkish traditions within a jazz framework, could find its true home there. And what would be the first tune he would play in a free Jerusalem?

'There will be a free Palestine,' he said assuredly. Then he laughed. 'It's going to happen for sure, and my ambition is to become the first Palestinian Minister of Jazz. Palestine will be liberated and the Israeli empire, the Bush empire, the Neo-Con. Empire will all have to clear the stage. And I will play the tune 'Al-Quds' in the new Jerusalem. It's a Hebrew song, but we have Palestinised it! For it is not only about liberating Palestinians, it is about liberating Israelis from themselves. It is about liberating the world!'

1

working man and strugglin' woman blues

When the people came from south to north, the music came with them. When they arrived and settled and found jobs and places to live in the northern cities like Chicago and New York, they called for their musicians to join them. The movement of millions of people provoked thousands of musicians to follow in their wake, to reflect and affirm the new life that they were building and to remind them of what had been left behind; to be their entertainers and commentators, their artists and their critics, the expression of their daily experience and its problems and hopes; the voice of their protests and their dreams; the sound of their era, the melodies of their moments; their chroniclers and historians, their storytellers and their poets.

Jazz was born in the Mississippi Delta and its crucible was in its Crescent City, a port at the end of the great Mississippi facing the Gulf of Mexico. In New Orleans, African-American and Creole workers found the instruments, tunes, hymns and marches of Europe and the Caribbean and used them in their funerals, their church services, their strip clubs, brothels, vaudeville shows and cabarets, and made their own huge musical adaptations. They found sounds in these instruments unknown in Europe, and made rhythms and harmonies with them that were utterly original, taken from their provenances in a city of cosmos which syncretised many musics into one. The New Orleans-born drummer of the Lincoln Center Jazz Orchestra, Herlin Riley, who learned his drumming from his grandfather, a member of the same orphanage band as Louis Armstrong in 1913, explains in the sleevenotes of his album *Watch What You're Doing*:

> During the time when jazz was being developed, New Orleans was a melting pot of French, African, Spanish and Italian culture; Congo Square was the only place in America where Africans could play their drums during slavery. From that experience came a connection to the drums that's different from anywhere else in the country. The dialogue between the bass drum and the snare drum which is mostly prevalent in brass bands is an undercurrent that permeates all New Orleans drummers – the bass drum may have a question, and the snare drum will answer it.

But there was little comfort or security for these musicians, as they struggled to find livelihoods, housing and family stability in New Orleans. The story of the early years of the city's greatest musical genius, Louis Armstrong, is fraught with hardship in many severe forms. On New Year's day 1913, the boy Louis, twelve years old and convicted of discharging a revolver at the intersection of Rampart and Perdido Streets, was sent to the Colored Waif's Home. Louis, from a district notorious for its 'honky-tonks, toughs and fancy women', came under the tutelage of the stern director of the home's music program, 'Professor' Peter Davis – who once gave Louis 'fifteen hard lashes on the hand'. Louis had worked at playing the cornet before his entry in the home – even becoming a student of the famous brassman Bunk Johnson – and accepted the band's discipline so that he was soon marching with them, even around his own neighbourhood in the Perdido/Liberty streets area.

In 1914 Louis left the home and found a job working long hours at Henry Ponce's saloon, playing his cornet for local whores, pimps and their clients. Despite the tips he made, his income was cruelly insufficient, and he found an additional job working for the C. A. Andrews Coal Company, hauling coal from seven in the morning until 5 p.m. A short rest and then he was back playing until three or four in the morning. Jazz was born from the hardest of lives; the most exhaustive toil. He had to shovel a ton of coal into his wagon, and deliver it at fifteen cents a load.

Coal Cart Blues

The words of his 'Coal Cart Blues' express the physical labour and mental alienation from such work in equal measure. Armstrong first recorded the tune in 1925 with pianist/composer Clarence Williams' Blue Five, sharing the front line with clarinettist and soprano saxophonist Sidney Bechet, who had sprung to fame in 1919 as a member of Will Marion Cook's touring orchestra in Europe, where he was feted by the French classical conductor Ernest Ansermet. Ansermet wrote of him, 'his own way is perhaps the highway the whole world will swing along tomorrow.' These sides with Clarence Williams and Armstrong, recorded in New York, were among Bechet's first recordings. Williams was a New Orleans man who was as much a vaudeville player as he was a musician. His Blue Five version of 'Coal Cart Blues' is taken at a sprightly pace with Charlie Irvis opening the theme. Irvis was Duke Ellington's first trombonist, whom the Duke described as having 'a great big fat sound at the bottom of the trombone – melodic, masculine, full of tremendous authority'. Known as a strong blues player, he begins with a powerful assurance, followed by two choruses of Armstrong's ringing ensemble lead. Vocalist Eva Taylor sounds routine and unconvincing, but Bechet's ensuing solo is wondrous – soaring with sound muscles as Irvis plays below him. The performance ends in a crisp New Orleans manner, with the combined hornmen taking it out in parade-style joy.

By the time that the two New Orleans hornmen recorded the tune again in 1940, they were perhaps the two most famous and legendary figures in jazz. They were also its first two great soloists, and were jointly responsible for changing jazz from an ensemble-propelled music to one where individuals began to achieve astonishing sounds through solo endeavour. Bechet had been an endless traveller, as far as Russia but having a particular love for France, although he endured a period of time in prison there, eventually being deported. Despite his fame and virtuosity, the thirties had shown him some rough times (he had even resorted to tailoring to supplement his meagre income as a jazz musician), but in 1938 his luck changed with a hit record of 'Summertime', the sponsorship of French jazz critic Hugues Panassié and a recording contract with Bluebird. Louis' rise was much more stellar. Following his 1923 migration to Chicago to play in King Oliver's Creole Jazz Band, he moved to New York to join Fletcher Henderson's orchestra, recorded with Clarence Williams, accompanied some of the great female blues singers and then returned to Chicago in 1925 to head the Hot Five and Hot Seven sessions which established him as the first virtuoso jazz soloist. Through the thirties he fronted a series of his own orchestras that were playing largely as a background to the leader's astonishing solos and his gravelly and frequently humorous singing. He also took small and often stereotyped roles in movies.

Thus by the time of the second recording of 'Coal Cart Blues' in May 1940, Armstrong and Bechet were in their musical maturity, both playing with extraordinary bravura, celebrated and renowned beyond the world of jazz. The blues was played by a quartet, with guitarist Bernard Addison and bassist Wellman Braud. Annapolis-born Addison had been in Louis' 1930 orchestra and had also played with another New Orleans man, Jelly Roll Morton, as well as with Fletcher Henderson and Coleman Hawkins. Braud had migrated from the Crescent City to Chicago in 1917 and played with Charlie Elgar (1920–22) before moving to New York to become a pioneer member of the Duke Ellington Orchestra (1927–35), and the bassist on all of the Duke's early recordings. This quartet knew each other's music instinctively and empathetically, yet two of the great egos in jazz were playing their horns side by side.

The tune begins with Louis taking a strong lead and gaining more strength through the bridge, Bechet meandering beside and behind him; then taking a short break before the agonizing, lived-out vocal:

> I've got these coal cart blues
> I'm really all confused.
> I'm about to lose my very mind
> It always worry, worry me all the time.
>
> These blues will make you cry
> Feel like you'll want to scream.
> Of course the cart was hard
> And it almost kill me up
> But just to leave it go boys
> was my cup.
>
> I've got these coal cart blues
> Till I really don't know what to do.

It was more than a quarter of a century since Louis' time with the Andrews' coal company, yet he sings these words as if he were returning to the cart at the end of the session: with passion and the testimony of real life, real work, real pain. After, Bechet briefly soars before the two horns interlock with a fearsome power and narrative. At the end, Bechet adds a decisive coda with the bass/guitar rhythm still pounding.

Pickin' on You Baby

Earlier in 1925, Williams' Blue Five, again with Armstrong featured, but with Eva Taylor adding the vocal, had recorded 'Pickin' on You Baby', a genteel enough, considering its subject, song about racism. Taylor's vaudeville presentation of the lyrics, almost polite in the scale of her protest, tell the story of a 'piccaninny rose' being discriminated against, mistreated and excluded by a group of white children. The words sometimes spark the indignation and flavour of a child's playground protest rhyme and are strangely contemporary and touching:

Mammy why this piccaninny
Crying to his mammy Ginny,
Do the white boys pick on me
And they never let me be?
And I must not play in their yard,
Ain't I just as nice as they are –
They won't let me in their games
And they call me names.

Are they picking on your baby
'cos I'm a piccaninny rose?
Mammy don't they know
That they should not treat me so?
Why don't they know that every dark cloud
Inside is silvery line?
Mammy why are they picking on me
All the time?
Oh, won't you tell them all about me,
Ain't I the sweetest rose that grows?
That's what you said
And I suppose you know,
Now ain't that so?
Day by day in every way
When they get together,
They go from bad to worse

Instead of getting better,
Are they picking on your baby
'cos I'm a piccaninny rose?

The key word 'black' is not used, substituted instead by the more sentimental 'piccaninny' (from the Spanish *pequeno nino*, or small child), thus partially disguising the nakedness of the racist bullying, but the truth is still set down, no matter how codified in 'acceptable' and sometimes saccharine language. There is none of the raw eloquence and beauty of Bessie Smith and her women blues sisters – Eva Taylor's voice is prim by comparison. But Armstrong's ensemble lead that follows the vocal adds power to the pathos, particularly in his brusquely-controlled stop-time chorus towards the end of the track, enhancing the anti-racist message of the song.

In 1995 this most intractable of issues still persisted. Tenorist David Murray, probably the leading saxophone virtuoso of his generation, recorded 'The Desegregation of Our Children' on his album of 2001, *Live at the Village Vanguard*. A slow, burning theme is accompanied by the New York pianist with Puerto Rican roots, Hilton Ruiz, drummer Pheeroan akLaff and Kelly Roberty on bass. Murray employs his characteristic notes beyond the upper register of his tenor horn to express the sense of stress and agony felt by black children still facing racism and separatism in American schools, and there is something especially moving in this extraordinary sound being linked to the pain of children. Ruiz' solo favours quietude in a cascade of troubled yet subdued notes, and akLaff's powerful brushes seem to intensify the sense of infant hurt. Roberty's solo recounts blow after blow through a tempest of plucked bass strings. The sound of the track's fearful climax in the twentieth minute is a long, long way from the lyrics of 'Pickin' on You Baby' of seventy years before, but Murray's message and aspiration carry a similar truth.

Northern Drive

Between 1910 and 1970, six and a half million black Americans moved from the Southern rural states to the Northern cities. It was one of the great migrations of the twentieth century, made even more astonishing by the fact that it was an internal migration, one made within the national borders of one of the world's largest countries. They moved from the Delta states of Louisiana, Alabama, Arkansas and Mississippi, the home of the cotton plantations and the sharecropping system. In May 1917 'The Great Northern Drive' to recruit southern black labour was begun by the proprietors of the Chicago-based cattle stockyards and packing houses, which had been left with acute labour shortages during the US participation in the war in Europe. As the country's leading black newspaper, the *Chicago Defender* set out to support the labour drive and biblical slogans and black preachers were employed to make the migration seem like a new Exodus: 'The flight out of Egypt' or 'Bound for the Promised Land'. Thus the black population of Chicago increased from 44 thousand in 1910 to 109 thousand in 1920, and to 234 thousand by 1930. During the final eighteen months of the 1914–18 War, some fifty thousand southern black people made the migration.

The 'pull' factors of jobs, better wages and the promise of an end to Jim Crow racism was balanced by the push factor of a final release from the heartbreak and injustice of the share-cropping system. The white planters provided a small stipend of 'furnish' and 'seed money' to the tenant families, whose smallholdings varied from fifteen to forty acres. With this money, the black sharecropper bought seeds and maintained equipment to plough, plant, weed and harvest – as well as buy seeds and tools for the cultivation of fruit and vegetables to sustain his family on a small garden plot. Any extra money needed could be borrowed from the planter-owned commissary (the average yearly interest was twenty per cent). After the cotton was picked by the sharecropper's family and separated from its seeds and weighed at the planter's gin, it was baled and sold. At the 'settle', the sharecropper frequently discovered that he had made only a very small amount of money, or often that he was in debt to the planter. Cheating by the planter was routine: remedy for the sharecropper in a violent and racist South was virtually impossible.

There was nothing surprising in the fact that millions of black Americans, struggling and suffering under such conditions, should want to leave and take their families to an urban life in the north. Big Bill Broonzy, who was born in Scott, Mississippi in 1893 and began his recording career in Chicago in 1927, reflected this huge sense of the abandonment of cotton cultivation for the migration northwards in his 'Plough-Hand Blues'. This was first recorded in 1940 and strongly featured in his 1955 autobiography, *Big Bill Blues,* told to Danish jazz writer Yannick Bruynoghe.

> Plough-hand has been my name, Lord
> > for forty years or more,
> Plough-hand has been my name, Lord
> > for forty years or more,
> Yes I declare I did all I could,
> Oooh Lord, trying to take care of my so and so.
>
> I ain't gonna raise no more cotton, Lord
> And I declare I ain't gonna try to raise no corn,
> I ain't gonna raise no more cotton Lord
> And I declare I ain't gonna try to raise no corn.
> Now if a mule starts running away with the world,
> Oooh Lord, I declare I gonna let him go right home.

> I wouldn't tell a mule to get up Lord
> > if he'd sit down in my lap,
> I wouldn't tell a mule to get up Lord
> > if he'd sit down in my lap,
> Lord I declare I'm through with ploughing
> Oooh Lord, that's what killed my old grand' pap.

Broonzy, a giant of the Southern blues, tells that he handled his first plough in 1900 when he was seven years old. He tells a similar story of working pain and alienation to Armstrong in his 'Coal Cart Blues', except the location is rural rather than urban. But the same urge to escape a living hell of body and mind is completely lucid in 'Plough-Hand Blues'. It is a good-bye to the land and its irksome labour, and a good riddance to the sharecropping system that had blighted the lives of black families like that of Broonzy for generations.

Washwoman's Blues

Another blues-based singer who frequently crossed over to jazz was the great Bessie Smith, born in Chattanooga, Tennessee in 1894 and dubbed the 'Empress of the Blues'. Her early years as a vaudeville dancer were as a prelude to being recognised as a singer of great potential by blues artiste Ma Rainey, who brought her into her Rabbit Foot Minstrels. By 1923 she was living and performing in Harlem and her first record, 'Downhearted Blues' and 'Gulf Coast Blues' with pianist Fletcher Henderson, sold 780 thousand copies in under six months. This success led to her touring years on the Theater Owners Booking Association (TOBA) circuit, generally known by black performers as 'Tough On Black Asses'. She performed with some of the most esteemed jazz musicians from Louis Armstrong, stride pianist James P. Johnson, tenorists Coleman Hawkins and Chu Berry to her own 'Trombone Cholly' – Charlie Green.

In February 1927 she recorded one of her most powerfully

tragic compositions, 'Backwater Blues'. The recording made a terrible coincidence with the Mississippi floods of the same year, when 600 thousand people, more than half of whom were black, lost their homes, prompting large numbers of black victims to migrate northwards. As Angela Davis writes in her revelatory account of Bessie Smith's music, *Blues Legacies and Black Feminism*, this natural disaster had consequences markedly attributable to Southern racism:

> Black people were often considered expendable, and their communities were forced to take the overflow of backwaters in order to reduce the pressure on the levees. While most white people remained safe, black people suffered the wrath of the Mississippi, nature itself having been turned into a formidable weapon of racism.

While I watched the newsreels of the deluge caused by Hurricane Katrina which smashed so many poor neighbourhoods of New Orleans in 2005, drowning hugely disproportionate numbers of the city's black residents, I remembered Bessie Smith's lyrics to 'Backwater Blues':

> When it rains five days and the skies turn dark as night,
> When it rains five days and the skies turn dark as night,
> Then trouble's takin' place in the lowlands at night.

> I woke up this mornin', can't even get out of my door,
> I woke up this mornin', can't even get out of my door,
> That's enough trouble to make a poor girl wonder
> where she wanna go.

> Then they rowed a little boat about five miles
> 'cross the pond,
> Then they rowed a little boat about five miles
> 'cross the pond,
> I packed all my clothes, throwed 'em in and
> they rowed me along.

When it thunders and lightnin', and the wind begins to blow,
When it thunders and lightnin', and the wind begins to blow,
There's thousands of people ain't got no place to go.

Then I went and stood upon some high old lonesome hill,
Then I went and stood upon some high old lonesome hill,
Then looked down on the house where I used to live.

Backwater blues done caused me to pack my things
                                        and go,
Backwater blues done caused me to pack my things
                                        and go,
'Cause my house fell down and I can't live there no mo'.

It was a Southern blues accompanied by the greatest of the
Harlem stride pianists, James P. Johnson, a meshing of South
and North, as were the majority of Bessie's recordings. Her
most potent song of work, for example, 'Washwoman's Blues',
told of the labour of many black mothers when they arrived in
the northern towns and cities. It was the destiny, for example,
of Lilly Ann Basie (mother of Count Basie) and Barbara Monk
(mother of Thelonious). 'Washwoman's Blues' has the sense of
alienated outrage of 'Coal Cart Blues', but the difference is
that this woman is already a migrant, working in what we
assumed she had once thought of as a city of hope. But no
longer; the labour is relentless:

All day long I'm slavin', all day long I'm bustin',
All day long I'm slavin', all day long I'm bustin',
Gee, my hands are tired, washin' out these dirty duds.

Lord, I do more work than forty'leven Gold Dust Twins,
Lord, I do more work than forty'leven Gold Dust Twins,
Got myself a'achin from my head down to my shins.

Sorry, I do washin' just to make my livelihood,
Sorry, I do washin' just to make my livelihood,
Oh, the washwoman's life, it ain't a bit of good.

Rather be a scullion, cookin' in some white folks' yard,
Rather be a scullion, cookin' in some white folks' yard,
I could eat aplenty, wouldn't have to work so hard.

Me and my ole washboard sho' do have some cares and
woes,
Me and my ole washboard sho' do have some cares and
woes,
In the muddy water, wringin' out these dirty clothes.

A universal woman's story is told in these hard lines woven
between the looping reeds of Bob Fuller and Ernest Elliott. I
could recognise this woman as my own grandmother from a
poor farmworker's family in East Anglia, being sent to London
to work in service at the beginning of the twentieth century. It
was endless urban drudgery for her too. But Bessie's lyrics
mark also the added dimension of racism to the pain of
poverty that she set down with so much naked poignancy in
her 'Poor Man Blues':

Mister rich man, rich man open up your heart and mind,
Mister rich man, rich man open up your heart and mind,
Give the poor man a chance, help stop these hard,
hard times.

While you're livin' in your mansion, you don't know
what hard times means,
While you're livin' in your mansion, you don't know
what hard times means,
Poor working man's wife is starvin', your wife's livin'
like a queen.

Please listen to my pleading, 'cause I can't stand
these hard times long,
Please listen to my pleading, 'cause I can't stand
these hard times long,
They'll make an honest man do things that you
know is wrong.

Poor man fought all the battles, poor man would fight
again today,
Poor man fought all the battles, poor man would fight
again today,
He would do anything you ask him in the name of the USA.

Now the war is over, poor man must live the same
as you,
Now the war is over, poor man must live the same
as you,
If it wasn't for the poor man, mister rich man,
what would you do?

Bessie's words are punctuated by Joe Williams' growling trombone slides and the wails of Elliott and Fuller, all adding to the sense of agony and humiliation of those in the basement of the American class system. Were these the thoughts of Count Basie's mother as she looked at her migrant husband who was coachman, caretaker and flunkey for Judge White, owner of one of the biggest estates and mansions along the Shrewsbury River, near Red Bank, a resort town which attracted the affluent and the powerful?

The song has its moments of apparent 'pleading' and obedience, but also a message of defiance in its culminating verse. And how much does the penultimate verse about patriotic soldiering clash with the messages from jazzmen dealing with the war in Vietnam two generations on? Recorded a year before the Wall Street crash and the subsequent depression, it resounds in the ears like a prophecy of the hard times to come for working people throughout the USA, and the even greater pressure and visibility of the glaring differences in class. And the song is imbued with a sense of impending resistance and class conflict – the poor man challenging inequality in a final understanding of his necessity to those who exploit and oppress him. In every sense, 'Poor Man Blues' takes a moment in history, analyses it and looks towards a prognosis of struggle.

And 'struggle' too is the key titular word in Clara Smith's 1927 waxing of 'Strugglin' Woman's Blues'. Very little is known about Bessie's namesake and sometime singing partner. She was born in Spartanburg, South Carolina in 1894 and by 1910 she was also a part of the Southern vaudeville TOBA circuit. In 1923 she migrated permanently to New York, working in Harlem speakeasies and cabarets and forming her own theatrical club. She performed in a series of musical revues and made 'race' records, playing with such early jazz virtuosi as Armstrong, Hawkins, Henderson and James P. Johnson. 'Strugglin' Woman's Blues' finds her accompanied by Bob Fuller, Gus Aitken's cornet and pianist Stanley Miller. Clara's voice is lucid and suffused with sadness, both about the work which is filling her with despair, and a man who is leeching off her. The blues is slow and Clara sings right through its lyrics, verse after verse:

> Every morning, early every morning
> I have to rise with the rising sun,
> A poor struggling woman
> My work ain't never done.
>
> Don't say I'm a fool, just a working fool
> Working for that man of mine,
> But what he's done to me
> Will come back on him in time.

My man don't want me, trouble haunt me
I always knew,
Hard working hurting me,
But I'll just die with the blues.

But I'll keep on struggling, always struggling
With my heavy load,
I may find a happy home
But far on down the road.

There is more stoicism here than defiance, more acceptance than resistance with some hope for an ending, but it is a stark and naked song and a part of the foundation of the stories in music which both precede and follow it. For the woman was always the bedrock of the jazz life dominated by men, the underpinning of their creations and musicianship achieved by women's work and relentless struggle. Perhaps Clara Smith is saying something like this in her hard and beautiful song.

Stockyards Strut

A new optimism and jauntiness suffuses much of the music of the migrant jazzmen who found their new homes in Chicago. Freddie Keppard was a folkloric trumpeter, even within his own mysterious and aborted lifetime. Born in New Orleans in 1890, he became one of the city's most formidable brassmen and leader of the Olympia Orchestra. He moved to Los Angeles in 1914 with his Original Creole Band and become one of the primary West Coast jazz influences. Both Bechet and Morton regarded him as a brilliant hornman, but his musical genius sparked at a time in jazz history when the onset of commercial recording was regarded with suspicion. The legend was that Keppard would not record because he wanted no one to copy his sound and technique; others assert that he insisted upon payment for test recordings which record companies would not pay. Consequently his recorded canon is relatively slight, but sufficient still to reveal his extraordinary artistry. His contributions to the 'Doc' Cook sides recorded by the bandleader's Dreamland Orchestra, 'Cookie's Gingersnaps' and 'Doctors of Suncopation' (even the outfit's ever-changing titles express a sense of arrivant exhilaration and hope), recorded between January 1924 and June 1927, breathe life into the somewhat supine arrangements. Jimmie Noone's New Orleans clarinet is the other exciting presence. Listen to them together on 'Messin' Around' and the two recordings of 'High Fever' – the huge energy, confidence and musicianship of the Crescent City parades have come full pelt to Chicago's South Side and burst through Cook's full twelve-piece Dreamland Orchestra. Keppard's horn is fierce and proud, particularly as he leads home in his final choruses, as if this is his city now, here and definite! Arrival complete.

But it is in the one recorded session under his own name and leadership, in September 1926, that Keppard fully extols this new destination. Many thousands of black southerners found new forms of work in the stockyards, changing from rural peons and virtual slaves without wages or expectations to become a part of the working class – urbanites and holders of new freedoms. Where they weren't compelled to sit at the back of a bus, bow their heads or make way for passing whites; where they could earn a living wage, vote and unionise and read their own black nationalist newspaper. In a brief momentary transition of arrivant illusion, they could look aside from the reality of a new municipal racism – the segregated and overcrowded schools operating on a double-shift system using trailers in playgrounds temporarily converted into makeshift classrooms, or the high-rise ghettoes being built in black neighbourhoods – and exercise their 'attitude' of new-found hope and confidence.

Keppard's Jazz Cardinals included the greatest of New Orleans' clarinettists, Johnny Dodds, born in 1892, whose liquid and spiky tone had enriched the historic 1923 recordings of Joe 'King' Oliver's Creole Jazz band and whose reed contributions were to be significant in the new solo virtuosity of the Louis Armstrong Hot Five and Hot Seven between November 1925 and December 1927. The notion of a 'strut' suggests walking certainly with an affected, if not a cocky or over-confident gait. The new Chicagoans, new urbanites and wage earners at the city's giant stockyards, may have felt they could suddenly afford new habits, modes and attitudes. Keppard and Dodds catch their historic moment with virtuosity and brilliance in the Jazz Cardinals' 'Stockyards Strut'. With trombonist Eddie Vincent completing the frontline, and with pianist Arthur Campbell and Jasper Taylor striking sparks from the woodblocks, the New Orleans pair play off each other with an empathy and vitality which implants the Crescent City's excitement and boisterousness in the heat of Chicago's formidable industrial heartland, while Vincent churns his slides below them. Keppard leads with fire and wit, his trumpet break soars across the autumn Lake Michigan shore and Dodds' solo moments cut the northern studio air like a factory whistle. Only two and a half minutes long, 'Stockyards Strut' is as much a commentary on and celebration of the end of a journey and the beginning of a settlement as any thematic poem or song. Its sound is full of arrivant voices, cocksure and determined.

As is another epochal jazz anthem recorded on October 5 1923, 'Working Man Blues', by King Oliver's Creole Jazz Band. Joe Oliver had been born in New Orleans in 1885 and his first instrument was the trombone. By 1905 his cornet playing was achieving considerable recognition across Crescent City jazz circles and his 'King' title came to him in 1917, offered by the trombonist and bandleader Edward 'Kid' Ory. In 1919 he made his first sojourn in Chicago, becoming a part of Bill Johnson's band at the Dreamland. Like Keppard, he spent some time in California, but returned to Chicago in 1920 to lead his own band at the Lincoln Gardens. He chose Johnny Dodds as his clarinettist and his trombonist was one of Louis' parade heroes from his boyhood years, Honoré Dutrey, who suffered badly from breathing difficulties due to inhaling gas in the 1914–18 War's European battlefields. Louis recalls in his *My Life in New Orleans* that he played 'one whale of a trombone. Whenever he had a hard solo to play he would go to the back of the bandstand and spray his nose and throat.' In 1923 Oliver sent to New Orleans for his protegé Louis Armstrong, and thus began Louis' career as a fully professional musician and the future first jazz virtuoso. But in the Oliver band, Louis' role was not as a soloist, but as a second cornet to Oliver. With Warren 'Baby' Dodds, the first great jazz drummer, pianist Lil Hardin and alternating guitarists Bud Scott and Johnny St. Cyr and the occasional support of Bill Johnson's bass to provide the rhythm, the Oliver band made a succession of recordings which were truly the first precious waxings of jazz history.

'Working Man Blues' is taken at a brisk tempo with breaks first by Dodd's clarinet and the two cornets in unison, then by Dodds again, a few notes from the C melody saxophone of Stump Evans and a final muted interlude by Oliver himself. But the performance is guided by New Orleans ensemble traditions: playing together, a collective act of musicianship, the whole being the sum of parts.

The Creole Jazz Band recorded 'Working Man Blues' twice, the second slightly longer and more familiar version was cut on October 23 1923, some three weeks after the first. The personnel was slightly different. Evans was absent and Charlie Jackson plays bass saxophone. The tempo is slower and Jackson's bass notes give the rhythm a fuller, thicker and more subliminal sound. The clarinet timbre sounds more defiant particularly the lingering notes in the fourth and fifth breaks and Dutrey's slides are much more emphatic, pressing the ensemble forward from below until he makes his own final solo break. There is a short cornet coda, presumably by Oliver, before the performance ends. I first heard 'Working Man Blues' as a teenager. It was one of twelve tunes on a Philips Minigroove LP that I bought in the late fifties, and was the first twelve-inch long playing record that I ever bought. It still has the price, thirty-five shillings and nine pence, inscribed in Biro pen on the back of the sleeve.

Ever since then I have marvelled at the achievement of the Oliver band, and at 'Working Man Blues' in particular. New Orleans musicians playing the blues, but not sadly, instead with the sense of a new beginning, with thousands of their compatriots of the South, formerly tied to the land in small isolated family plots, working separately and individually, cut off from each other and in constant jeopardy of fraud, naked exploitation and murderous racist violence, now working in a new city, close to each other, next to each other as a part of the American working class, with new possibilities of both defence and initiative. The New Orleans ensemble tradition had been implanted in Chicago by its own musicians, and it reflected the new class that those arrivants who loved the music were now part of. The solidarity of the Crescent City marching bands, the community of musicianship and mutuality of sound had found its way to the urban North.

Savage City

Yet the prime birthplace of jazz was anything but a comfortable city for the generations of jazz musicians who were born and raised there. Despite the artistry and genius that arose from its streets and the gush of sentimental songs that were written about them, they were often savage and hellish places which bred alienation, fear and a dimension of self-loathing in the minds of their black citizens. Louis Armstrong became the city's most famous and precious artiste, but it was no easy journey for him. And for many others less celebrated too. A persuasive account of the early life of a New Orleans jazzman in the first years of the twentieth century when the music was flourishing with the unrecorded pioneers of jazz – from the trumpeters Chris Kelly and Buddy Bolden to legendary clarinettists Alphonse Picou and Lorenzo Tio – is to be found in Jay Allison Stuart's 1961 life of the clarinettist George Lewis, born nine days after Louis Armstrong in 1900, *Call Him George*.

Stuart was writing at a time when the South was ablaze with the Civil Rights movement and violent racism was still a dominant factor of black life. He seeks to chart the life of Lewis' ancestors, from his great-grandmother Zaier, who made the crossing from Senegal to New Orleans in the mid-nineteenth century as an eight-year-old girl, and was bought as a slave to a white Catholic family. She immediately became subject to Louisiana's 'Black Code' a raft of racist legislation to ensure that nothing could 'endanger the absolute supremacy of the white race' and which forbade any gatherings of blacks who worked for different masters. Those who disobeyed were to be whipped, branded and in the event of 'aggravated circumstances', killed. The formal end of slavery did not erase the spirit of the 'Black Code', which continued until and in some places beyond the measures won by the Civil Rights movement. In his sleevenotes to Wynton Marsalis' album of 1985 *Black Codes (from the Underground)*, the critic Stanley Crouch refers to the Black Codes as the 'prohibitive nineteenth century slave laws which emphasised depriving chattels of anything other than what was necessary to maintain their positions as talking work animals.'

Stuart tells how Lewis' fourteen-year-old cousin was shot down and killed in cold blood by a white boy for no clear reason beyond racial hatred and contempt. There were several black eye-witnesses yet none dared to come forward and speak in court against the murderer. Lewis' most vivid childhood memory was walking past the surgery of a white vet who was notorious for his antipathy to local black people. The man, engaged in surgery on a pet dog, slung out a full basin of the dog's blood and innards over Lewis and his friend, who were dressed in their best laundered and starched clothes for Sunday School. Such incidents told of a strictly and violently segregated city, savage in its separatism, which even the communally minded musicians could not break. At Mardi Gras, both white and black bands marched and played, but always separately. In his story of black New Orleans' jazzmen, *Bourbon Street Black*, the banjoist Danny Barker asserts:

> Around the turn of the century in New Orleans, whites practically never worked with black organisations, and it was usually only some of the lighter Creoles of Color who were able to 'pass' who worked with the white bands.

My Only Sin

Arvell Shaw, for many post-war years the bassist of the Louis Armstrong All-Stars, once said of his leader:

> Louis was very serious about music, it was his life. By that I mean he expressed his whole life through his music – the good times and the not-so-good times. What you heard through the horn was the truth.

And inside the prodigious exuberance and artistry of his music were also the deeply-laid complexes and absurdities about his life and meteoric rise to fame and idolization in Chicago, New York and right across the US and beyond. In July 1929 he recorded the song '(What Did I Do to Be So) Black and Blue' with a full orchestra. This was a song written for the 1929 revue *Hot Chocolates* by the extraordinary twosome of Fats Waller and Andy Razaf. Louis recognised its terrifying brilliance and recorded it virtually as soon as it came out. Waller was a New Yorker born four years after Armstrong in 1904, and like him a multi-talented entertainer – brilliant stride pianist, singer, composer and humorist. His partner, mainly responsible for the lyrics of their songs was, in truth called Andreamentena Razafinkeriefo (which means 'noble child of wisdom'), the nephew of Ranavaoina III, the last Queen of Madagascar who was killed in the anti-colonial war against the invading French forces in 1896. His pregnant mother, the Duchess, managed to find asylum in America, and 'Andy Razaf' was born in Washington that year. As a young man he aspired to be a poet and dramatist, and moved to New York, finding work as an elevator boy in the New Amsterdam Theatre. Unbeknowingly, he found a place to live very near Waller. They met at a Harlem theatre piano contest and began a collaboration that produced hundreds of songs which achieved huge popularity – from 'Honeysuckle Rose' to 'Blue Turning Grey Over You' and 'Keepin' Out of Mischief Now'.

None however, carried the power and internal agony of 'Black and Blue', and when Armstrong, the young black prodigy of New Orleans, sang and played it, its forceful revelation to white and black audiences became completely direct and explicit as a message of the brutal effects of a racist society. Perhaps Razaf, the black son of an African aristocrat, found his American dismissal as just another inferior black man who had to seek and strive to live a white life in order to prosper and achieve in the United States of America, as clear cut and intolerable. When Louis sang his words and blew Waller's poignant theme in his first recording of the song, nothing like it had been heard before from the mass recording industry. Yet the song had arisen when a producer of *Hot Chocolates* had said to Razaf: 'Andy, here's what we want. When the curtain rises this little gal will be in bed under a white counterpane with only her face sticking over the sheets. Now we need a number for her to sing – something about how tough it is to be coloured. You know what I mean – something funny.'

Razaf responded and at last nothing was being hidden, made into bathos, sentimentalised or rendered oblique. Its message was as direct as it was possible to be. The physical rejection and loneliness was only the outward expression of the song. The more terrifying theme was the imprisonment of the mind, held in thrall by the racist society, where there seemed to be no alternative to pursuing the white American dream, the white route to a pursuit of white happiness, trapped within the black skin. Nothing had revealed such truth before in the popular domain with so much strength, clarity and authority. It was New York, New Orleans and anti-colonial Africa in unison to articulate its message with such artistry and absolute lucidity.

> Cold empty bed
> Springs hard as lead
> Feel like Old Ned
> Wished I was dead
> What did I do
> To be so black and blue?
>
> Even the mouse
> Ran from my house
> They laugh at you
> And scorn you too
> What did I do
> To be so black and blue?
>
> How would it end
> Ain't got a friend
> My only sin
> Is in my skin
> What did I do
> To be so black and blue?

Perhaps Armstrong's recording of this song and its theme is only challenged in its simple yet complex brilliance by the 1938 publication of the Martinican Aimé Césaire's *Return to My Native Land* where, in an allusion to the Haitian Toussaint L'Ouverture's rebellion against French colonialism (1794–1801), he wrote:

A man alone, imprisoned by whiteness
A man alone who defies the white
    scream of a white death.

And his compatriot, the psychologist Frantz Fanon, who dedicated his life to the Algerian Revolution, in 1952 wrote his epochal study, *Black Skin, White Masks*, to reveal and remove the consciousness of whiteness that he saw internalised in millions of colonised black people in the Caribbean, Africa and the Americas: 'A shameful apprehension of something and that something is *me*. I am ashamed of what I *am*.' When Fanon declared that his intention was 'to help the black man to free himself of the arsenal of complexes that has been developed by the colonial environment', he had an able ally in Armstrong's 1929 performance of 'Black and Blue': 'Willy-nilly, the negro has to wear the livery that the white man has sewed for him.' Waller, Razaf and Armstrong revealed that, and raised questions in the minds of millions of ordinary listeners, manifesting Fanon's final prayer in his book: 'O my body, make of me always a man who questions!'

But such questions went beyond 'Black and Blue' in Armstrong's ever-expanding canon. By 1930 he was recording in a Los Angeles studio with his 'Sebastian New Cotton Club Orchestra', the house orchestra at Frank Sebastian's New Cotton Club in Culver City. His recording on March 31, of the Irving Caesar/Leonello Casucci song, 'Just a Gigolo', became a sensation to those who listened to it very closely. As he sang the final verse of the vocal he seemed to change the words. Instead of 'just another gigolo', there was:

When the end comes, I know
They'll say 'just another jig', I know
And life goes on without me.

When you listen to the track the change in diction is very clear, and gives a whole new meaning to the song. 'Just a Gigolo' was recorded a few weeks after the Los Angeles session that waxed such light-hearted romps like 'You're Driving Me Crazy', 'Sweethearts on Parade' and 'The Peanut Vendor', but something else was in Louis' mind on March 31. Lionel Hampton's vibes, Bill Perkins' acoustic guitar and Joe Bailey's tuba bass are all to the fore as Louis plays a restrained and delicate trumpet solo around the theme, followed by his purposefully ambivalent vocal. Then it is as if his audacious pun has suddenly lifted him up on a wave of resistance. The tempo quickens into double time, he abandons his previous almost fragile lyricism and tears into the melody with a confident stride, his second chorus reaching for high notes and ending with a soaring coda.

Shine

One of the foremost trumpeters of the next generation, the Kansas-born, Basie-ite horn, Buck Clayton, remembers in his 1986 autobiography, *Buck Clayton's Jazz World*, the impact of first hearing Louis' 'Just a Gigolo' in California, where he was working. At the time, so devoted to Armstrong was he, that he 'learned note for note and word for word' his recordings. He continued speaking of 'Just a Gigolo':

> Louis changed the words a little bit at the end. It kind of stirred up some people, especially the NAACP [National Association for the Advancement of Colored People] back home. Well, you know the word 'jig' often means a coloured person, which isn't too bad a word really; we use 'em, words like 'spook' and 'jig', or at least we used them in those days, not so much now. But that's just the way Louis was; he put his own little version in there.

And this 'own little version' more than anything else made people listen. Jazz was synonymous with dancing at that time, not careful listening, yet Louis had punned and codified his way into creating a subtle protest in the heart of a familiar and sentimental item from the American songbook.

Perhaps it was a sense of freedom and daring provoked by the new location of California that was inspiring him, but on the very same day that 'Just a Gigolo' was recorded, along came 'Shine' with its differently ambiguous message. Armstrong attacks the jaunty theme with rapid-fire gusto and energy for a joyous opening chorus. Then he slows down and breaks into the vocal, with Hampton's tinkling vibes behind him. He lampoons a caricatured black identity. He is the curly-haired, pearly-teethed black entertainer, his face always wearing a smile, his clothes always in the 'latest style'. He affirms he takes all his troubles 'with a smile', never a protest. 'Shady' and 'different', and that is why, he declares, 'they call me Shine'.

What to make of these lyrics? The ever-smiling shoeshine boy? The portrait of a black minstrel? The emphasis on sheer human surface without touching the inside? Wearing rather than being? Smiling to keep from crying? Style over all? The disguise of hardship and emotion with the veil of a smile? The expression of colour as a definition of difference? Visible skin but invisible man? Every word invokes a question, an enigma, an ambiguity, a provocation – for what is this man really thinking, feeling, dreaming, planning? Who knows, as Louis soars into a scat reprise of the vocal which creates more doubts about the truth of its words then heads for the stratosphere in the final trumpet chorus, bending his notes and taking a break of the most intense sound and finishing on a summit. After this, 'Shine' became one of his showstoppers ecstatically cheered by huge and mostly white audiences all over America. 'We used to get out in those little towns in the Midwest where people didn't know him so well,' recalled drummer Harry Dial: 'He'd hit as many as 350 high C's on 'Shine'.' As Louis sang out

Double · Conciousness

his layered life and nearly squandered his lip on his trumpet choruses, how many in his audiences understood the cruel pain and meaning in the import of the message that he gave to them?

By April 20 1931 Louis was recording in Chicago again. Perhaps he had left his appetite for irony and ambiguity back in California, for this was the date he cut his first version of 'When It's Sleepy Time Down South', the first of endless recordings and performances of the song, so much so that it was frequently referred to as his signature tune and became the most common opener for his concerts all over the world. It evoked a mythical heaven of Southern life in a paradisical plantation. It begins with an ensemble chorus, then a dialogue between Louis and his pianist, Charlie Alexander, whom Louis pretends is from his 'home town.' They chat about how long they have been 'up here' (in Chicago), and Louis begins to reminisce about what he is missing (red beans etc.). Then he breaks into the vocal, recalling

> Soft winds blowing in the pinewood trees
> The folks down there live a life of ease
> When old Mammy falls on her knees . . .

or

> You hear the banjos ringing
> And the darkies singing
> And they dance to the break of day.

Unlike 'Just a Gigolo' and 'Shine', neither the vocal nor Louis' chorus have any surge, edge or ambivalence, and the performance veers towards the mawkish and maudlin. Of course it was a portrait of the South which never existed except in dreams and fiction, and it was frequently to be challenged by jazzmen, poets, novelists and dramatists in the years to come. Subsequently, Louis slightly changed the words, and 'darkies' became 'the folks' in versions of 'When It's Sleepy Time Down South', but never in the decisive way in which Paul

Robeson changed the stoical 'Ol' Man River', which became intimately associated with his performances in a similar way that 'Sleepy Time' stuck like glue to Armstrong. 'I'm tired of living and scared of dying,' sang Robeson in the last verse of the 'Show Boat' song in 1927, and the performance he gave was widely condemned as one – as the New York *Amsterdam News*, put it – which portrayed black people as a stereotype of the 'lazy, good-natured lolling darkey that exists more in white men's fancy than reality.' When the film of *Show Boat* eventually found the screen in 1936, Marcus Garvey's United Negro Improvement Association's monthly journal, *The Black Man* criticised Robeson severely for exploiting 'his genius to appear in pictures and plays that tend to dishonour, mimic, discredit and abuse the cultural attainments of the black race.' By 1949 Robeson was explaining how the song's message of subjection and passivity needed change, how it needed to reflect 'the lack of rights of the negroes in the southern states, of the politics of a government that throws fighters for freedom and democracy into prison. The modified words of this song called for struggle and resistance.' And the old words were transformed, with new meaning, and became his rallying anthem. In one of his last messages – to the audience at New York's Carnegie Hall in April 1973, he declared:

> Though ill health has compelled my retirement, you can be sure that in my heart I will go on singing:
>
> > But I keeps laughing
> > Instead of crying,
> > I must keep fighting
> > Until I'm dying,
> > And Ol' Man River
> > He just keeps rolling along!

Of course Armstrong was Armstrong and Robeson was Robeson, men of very different ideas, consciousness and experiences – contemporaries and in many ways foils who were struggling against the same cruel American racist realities. But whereas Robeson, the singer and militant, had the huge progressive forces of the Popular Front to buoy him up – trade unions, black, liberal and socialist intellectuals, black groups and a wide international movement – Armstrong the jazzman was isolated, an individualist and brilliant virtuoso feted and besieged by white, commercially-minded impresarios, agents, theatre owners, concert promoters, showbusiness opportunists and a manager who eschewed progressive political positions and projects. So 'When It's Sleepy Time Down South' remained as it was for four decades until Armstrong's death, despite the lynchings, murders, Ku Klux Klan outrages – and the uprising and black mass resistance of the Civil Rights years.

As for Robeson, despite his death in 1976, five years after that of his contemporary Armstrong, his influence upon jazz and its musicians continues into the twenty-first century. In September 2001, the free jazz multi-instrumental improviser, Joe McPhee, recorded his inspirational album, *Let Paul Robeson Sing!* for the CIMP lable, with reedman Joe Giardullo and two bassists, Michael Bisio and Dominic Duval. The album title reflected the 1954 slogan of the mass campaign which, as McPhee describes in his sleevenotes, 'flooded the State Department with petitions, letters and cables demanding the reinstatement of Robeson's passport', which had been removed from him because of his explicit support of revolutionary and socialist processes throughout the world. The passport was eventually returned in April 1958.

McPhee's tenor, flugelhorn and alto clarinet celebrate some of Robeson's most renowned themes in his 'Harlem Spiritual' and 'Epitaph' – the latter a solo tenor performance bleeding with emotive power. In the suite 'Peeksgill, 1949', the quartet remembers how the planned Robeson open-air concert of August 27 near Peeksgill in upstate New York was attacked by five hundred rioting American legionnaires and prevented from proceeding. The concert was rearranged for September 4 with an audience of twenty-five thousand, many of them black and Jewish residents, garment workers and other trade unionists from New York City, and Robeson sang his songs of the world's people, uninterrupted. His words to the writer Howard Fast, quoted in the pamphlet *Peeksgill, USA*, affirm the will of jazzmen and jazzwomen too always to make their music, tell their stories about the world and never be silenced: 'I will sing whenever the people want to hear me. I sing of peace, of freedom, and of life.'

Rocky Road

Compared to much of the recorded output of McKinney's Cotton Pickers between 1929 and 1931, 'Rocky Road', waxed in New York in 1930, seems in a different reality. I first heard it decades ago on a French RCA album, sandwiched between the sentimental routines and saccharine lyrics of 'Never Swat a Fly' and 'Do You Believe in Love at First Sight?', and it stood alone as a powerful statement of jazz realism during a period when jazz musicians faced enormous difficulties in exposing in their recorded music anything that was explicitly real about the racial injustice and inequality in the world in which they lived.

William McKinney was a former drummer who in 1923 turned to managing a big band which played regularly in the Arcadia Ballroom in Detroit. In 1926 he recruited the Fletcher Henderson Orchestra's brilliant arranger and reedman Don Redman, and the Cotton Pickers, despite their outmoded plantation name, were soon competing with Henderson and even the Duke Ellington Orchestra. Redman's artistry attracted guest sidemen of the calibre of Coleman Hawkins, Fats Waller and James P. Johnson to play with the band, and present on 'Rocky Road' are luminous trumpeters Rex Stewart and Joe Smith, future Ellington trombonist Quentin Jackson and the pioneer master of the alto saxophone, Benny Carter.

'Have you ever been in Dixie 'neath that burning, shining moon?' is the enigmatic preface to Stewart's artfully muted and powerfully emotive solo over the shuffle rhythm of Cuba Austin's drums, Billy Taylor's tuba and Dave Wilborn's banjo, straining every note for its maximum feeling before the onset of Redman's lyrics:

> Rocky is the road
> My spirit's kind of low,
> My sorrow burning
> Makes travelling mighty slow.
> Trouble makes me sad,
> Seems cloudy all the time,
> I'm praying, I'm sighing,
> Just hoping that the sun will shine.
>
> Life don't seem worth living,
> Everything goes wrong,
> You can't blame me for grieving
> 'cause the one I love done gone.
> Future holds no hopes,
> Heavy is my load,
> I'm tired and weary
> Travelling this rocky road.

The words cite a broken love affair but in their harshness seem to be telling of a world and a journey of life which are darkness itself, and so much in contrast with the playfulness and zest of the band's customary musical fare. Then there are two choruses of brassy ensemble, a soaring alto break by the fired-up Carter, Redman's repetition of the final two lines, and finish. 'Rocky Road' protrudes from the McKinney Cotton Pickers' recorded canon like a message of truth released, pricking through the skin of the superficial and assumed.

2

ALL

jump for joy

When Edward 'Duke' Ellington arrived in Harlem from Washington D.C. in March 1923 for his first sojourn, he was stepping into the most intense concentration of black citizens in the American city which had the largest black population of all. Between 1920 and 1930 the number of Harlem's black residents rose from 73 thousand to 165 thousand – all living in an area of twenty-five blocks long and six blocks wide. It was within this astonishing crucible that the 'Harlem Renaissance' thrived, in a context of continuous immigration, particularly from the South and beyond, from the Caribbean. Ellington made his first records in June 1926, and later that month he hired Joe 'Tricky Sam' Nanton, a New York-born trombonist whose parents had come from the West Indies. Nanton's gruff choruses are at the centre of 'Immigration Blues', recorded on December 29 1926, with Harry Carney's baritone opening, an enigmatic Ellington solo and some wailing, muted Bubber Miley towards the end – an early acknowledgment by Ellington of the scattered origins of the people in this city which was his new home and artistic base.

The orchestra which Ellington assembled for his opening at the Cotton Club in New York's Harlem on December 4 1927, was composed of brilliant musicians from North and South. Altoist Otto 'Toby' Hardwick was, like Ellington, a Washingtonian. Trumpeters Artie Whetsel (Punta Gorda,

Florida) and Bubber Miley (Aiken, South Carolina) were southerners – as were the New Orleans pairing, Wellman Braud (bass) and clarinettist Barney Bigard, and guitarist Freddy Guy was from Georgia. Sonny Greer, the drummer, was from Long Branch, New Jersey, and both alto and soprano saxophonist Johnny Hodges and baritonist Harry Carney were northerners from Boston, along with New Yorker Nanton and Chicagoan reedman Rudy Jackson. So these weren't all southerners migrating north – although some of the titles of the tunes they played invoked that 'Dear Old Southland' of Jim Crow and sharecropping, which Ellington in his autobiography *Music Is My Mistress* called 'that lions' den of terror', like 'Song of the Cotton Field', 'Birmingham Breakdown', 'Louisiana' or 'New Orleans Lowdown'.

1929 saw recordings of 'Black and Blue' and an opus with the grim title of 'Jolly Wog'. The latter drags morosely, with an almost tailgate-sounding oppressive trombone by Nanton, some spiky Bigard and a powerful trumpet chorus before Hodges' alto soars and Carney's baritone rumbles over the clip-clop beat. Anything but 'jolly', this tune may be another piece of Ellingtonian irony and an early example of his coded artistic intentions which were demonstrated in the 1941 revue, *Jump for Joy*: 'I think a statement of social protest in the theatre should be made without saying it, and this calls for the real craftsmen.' As for 'Black and Blue', it seems to be played on two separate levels. Bigard's low register clarinet introduces the theme before a punching trumpet solo is filigreed by whirling high-register clarinet notes which suddenly plunge back into the lower reaches. The reed ensemble takes over, pursued by Nanton's trombone growls and Hodges' simmering obbligatos. Then the tempo suddenly quickens as if Ellington is parodying himself with some rapid-fire stride piano and the soulful theme returns, ending with Bigard's low register coda. Ellington was habitually playing this wordless variant of 'Black and Blue' to an all-white, segregated, prosperous audience in a spoof plantation house setting, surrounded by black waiters attending to every whim of the elite customers. Only humour and musical mockery would serve artistic truth in such a context – the stark and pointed words would be wasted.

Harlemania

Ellington's pragmatism forced him all the time to confront the real world in which he lived and worked. Even his fantasies had roots in the truth he saw around him. 'Every one of my song titles,' he declared, 'is taken principally from the life of Harlem. I look to the everyday life and customs of the negro to supply my inspiration.' Between 1927 and 1932 that working life was in the racial divide of Harlem's Cotton Club. Another black bandleader, Cab Calloway, described this musical setting in specific terms in John Edward Hasse's biography of Ellington, *Beyond Category*:

> The bandstand was a replica of a southern mansion, with large white columns and a backdrop painted with weeping willows and slave quarters. The band played on the veranda of the mansion, and in front of the veranda, down a few steps, was the dance floor . . . The waiters were dressed in red tuxedos, like buffers in a Southern mansion and there were huge, cut-crystal chandeliers.

Such were the immediate surroundings where the Ellington orchestra played some of America's greatest and most innovative music: a stylised slave setting, an exclusive segregated audience in the USA's blackest city, an ornate and ostentatious chamber run by gangsters and patronised by the rich and the racist. Ellington's huge musical brain and deeply aware consciousness knew that economic and artistic survival required the most careful and subtle of musical strategies in this brutal plantation of artifice.

Yet the Cotton Club walls did not prevent Ellington from reflecting and describing in music the Harlem streets all around him. From 'Harlem River Quiver' in 1927 to 'Harlem Flat Blues' and 'Harlemania' in 1929, the Duke began to name his tunes with multiple references to Harlem. 'Harlem River Quiver' begins with some joyously unfettered Nanton, some forceful Louis Metcalf trumpet, Carney's plunging baritone and Bubber Miley, pure and unmuted, blowing over Greer's clopping percussion. It is a free, sauntering music, reflecting an ethos of the lifting of oppression and restriction. Wellman Braud's rhythmic bass pulse is central to 'Harlemania'. Nanton again sets the entirely positive, exultant tone; Carney swings his low notes and Freddy Jenkins' trumpet is straight and true. Johnny Hodges positively strolls through his alto solo as if worry were the last thing on his mind. This is Harlem, the Duke seems to be exclaiming, a new territory of freedom. Even 'Harlem Flat Blues', with its wailing opening ensemble, Nanton's superb growling and hooting chorus and Bigard's looping solo – with the final ensemble riff, all suggest that Harlem belongs to its musicians and the people whom they paint in sound.

These performances contrast starkly with that of 'Song of the Cotton Field', recorded before Ellington's Cotton Club debut, in February 1927. The opening muted trombone of Nanton seems to reflect a different life in the South: sorrowful, irksome, dominated by worry. The ensemble theme is heavy and blues-laden and when Nanton returns, there is a subliminal sadness in his notes. Bigard's low-register chorus seems to tell a similar mournful tale and Carney's solo digs deep, almost falling to the earth. North and South portrayed as different countries, divided realities in the messages of Ellington's profoundly new music.

In the Cotton Club he conceived and developed a whole new style of jazz. A part of this depended upon a stylistic notion of 'jungle' exotica. 'Echoes of the Jungle', 'Jungle

Jamboree', 'Jungle Blues' and the forerunner, 'Jungle Nights in Harlem' were all variants on this mode – and for a period, between 1929 and 1930, Ellington's orchestra was even called 'The Jungle Band'. Of course this style only bore an affectatious relationship to any sound that was truly African, but it became one of the characteristic effects of Ellington's music, created in particular through the astonishing muted trumpet and trombone skills perfected by both Miley and Nanton. From 1929 the style was continued and developed by Cootie Williams from Mobile, Alabama, who, at the age of nineteen, was Miley's replacement when the latter's alcoholism forced Ellington to fire him (he died two years later of tuberculosis, the first great Ellingtonian loss). Braud's rhythmic, thudding bass and Greer's relentless timekeeping added to the jungle effect – both are particularly prominent on 'Jungle Blues' (1930) for example, while in 'Jungle Jamboree', Braud enjoys an early joust with Carney's throbbing baritone before Bigard whirls around in high register and new man Williams delivers a muted solo that faithfully replicates the Miley sound, while retaining his own more forceful undertow.

Jungle Nights in Harlem

'When I began my work, jazz was a stunt, something different,' Ellington once declared. 'Not everybody cared for jazz and those who did felt that it wasn't the real thing unless they were given a shock sensation of loudness or unpredictability along with the music.'

Ellington was alive to the need to ensure that his livelihood and that of his entire orchestra were sustained. The jungle theme to his music was a strategy that worked powerfully for his white patrons and listeners. The reality of Africa or Harlem was far from their lives and even further than their thoughts, but a superficial, exotic caricature of Africa played by black men in European suits and with familiar European instruments

was more than tolerable. That they played these instruments
with such 'new' sounds made their music even more compul-
sive. It was Bubber Miley who first defined the jungle sound
with his brilliance with the plunger mute, but to Ellington he
was also a skilled griot and storyteller. In *Music Is My Mistress*,
Ellington writes:

> Before he played his choruses, he would tell his story and he
> always had a story for his music, such as: 'This is an old man,
> tired from working in the field since sun up, coming up the
> road in the sunset on his way home to dinner. He's tired but
> strong, and humming in time to his broken gait – or vice
> versa.' That was how he pictured 'East St Louis Toodle-oo'.

Ellington called Nanton 'Bubber's plunger mate', and he
described how the trombonist developed these new sounds
with sophistication and precision – 'there were certain dis-
tances the plunger had to be away from the mute inside the
bell, and there was the matter of when you squeezed it.' And
for Ellington, Nanton had a whole family story to tell in his
sound: 'what he was actually doing was playing a very highly
personalised form of his West Indian heritage. Tricky and his
people were deep in the West Indian legacy and the Marcus
Garvey movement.' So, behind the so-called jungle sound were
not only countless stories of hardship in the South. There was
a distinct Caribbean tradition too pouring out of Nanton's
horn. The Cotton Club audience thought that they heard one
kind of exotic, fantasised black music: Ellington, Miley,
Nanton and their band knew that they were telling an entirely
different story of their own people and their history. The two
meanings co-existed in ambivalence and irony.

Take 'Jungle Nights in Harlem', for example. Even the title
is laden with contradictions: the unreal and the real, the
invented and the raw streets simmering outside the Cotton
Club doors, full of new, black New Yorkers, brilliant writers,
poets, painters and more and more musicians challenging

every notion of white exclusivity that prevailed within the club's luxurious confines. In 'Jungle Nights' it is as if the men and women in the streets, the apartments, the shops, the hairdressers, the bars, the riverside, the workplaces are all conferring, their diversity of speech heard within the diversity of instrumental voices – soloists and ensembles, that crackle through the performance. Ellington's thumping stride piano starts off the colloquy, followed by Nanton's gruffly muted trombone making its points with force and pertinence. In comes Miley, wailing, squealing as if in disagreement or protest, with Carney's deep baritone rhythms beneath. This is dramatic speech, a dialogue of voices below the apparent exoticism. Bigard joins in, swirling with his alto. The finale pits the voice of Miley again, crying out the story of his pain or derision against the ensemble riffs as the pace gradually decelerates, down to the voices of silence. It is an astonishing listening experience, and one not easily forgotten that persuades you directly to take up the words of Harlem's great black writers: from Langston Hughes to Claude McKay, from Countee Cullen to Zora Neale Hurston. For their voices and their provenances – from the South, to the Caribbean, and black life all over the Americas, are all telling their stories alongside Ellington and his confreres.

A story which affected the entire orchestra as well as ordinary working people in cities all over the Americas was that of the violent downward perturbations of the New York Stock Exchange in the critical year of 1929. Many of the Cotton Club's regular clientele saw their fortunes tumble, but more significantly were the lasting effects on millions of many poor Americans, and their messages of deprivation which were poured out in countless blues, and sung thousands of times in songs like 'Nobody Knows You When You're Down and Out' or 'Brother, Can You Spare a Dime?' As Joseph North described the American years that followed in the introduction to his *New Masses* anthology:

The hunger. The wrecked home. The family on the city pavement. The grandmother in her rocking chair, dry-eyed, on the sidewalk. In rain. Hopelessness. The crying child. The staring, anguished mother. The shamed, bitter father. The jots of life on the outskirts of every city. Waste, refuse; humankind on the dump. I repeat: the hunger. A continent in starvation. 17,000,000 jobless. Milk dumped into rivers, obscene, like a social onanism. Oranges burned, wheat burned . . . to keep the prices up.

And Ellington faced the stockbroking elite in the Cotton Club with his 'Wall Street Wail' in December 1929: direct, confrontational, his reed and brass sections riffing like fury as if facing each other across the stock market floor of Braud's tireless bass. The clarinet twosome of southerner Bigard and northerner Carney braced to blow out the clarity of their message, and the New York trumpet of Freddy Jenkins storming out his chorus. What did those who listened think?

Black Beauty

So, considering the kind of cultural prison and Yankee plantation that the Cotton Club actually was, Ellington's musical strategies not only of survival, but of musical and social invention, were both astonishing and courageous. He enabled the sound of black genius to soar from a northern cultural and racist corral. And nothing expresses that musical bravery more than one of his early recordings (recorded in March 1928 after he had been playing in the Cotton Club for a mere three months), the tribute to the black singer and dancer Florence Mills, called 'Black Beauty' and subtitled: 'A Portrait of Florence Mills'. Mills was hugely popular and her early death at the age of thirty-two provoked some fifteen thousand people to attend her funeral in Harlem. The public identification of blackness with beauty to an audience that was white, powerful and unpredictable was unusual enough, but Ellington also unwittingly pioneered a truth and slogan that was to be at the centre of political struggle decades into the future. There was nothing hidden or coded in 'Black Beauty': it was a musical poem of love and pride for a resplendent and beautiful black woman and the thousands of other black women everywhere who walked in the Americas, in Africa or anywhere in the world. Artie Whetsel's muted trumpet begins the melody, played with a beautifully lyrical timbre, and section-mate Louis Metcalf takes over for the middle eight bars. Nanton growls a characteristically surly solo before Ellington himself makes his own personal salutation, accompanied only by the regular breath of Braud's bass and the almost inaudible cymbal touch of Greer. Bigard's solo is tender, like a gentle sound of birdsong in his rises and cadences, and Whetsel closes a performance of perfection by playing in the way in which he began.

After leaving the Cotton Club in 1931, Ellington's evocations of Africa changed radically. He could now openly attest to his love for the continent without any coding, gimmicks or ambiguity. Later in life he would write compelling long musical tributes to the continent like the 'Liberian Suite' (1947) or the 'Togo Brava Suite' (1971). But his most dramatic dedication to Africa came while playing piano in February 1940 as a member of one of the 'small groups' of Ellington musicians that were formed by prominent members of his orchestra, this time by his trumpeter and cornetist Rex Stewart. In October 1935, 120 thousand Italian troops supported by 350 planes and reinforced by 100 thousand irregulars from Eritrea and Somalia made an unprovoked invasion of Ethiopia, the last African state to be confronted by the unleashed power of European conquest and colonization. The Italian tyrant, Mussolini acknowledged the outrage as 'a war waged and won in the very spirit of fascism,' and the invasion was met with only very limited sanctions by the Assembly of the League of Nations.

Stewart said of 'Menelik': 'I tried to depict an African motif, while at the same time sort of saluting the courage of Haile Selassie. Hence the so-called "lion" tones in the piece.' The Ethiopian emperor had made an indignant presentation to the League of Nations with very little gained in return, and this had lodged in the Ellingtonian's consciousness, as had the barbarism shown by the Italian occupiers against the Ethiopian people, such as the murderous reprisals taken against Ethiopian patriots in 1937, after an abortive bomb attack in Addis Ababa.

'Menelik' was named in memory of Haile Selassie's predecessor, whose army of 100 thousand men had defeated three Italian brigades in March 1896, as they attempted to advance on the northern Ethiopian town of Adowa. The victory, as well as provoking a wish for revenge by the Italian rulers, created a sense of legend and pride around the Ethiopian people, which Stewart and Ellington express manifestly in 'Menelik'. For the tune and its performance was not a piece of 'jungle' exoticism looking for the superficial approval of Cotton Club customers. It was an act of musical solidarity for a struggling African nation, focusing on the story of one of its past leaders who had successfully resisted European expansionism into Africa. Stewart, a profoundly vocal trumpeter and mute expert in the Bubber Miley and Cootie Williams tradition (his tribute to Miley, 'Poor Bubber', and to Williams too, 'Mobile Bay', were also recorded at this session) uses his skills audaciously in 'Menelik'.

The performance begins with Stewart blowing his horn to simulate the sound of a breathy, roaring lion. But this is no mere effect to humour a white Cotton Club audience. It is the fusion of artistry and solidarity. Greer pounds his tom tom, Carney and Ben Webster offer a low rhythmic reed background before Stewart comes back on clear and resplendent open horn, leading the ensemble, with Ellington's comping piano and the young Jimmy Blanton on bass providing thudding relentless time. It is an all-round performance featuring

some of the greatest jazz innovators of the epoch, brilliantly
realised as a trans-Atlantic message of hope and brotherhood,
borrowing genuinely from the sounds and spirit of Africa.

1940 and the following year formed a key period for
Ellington and perhaps his greatest orchestra. Blanton, born in
Chattanooga, Tennessee, had taken over the bass in 1939 when
he was twenty-one and, like Louis Armstrong, he was an ex-
member of Fate Marable's Mississippi riverboat bands.
Webster, the sublime tenor saxophonist, born in Kansas City
in 1909, arrived in 1940 after a decade spent in the big bands
of Fletcher Henderson, Benny Carter, Cab Calloway, Andy
Kirk and Teddy Wilson. These two outstanding recruits coin-
cided in their membership of the orchestra with Ellington's
greatest years, and the orchestra's most committed involve-
ment in political life. Its activities were in broad support of
the cultural work of the Popular Front movement – centred
around anti-fascism (focusing in particular upon a broad movement against lynching in the South) and the industrial trades
unionism of the CIO, millions of whose rank and file members
were from the families of black and migrant workers. In New
York, where jazz and big band swing had such mass popular
support, the Popular Front was held together by informal and
perpetually shifting alliances between the unions of garment
workers and needle trades, white collar unions and the organisations of the Harlem community. A prime motivation for
community unity and solidarity was around the campaign to
free the 'Scottsboro' Boys'. The case began in 1931 when nine
black youths from Alabama, one barely twelve years old, were
accused and convicted of raping two white girls while in
Tennessee. They were sentenced to death and the sentence
(called by Robeson 'legal lynching') provoked a mass defence
campaign, led by the International Labor Defense and the
Communist Party. The young men were reprieved, but they
were held in prison for many years, despite clear evidence that
they had been falsely charged. Other significant campaigns

were waged around support for republican Spain against the Franco pro-fascist uprising and, as we have seen, the Ethiopian people.

The Ellington Orchestra played benefit concerts alongside other artistes such as Robeson, folk singer Josh White and other jazzmen like Fletcher Henderson, Sidney Bechet, Count Basie, Benny Carter, Teddy Wilson and Frankie Newton, for these causes and for others too, for example, Russian War Relief or the campaign to elect the black Communist candidate Benjamin Davis to the New York City Council in 1943. Teddy Wilson chaired a committee of cultural figures who supported Davis, which received support from significant jazz musicians such as Mary Lou Williams, Coleman Hawkins, Art Tatum, Count Basie, Ella Fitzgerald, Jimmy Lunceford and Billie Holiday.

Stevedore Stomp

Another major cause supported by Ellington was the campaign for civil rights in employment practice, launched around the Fair Employment Practices Commission. In 1934, the play *Stevedore*, with a theme of racial and trade union conflict, opened successfully in New York, produced at the Theater Union – a company which had been formed to stage plays on working class themes, with much reduced admission charges to attract working class audiences. *Stevedore* was the story of a young black dock worker falsely accused of raping a white woman – a northern parallel to the Scottsboro' Boys narrative. The protagonist, one Lonnie Thompson, escapes lynching, successfully campaigns for and engages the support of black and white workmates and the racist mob is defeated at the cost of Thompson's life. The play was strongly supported by Robeson and produced in London a year later with Robeson taking a major role. Perhaps Ellington's classic recording in 1929 of his tune 'Stevedore Stomp' was a pointer of the drama to come, as well as a strong identification with black workers in the Port of Harlem. It communicates something of the same sense of jaunty confidence of the black migrant worker in a northern city as Freddie Keppard's 'Stockyards Strut' of three years before, and another musical commentary of the 'southernisation' of American urban life and the astonishing statistic of movement which reveals that between 1920 and 1984 the number of black Americans who lived on farms had dropped from fifty to one per cent of the total black population, and that ninety per cent of migrants moved to urban locations in six states: California, Illinois, Michigan, Pennsylvania, Ohio and New York.

Ellington's musical portraiture of New York stevedores struts with pride, largely due to the basswork of Braud, who plucks his strings with such force and twang that he urges on every soloist, fully supported by Freddy Guy's ringing banjo chords. Whetsol skims his muted notes while still keeping their picked-out clarity and lightness; Carney's baritone solo races with the sense of a heavy dockworker speeding to complete his tasks; Nanton charges through his chorus in gruff voice with breathless slide-work and Bigard chirrups away like a migrating bird before Hodges swings in with the final bridge and the ensemble takes it out. A triumph of Ellington's musical picture-making, but a statement too about the thousands of new black workers and urbanites in the Big Apple: there to live, there to work, there to stay.

Eleven years later in Harlem, Ellington is happily laughing with these workers. The humorous narrative ballad, 'The Five O'Clock Whistle' tells the story of disorder in a factory and family when the whistle to end the day shift fails to work. Ivie Anderson sings of her father caught in this confusion:

The five o'clock whistle's on the blink
The whistle won't blow, and what do you think?
My Papa's still in the factory
'cos he doesn't know what time it happens to be.
You want to hear what my Mama said
When Papa came home and sneaked into bed
And told her he worked till half past two
'cos the five o'clock whistle never blew.

Nothing could be further from the oppressive stories of the rural and sharecropping South contained in Ellington's early Cotton Club waxings like 'Song of the Cotton Field' (1927) or 'Louisiana' (1928) than this sprightly and entirely proletarian ditty. Some of Harlem's most brilliant musicians came together in April and June 1939 to form The Port of Harlem Jazzmen and to make some of the first recordings for Blue Note, a record label that one and two decades later would wax some of the greatest postwar jazz sessions. The frontline consisted of the talismanic Bechet of New Orleans, and two other Southerners – the trumpeter Frankie Newton, born in Emony, Virginia, in 1906, and the trombonist J. C. Higginbotham, born in the same year in Social Circle, Georgia. The 'Port of Harlem' tracks are arguably the finest recordings by both Newton and Higginbotham. Newton could be as hot as any big band trumpeter, as he showed when he was the featured horn in 1936–37 in the Teddy Hill Orchestra between the periods of Roy Eldridge and Dizzy Gillespie, but it was as subtle trumpet colorist with a dextrous use of bent notes and mutes that he achieved a true uniqueness. Listen to the sonic shades and note perfection on 'Daybreak Blues' or 'Port of Harlem Blues'; and on 'Mighty Blues' his sublime control delivers whooping, springing sounds unheard in recorded jazz before this time.

Higginbotham liberated the trombone from its restricted tailgate persona and was the pioneer of a more delicate, richer, modern sound. His solos on 'Wearyland Blues' and 'Port of Harlem Blues' sound as if they were blown on a different instrument to that played by Ory or Dutrey, even when he is leading the melody of the New Orleans-inspired 'Basin Street Blues'. 'After Hours Blues' is another brass essay exquisitely performed by Newton with three northern virtuosi – pioneer solo guitarist Teddy Bunn of Freeport, New York; Chicagoan boogie woogie pianist Albert Ammons; and drummer Sid Catlett of Evansville, Indiana. Yet perhaps the two most memorable tracks are 'Blues for Tommy' and 'Pounding Heart Blues'. In the former, dedicated to Crescent City trumpeter Tommy Ladnier who had died three days before, Bechet swirls provocatively into the opening bars and ensuing choruses on soprano saxophone; Newton fashions his solo high and going higher; Bunn's bluesy statement follows and Higginbotham sounds mournfully beautiful, eschewing any rawness. The final ensemble is a collective statement of Harlem genius. Finally 'Pounding Heart Blues' expresses the surging life of the Black city. Slightly pacier than 'Blues for Tommy' and with Bechet on clarinet, Sid Catlett's relentless drumbeat is the swinging heart of Harlem, below Higginbotham's growling chorus and then Newton's astonishing solo, resplendent with collapsing cadences and forthright melody before Bechet enters swooping and moaning and the ensemble takes out the theme with a proud assertiveness. Black America never to be turned back.

Pastures Groovy

As Michael Denning shows in his illuminating study of the era, *The Cultural Front*, the stage success of *Pins and Needles*, a hugely popular musical revue which opened in the New York auditorium of the International Ladies Garment Workers Union (ILGWU) in November 1937, was part of the inspiration that Ellington needed to forward his own musical revue, eventually titled *Jump for Joy*. The ILGWU had sponsored *Pins and*

Needles, which combined satire and romance, sometimes through ambivalent lyrics, paralleling human relations with factory and labour relations. The stage venue for *Jump for Joy* was to be not in New York, but in the metropolis of the Californian coast, Los Angeles, where Ellington collaborated with a group of Popular Front Hollywood writers. The fifteen writers, as Ellington describes in *Music Is My Mistress*

> decided to attempt to correct the race situation in the USA through a form of theatrical propaganda . . . a show that would take Uncle Tom out of the theatre, eliminate the stereotyped image that had been exploited by Hollywood and Broadway, and say things that would make the audience think.

This intention was, of course, worlds away from the 'black' revues of the twenties staged in both Harlem and on Broadway such as *Chocolate Dandies*, Fats Waller's *Hot Chocolates*, Eubie Blake's *Shuffle Along* or Ellington's own *The Chocolate Kiddies*, with their repeated scenes of southern plantations and characters drawn as black caricatures. By 1941, Ellington was determined to confront and write a riposte to such theatre which he now saw as a curse on black Americans. As he pointed out to the *People's World*:

> There was the first and greatest problem of trying to give an American audience entertainment without compromising the dignity of the negro people. Needless to say, this is a problem that every negro artist faces. He runs afoul of offensive stereotypes, instilled in the American mind by whole centuries of ridicule and derogation. The American audience has been taught to expect a negro on stage to clown and 'Uncle Tom', that is to enact the role of a servile, yet lovable, inferior.

By the time of *Jump for Joy*, Ellington's directness now knew no codes, either in his commentary or his music. 'The negro is the creative force of America,' he declared during his 1941 Lincoln Day Speech: 'we fought America's wars, provided her labor, gave her music, kept alive her flickering conscience, prodded her on towards the yet unachieved goal, democracy.'

And the title song, played by the full Ellington orchestra, and recorded in two versions, in Hollywood on July 2 1941, with two very different singers, firstly Herb Jeffries and secondly Ivie Anderson, carried the message joyously:

> Fare thee well, land of cotton
> Cotton lisle out of style, honey child
> Jump for joy.
> Don't you grieve, little Eve
> All the hounds I do believe
> Have been killed, ain't you thrilled
> Jump for joy.
>
> Have you seen pastures groovy?
> Green pastures was just a technicolor movie.
>
> When you stomp up to heaven
> And you meet old St Pete, tell that boy
> Jump for joy!
> Step right in, give Pete some skin
> And jump for joy!

In both cuts, Nanton carries the theme, muted above Carney's baritone undertow. Jeffries' crooning, unemotive vocal in the first is easily overcome by Ivie Anderson's joyous, buoyant delivery of the lyrics in the second. And then it is Hodges, until the ensemble, raucous and festive, take it out, dancing across their 'pastures groovy'.

The other triumph of *Jump for Joy* was Anderson and the orchestra performing the ballad 'I Got It Bad and That Ain't

Good'. This is, in essence, a romantic love song sung by a heartbroken, mistreated woman about her lover. She is alone and full of the blues, singing out her choruses in sadness and forlorn words:

> Never treats me sweet and gentle
> The way he should,
> I got it bad and that ain't good

or

> He don't love me like I love him,
> Nobody could

and later

> Like a lonely weeping willow
> Lost in the wood,
> I got it bad and that ain't good.

Anderson sings the words with restraint and powerful lamentation – and as a perfect complement to Hodges' swooping alto with Ellington's background tinkling on the celeste. Strangely, the song went beyond the orbit of romance and person-to-person love and was accepted as one of the most political messages of its era, with its lovesick title becoming a slogan and rallying cry, a statement of oppression and pain whilst refusing simply to agonise but also asserting itself to criticise – 'that ain't good'. The defiance is also implicit, as is the protest – jumping in joy but also in anger and wilfulness.

On October 28 1940, Ellington recorded his 'Across the Track Blues' in Chicago. It is a dramatic and continually astonishing performance, only curtailed by the three minutes or so that a ten-inch 78 rpm disc allowed. You want it to go on and on and on. It predates 'Jump for Joy' but it also, through its title and theme melody, gave a message about the American racial divide. The voice was coming clearly, brilliantly and relentlessly from those across the tracks, singing out through the instruments of Ellington's men. First there is the blues-laden introduction by the leader himself, then Bigard playing in the lower register, followed by a characteristic Stewart chorus, recollecting his sound on 'Mobile Bay' or 'Poor Bubber'. Then in comes the whole reed section – Bigard, Hodges, Carney, Webster and Hardwick. Then the creamy trombone slides of Lawrence Brown prelude more whirling Bigard with the trumpets riffing behind him, a phrase from Ellington's piano and that is the end. 'Across the Track Blues' – a peerless recording, and one with a prevailing message to last right into the Civil Rights struggles in Birmingham, Atlanta, Selma and Albany some decade and a half hence.

Deep South Suite

On November 23 1946 at a Carnegie Hall concert in New York, the Ellington Orchestra performed his *Deep South Suite*, which was later issued as a series of V-Discs, commemorating the end of the war. The same suite had also been performed and recorded two weeks before at a concert at the Civic Opera House in Chicago, but the recording was not released until 1994, twenty years after Ellington's death. He habitually saved the inaugural performances of his suites for significant occasions. The *Black, Brown and Beige Suite*, musically telling the story of the African-American presence in the USA, had been first performed at the momentous concert in aid of Russian War Relief in 1943, also at the Carnegie Hall.

The unveiling of *Black, Brown and Beige* was an epochal moment in both black history and jazz, with its proud assertion of the black contribution to the Americas. But the *Deep South Suite*, which has had much less attention and consideration by jazz commentators and critics, was an equally crucial musical creation. It was a direct and bitingly satirical criticism of the unreal and frequently mawkish caricatures of that 'Dear Old Southland' that Ellington and his men were pressurised to portray during their many years of work at the Cotton Club.

Now he was openly and artistically rejecting that cartoon of Southern life with its plantation house aura. The British jazz critic, Leonard Feather, made this clear during his recorded comments on the Carnegie Hall concert. He tells the listeners that the opening movement, called 'Magnolias Just Dripping with Molasses', is in effect a lampoon of the South aimed 'to reproduce what might be called the Dixie Chamber of Commerce dream picture of the South, with beautiful blue skies, Creole gals with flashing eyes, fried chicken, watermelons and all those good old nostalgic memories' that also scorned the real lives of all black Southerners.

As for the second movement, the sombre 'Hearsay', it ironically suggested the truth of Jim Crow, including rampant racist segregation and the horror of lynching. Such things, suggested Feather, 'were not at all in accordance with the Chamber of Commerce dream picture'. The third movement 'There Was Nobody Looking', says Feather, shows how 'many people of different extractions are able to get along in peace and harmony' when there is no 'interference' – a clear antiracist message. The final movement, another Ellington train classic, is the 'Happy-Go-Lucky Local', the story of a southern train whose black fireman 'hums, whistles and plays tunes on the train whistle', saluting everyone he passes 'on his side of the tracks'. It was another biting echo of 'Across the Track Blues'.

In 'Magnolias' the emphasis is on lush ensemble Southern portraiture overplayed for satirical effect, but Ray Nance and Lawrence Brown enjoy clipping brass choruses within the orchestral luxuriance, and Jimmy Hamilton's clarinet spikes its way towards the conclusion. The ominous 'Hearsay' has morose and violent rumorous undercurrents, with trumpeter Shorty Baker's vulnerable thematic line punctuated by Carney's baritone growls until a climactic and possibly tragic crescendo. 'There was Nobody Looking' is all solo Ellington, cockily vibrant and assured, a piano performance of a musical leader at his zenith. 'Happy-Go-Lucky Local' has more strident Ellington with his prodigious bass partner Oscar Pettiford, and sharp and optimistic contributions from Nance, Hamilton and the stratospheric specialist, trumpeter Cat Anderson. Nine years before the murder of Emmett Till, ten years before the Montgomery Bus Boycott, eleven years before the Little Rock confrontation – Ellington laid his prophetic musical marker.

Same Old South

When William Basie found himself stranded in Kansas City in 1927, he must have wondered why he, a northerner travelling southwards, had reversed the pattern of millions of his black compatriots. Basie had been born in Red Bank, New Jersey in 1904 and learned his piano from the stride pianists of New York – in particular from Fats Waller, with whom he played the silent cinema circuit. In K.C. he joined bassist Walter Page's Blue Devils, until the pianist and bandleader Bennie Moten offered him his own piano seat in his Kansas City Orchestra, with which Basie recorded between the years 1929 and 1932. In 1935 Moten died and Basie formed his own band, securing a radio programme which soon became hugely popular. Basie changed his piano style to become more sparse and spacious, and developed a buoyant and swinging rhythm section with Page, high hat cymbal-emphatic drummer Jo Jones and the eternally chinking acoustic rhythm guitar of Freddie Green.

By 1937 the Basie orchestra had achieved its own very original pulse and sound with a combination of musicians from the South and mid-West: Jones was a Chicagoan, altoist Earl Warren and trumpeter Harry Edison were from Ohio, but Green and tenorist Buddy Tate were from the Carolinas, North and South respectively, tenorist Herschel Evans and guitar/trombone man Eddie Durham were Texans, trombonist Dicky Wells was from Tennessee and trumpeter Buck

Clayton was from Kansas. The entirely original sound of tenorist Lester Young was from Woodville, Mississippi. So when the band, under the temporary name of Basie's Bad Boys, played their 'Going to Chicago Blues' during their first Vocalion recording session in New York in February 1939, their diverse migrations told another story. Basie remembers his Fats Waller tutelage, and begins with a chorus on organ, Buck Clayton comes in with some soft trumpet, and Oklahoma man Jimmy Rushing's vocal is restrained and uncharacteristically quiescent, without the whole band behind him. Young blows a clarinet obbligato between Rushing's lines, before trombonist Dan Minor takes over as Rushing sings:

> If you see me comin' raise your window high
> When you see me passing, hang your head and cry.

It's a powerful performance, but the listener thinks, why Chicago? Wasn't this waxed in New York?

So hearing 'Taxi War Dance', with the entire fifteen-piece orchestra including eleven horns, which was recorded a month later, is a different experience entirely. New York's urban sound, clatter and hugeness pound through the performance. This is a city sound, massive and metropolitan, redolent with traffic, confusion, bustle and working class life. A head arrangement, it begins with a Lester Young solo that generates swing and excitement before Dicky Wells picks up the challenge, rousing the horns to a stirring riff before Tate, then Young again and finally Basie – with breaks from Page and Jones – pass to the ensemble to see the taxi fleet home. The performance evokes the real life of New York cabmen and brings to mind accounts written of the 1934 strike of forty thousand of the city's hackies, who, in the words of Joseph North, the editor of the *New Masses*, writing in April 1934: 'abandoned their wheels for the sake of an independent union, and against the straitjacket of a company union . . . and the

New York hackie is a man in whom revolt has been festering for many years.'

North writes about a black cabman from Harlem, originally from Missouri, addressing fellow strikers at a meeting at Germania Hall:

> 'Boys,' he said, 'when you say you're with us, mean it! Mean it from the bottom of your hearts! If you show the boys up in Harlem that you mean what you say, then you're getting the sweetest little bunch of fighters in the world: for them spades driving the Blue and Black taxis up there can do one thing – and that's fight!' The hats began to fly in the air. He gestured for silence. 'And when we fights together, us black and white, man, they ain't nobody can stop us!'

'Taxi War Dance' and all its swing, rhapsody, brilliant solos, musicianship and pyrotechnics, carries the spirit of these words and the new New Yorkers who spoke them in an era when jazz itself signed up to a popular cultural front of struggle and betterment.

And these musicians had not forgotten whence many of them had come – and although Basie's first memories were of the backyard of his old house in Mechanic Street, Red Bank, New Jersey where his father was a caretaker and his mother a laundress, his parents had come north from Chase City, Virginia at the beginning of Basie's century. Basie lent his support to the causes of the Popular Front such as the Scottsboro' Boys, the Spanish republicans and Russian war relief on many occasions. He even preceded Ellington by recording a song on December 13 1940: 'It's the Same Old South', very much in the spirit of 'Jump for Joy', taken from the satirical labour revue *Meet the People* produced by the Front-inspired Hollywood writers of the Hollywood Theater Alliance. Clayton leads in the melody on open horn, with the Count's reed section taking over at the bridge. Then Oklahoma-born big band bluesman Jimmy Rushing swings in with:

It's the same old South
It's a regular children's heaven,
Where they don't start to work till
they're seven
It's the same old South.

It's the same old South
With those old-fashioned get-togethers
'Colonel, pass me the tar and the feathers,'
It's the same old South.

Honey, shut my mouth
Where the bloodhounds that once chased Liza
Chase a poor CIO organiser,
It's the same old South.

I Have Seen Black Hands . . .

'It's the Same Old South' was Basie's crystal clear refutation of the schmaltz-song with southern themes, and a strong identification with the burgeoning cultural movement hand-in-hand with the Popular Front. The impresario and record producer John Hammond, who had brought Basie back to New York in 1936 and who organised the epochal *Spirituals to Swing* concerts at Carnegie Hall in 1938, sponsored by the Popular Front journal *New Masses*, was a cultural dynamo. It was he who set up the session which combined Basie with Paul Robeson in New York in October 1941 to record the two parts of 'King Joe'. This was a powerful collaboration of black artistry. The lyrics were written by the foremost black novelist Richard Wright, whose novel *Native Son*, published in 1940, was the first novel by a black writer to be chosen for the Book-of-the-Month Club. Within three weeks of its publication, Wright's harrowingly critical book about a young black man in the South (Wright himself had been born in Natchez, Mississippi in 1908, and after a fatherless and desperate childhood in

Tennessee and Arkansas, he journeyed to Chicago as a nine-teen-year-old) had sold a quarter of a million copies and, after five months, half a million. So here was the greatest swing band in the land accompanying the country's most luminous black singer singing a song with lyrics by a renowned young black novelist about the most famous black man of them all, the World Heavyweight Boxing Champion, Joe Louis.

For Basie, the opportunity to work with Robeson 'was one of the great thrills of my life.' As he told Albert Murray in his autobiography *Good Morning Blues*:

> I was crazy about that guy. He was a great man. He stood for something, and I mean if he was all for something, he would take a stand on it, even if it cost him jobs or even his whole career. And he had a hell of a voice, one of the greatest you ever heard. But the strange thing was that he never had sung the blues.

As for Wright, he had become a member of the Communist Party, and a regular contributor to *New Masses*, which had published his first work, the Whitmanesque poem 'I Have Seen Black Hands', which transferred the vision of the labouring black man from the South to the northern cities, from share-cropping farms and ploughs to factories and their machines:

> I am black and I have seen black hands,
> > millions and millions of them –
> They were tired and awkward and calloused
> > and grimy and covered with hangnails,
> And they were caught in the fast-moving belts
> > of machines and snagged and smashed
> > and crushed,
> And they jerked up and down at the throbbing
> > machines massing taller and taller the
> > heaps of gold in the banks of bosses . . .

Heavyweight boxer Joe Louis knocked out Max Baer, the 'Nordic Menace' on September 24 1935. For Wright in his *New Masses* article of two weeks later, 'Joe Louis Uncovers Dynamite':

> Something had popped loose, all right. And it had come from deep down. Out of the darkness it had leapt from its coil. And nobody could have said just what it was, and nobody wanted to say. Blacks and whites were afraid. But it was a sweet fear, at least for the blacks. It was mingling of fear and fulfilment. Four centuries of oppression, of frustrated hopes, of black bitterness, felt even in the bones of the bewildered young, were rising to the surface . . . From the symbol of Joe's strength they took strength, and in that moment all fear, all obstacles were wiped out, drowned. They stepped out of the mire of hesitation and irresolution and were free! Invincible! A merciless victor over a fallen foe! Yes they had felt all that for a moment . . .

As for the Basie–Robeson performance, it carries an enigmatic power, with the huge voice of Robeson singing the lyrics something akin to a recitation after Buck Clayton's cutting and lyrical opening chorus over a clip-clopping beat with an emphatic walking bassline from Walter Page. Clayton gives out the obbligatoes between the lines before some slides by the trombone section and ensemble riffs after the second verse:

> Black eyed peas and cornbread
> What makes you so strong?
> Cornbread say 'I come
> From where Joe Louis was born.'

> Lord I know a secret
> Swear I'd never tell
> I know what makes ol'Joe
> hook, punch and roll like hell.

They say Joe don't talk much
but he talks all the time.
Now you can look at Joe
but you sure can't read his mind.

Rabbit say to the bee
'what makes your sting so deep?'
Bee say, 'I sting like Joe
and rock 'em all to sleep.'

I been in Cleveland
St Louis and Chicago too
But the best is Harlem
when a Joe Louis fight is through.

Lord, I'd hate to see
Ol' Joe Louis step down,
But I bet a million dollars
no man would wear his crown.

Bullfrog told Boll Weevil
Joe done quit the ring,
Boll Weevil say he ain't gone
And he is still the king.

Two generations after, similar sentiments grew around the
skill and courage of Muhammad Ali, but there was something
even more cohesive and profound, as three of America's most
esteemed black cultural icons wrote, sang and made music
about a fourth, and in doing so created a black unity that
inspired millions. As Wright concluded his *New Masses* essay
on Joe Louis:

Say Comrade, here's the wild river that's got to be harnessed
and directed. Here's that something, that pent-up folk consciousness. Here's a fleeting glimpse of the heart of
the negro, the heart that beats and suffers and hopes – for

freedom. Here's that fluid something that's like iron. Here's the real dynamite that Joe Louis discovered.

Scent of Magnolia

'Café Society Blues' is a July 1942 track with a Count Basie quartet playing a beautifully poised and laconic performance with Page, Jones and Green giving the customary unwavering and swinging support. It has both a hint of boogie-woogie and echoes of Basie's standby, 'One O'Clock Jump'. But its title tells another story, the narrative of the Popular Front taking a cabaret turn, with political satire and small-group jazz as its principal menu. Café Society (Downtown) was the invention of its proprietor, Barney Josephson and the opposite to its Big Apple predecessor, the Cotton Club. Integrated and unostentatious, its content challenged its audience directly, rather than assuaged it with exotic or escapist fantasies, and it regularly hired some of the sharpest and most highly-conscious, as well as most technically skilled, jazz musicians. The bartenders were veterans of the Abraham Lincoln brigade – Spanish Civil War internationalists; there was 'no girlie line, no smutty gags, no Uncle Tom comedy' and black and white customers relaxed within an ambiance of equal dignity. Café Society (Uptown) opened in October 1940, and the two venues employed not only some of the most brilliant female jazz artistes – including singers Billie Holiday, Sarah Vaughan, Helen Humes and Lena Horne, but also the versatile and audacious pianist who played just about every genre of jazz throughout her life, Mary Lou Williams. Other Café Society regulars were the so-called 'Marxist Mozart' of jazz, Teddy Wilson, who led so many of Holiday's brilliant late-thirties sessions and trumpeter Frankie Newton, with his reputation of being a radical socialist intellectual, as well as an outstanding jazz musician.

In 1939 Billie Holiday was shown some lyrics written by the Bronx English teacher, poet, composer and communist Abel

Meeropol, whose pen name was 'Lewis Allan'. He and his wife Anne were later to adopt the orphaned children of Julius and Ethel Rosenberg after their execution by the US government in June 1953 for alleged 'conspiracy with the aim of espionage'. The song was called 'Strange Fruit' and its subject was lynching, one of the most dedicated causes of the Popular Front. (It was estimated, conservatively, by the Tuskegee Institute, that some 3,833 people were lynched, mostly black southerners, between 1889 and 1940). Its lyrics centred around a single stark metaphor:

> Southern trees bear a strange fruit,
> Blood on the leaves and blood at the root,
> Black body swinging in the Southern breeze,
> Strange fruit hanging from the poplar trees.
>
> Pastoral scene of the gallant South.
> The bulging eyes and the twisted mouth
> Scent of magnolia sweet and fresh,
> And the sudden smell of burning flesh.
>
> Here is a fruit for the crows to pluck,
> For the rain to gather, for the wind to suck,
> For the sun to rot, for the tree to drop,
> Here is a strange and bitter crop.

It was in the Greenwich Village Café Society that Holiday first sang 'Strange Fruit', burning the consciousness of all who heard it. No mainline recording company dared to put it on disc, particularly Columbia, for whom she was recording at the time. It was left to Milt Gabler, who owned the small and struggling label, Commodore Records, and who sold his records from his legendary Manhattan record shop, to wax Holiday's two agonising renditions, accompanied by Newton's resident Café Society band. Newton's notes, harrowingly pitched, hauntingly poised, are followed by a phrase of Sonny

White's piano, creating such awesome expectation, before Billie begins to sing. 'She didn't like to sing it because it hurt her so much,' said drummer Lee Young, brother of Lester, Holiday's great friend, 'and she would cry every time she would do it.' Once when she performed 'Strange Fruit' at the Apollo Theatre in Harlem, which she did several times to large majority-black audiences, the theatre owner, Jack Schiffman wrote: 'When she wrenched the final words from her lips, there was not a soul in the audience, black or white, who did not feel half-strangled.'

As we listen to it even now, in England, through the years of Stephen Lawrence, Ricky Reel, Michael Menson or Anthony Walker and those who are still lynched by racism in our own times in our own green and pleasant land, we cannot hear Billie Holiday's vocal as cultural history or a sound of a bygone jazz era. We see the stunted branches of racist murder around us still.

3

now's the time

In December 1944 the most innovative and luminous individual voice of the startling pre-war Count Basie Orchestra was released from Fort Gordon detention barracks in the segregated confines of Georgia, and given a dishonourable discharge from the US Army. It seemed like a transitional moment in the history of jazz.

39729502 Private Lester 'Prez' Young was, of course, anything but soldier material and soon after joining the army he had found himself under the command of a white major from Louisiana who had shown great interest in a photograph he had seen of Young's white wife. Prez was thirty-four years old, suffered from alcoholism, syphilis and drug dependency, and three months after drafting he was designated for 'minor rectal surgery'. Arrest for possession of marijuana and barbiturates followed, which resulted in court martial and a ten months sentence, surrounded by racist armed guards.

As Young tried to make sense of the unnerving experiences of his previous year, the bebop jazz movement was carrying all before it in New York, led primarily by the scintillating horns of Charlie Parker and Dizzy Gillespie. But in October 1945 Prez entered a Los Angeles studio with a group that included two other Basie veterans – trombonist Vic Dickenson and guitarist Freddie Green, bassist Red Callendar who had played with Prez in 1942 and nineteen-year-old West Coast piano bopper Dodo Marmorosa. They recorded for the first time the astonishing 'D. B. Blues' (Detention Barrack Blues). More than anything, Lester's saxophone is singing out against US militarism – which was to haunt Americans for the next five post-war decades, and into the new millennium too. Its sound became a vital signal to the lighter, more buoyant and 'cooler' sound of the tenor – as distinct from the fuller, deeper and more soulfully combustive sound of Lester's two contemporary saxophone geniuses, Coleman Hawkins and Ben Webster.

Thus 'D. B. Blues' had a strong impact on the changes that were to fire through jazz musicianship during the oncoming years. But a tune that was deliberately named by its creator to signal the deformed military authoritarianism and racism that he had endured at Fort Gordon was also an omen of the cosmic role that US military aggression would play over the next sixty years. From Korea to Cuba to Guatemala to Vietnam to Chile to Nicaragua, to Panama, Grenada, Afghanistan, Haiti and Iraq the 'D. B. Blues' would have its echoes. Henry Tucker's cymbal-emphatic rhythm introduces Lester's opening solo, floating mesmerically above the beat: Dickenson comes in with his characteristic gruffy wit and directness, before Marmorosa teases with a boppish chorus. Lester returns, riffing on the theme and forging a question-answer dialogue with Dickenson, almost as if he is at last finding replies, one by one, to the humiliating and demeaning questions that he faced during his court martial.

Parker's Moment

In his book *Quintet of the Year*, the English jazz writer Geoffrey Haydon describes a trip that he took in the 1980s with the great jazz drummer Max Roach to the bop pioneer's boyhood home in Dismal Swamp, North Carolina. He tells how they entered a local motel, to be 'met by a wall of white staring faces' and a spokesman who announced to Haydon: 'we don't like your friend and we don't want people like that coming here.' He quotes Roach's words: 'We have proved we're masters of our instruments. Now we have to employ our skill to tell the story of our people and what we've been through.'

Haydon also quotes the white saxophonist Davey Schildkraut's story of Roach's fellow bop inventor Charlie Parker waiting in a car park while the Stan Kenton band, with whom he was appearing in a tour of the South, stopped at a whites-only restaurant: 'Bird had to wait in the bus while the rest of us were wolfing down steaks . . . I brought him out a big steak sandwich and he grumbled: "what, are you trying to be good to me?"'

And this was the greatest jazz genius of his era, possibly any era, speaking. No wonder then, as Roach told Haydon, that when Parker renamed a familiar blues riff (sometimes called 'The Hucklebuck') 'Now's the Time' in 1945, Bird was saying 'now is the time for black Americans to claim their rightful inheritance,' and was thus directly anticipating the Civil Rights' struggle of the following decade.

In the same book, Dizzy Gillespie, Parker's fellow soul-mate of bop, told Haydon about an incident of 1933 in Cheraw, South Carolina, when the trumpeter was sixteen and playing in his first band. Haydon writes:

> What happened next was horrific but not unprecedented. The band's trombonist was kidnapped by white vigilantes who claimed he had been peeping into a white person's home. His body was not found. 'Our band never sounded the same again, but it made us want to improve ourselves so we could get the hell out of Cheraw.'

So when Parker blows in for his blues-based choruses on the two versions of 'Now's the Time', recorded by Savoy in November 1945 – a month or so after Lester Young's

'D. B. Blues' – it is an annunciation, as Roach said it was. There are two brief scuffed and aborted versions, with the musicians hardly getting into the groove before the real message begins. Bud Powell chimes out a brief piano intro, bassist Curly Russell has a few lone bass notes, the two horns lock together for the theme, and then it is all Parker. On both complete takes his blues statement seems like a testimony and prophecy fused together in the glory of his phrases, curling and twisting in felicitous patterns. Miles Davis' trumpet solo seems restrained and tethered after Parker – in other circumstances it might seem stronger. Russell's walking bass ushers in the theme again, with both horns in harmony. On the second take Roach is stronger, dropping his bombs and Bud Powell's piano comping is louder but, again, Parker seems irrepressible, auguring an era, a time beginning 'now', when his people will expose and challenge everything in America which demeans them. And they will use their music, and in particular jazz, their most powerful and beautiful genre of music, to make their case and form their protest, and in doing so make it the prime artistic narrative of their real and struggling lives. In that way, now was the time!

Dizzy and Jazz Internationalism

The lifelong achievement of John Birks 'Dizzy' Gillespie in jazz was not only as co-inventor of bebop and disseminator of its sounds and techniques and as an astonishing stratospheric trumpeter who soared to high note virtuosity and creative brilliance with instantaneous passion, but as one of the most influential big band leaders in the story of jazz. Bebop began as a small-combo phenomenon: Gillespie made it also the territory of the touring jazz orchestra. And in doing so he incorporated the sound not only of the black music of the USA, but also of the other Americas and the pulse of Africa too. Gillespie had replaced his trumpet idol, Roy Eldridge, in the Teddy Hill orchestra in 1937, and soon befriended Mario Bauzá, the Cuban trumpeter/composer, who recommended him to Cab Calloway. After two years with Calloway and many an after-hours session in New York with Thelonious Monk, Kenny Clarke and Charlie Christian, fellow bop progenitors, in 1944 he was playing with Charlie Parker in the Billy Eckstine Orchestra. By 1945 Gillespie and Parker were blowing together in small combos on 52nd Street, and the sound of bop was staggering the jazz world.

By 1947 Gillespie had tired of Parker's erratic and unpredictable behaviour fuelled by his addiction, and changed the sound of his music by hiring the Cuban percussionist Chano Pozo (born in Havana in 1915) who introduced influences of Cuban folk and religious music into his newly-formed big band, with arrangements by some of jazz's most powerful orchestrators – Tadd Dameron, Gil Fuller and George Russell. Gillespie's band thus became the first incubator of US, Latin and African notes and, as a touring outfit, it was taking these sounds to many new jazz places of the world.

February 1948 found Gillespie's orchestra at the Salle Pleyel in Paris, with musicians such as Benny Bailey on trumpet, Cecil Payne on baritone, pianist John Lewis, drummer Kenny Clarke and Pozo playing his congas. A concert highlight was the 'Afro-Cuban Drum Suite', an adaptation of a previous Gillespie tune 'Cubana Be', but arranged by Russell. It begins with a solo conga fanfare by Pozo, before the trombones enter, pursued by the full ensemble. Gillespie's potent high notes dominate the theme melody before the orchestra recedes and there is a dramatic duet between Dizzy and Pozo. The trumpet climbs, then descends and Gillespie breaks out into scat, responded to by other voices while Pozo drums on. The audience response is massive.

The importance of such performances cannot be underestimated. For not only did they portend huge political movement and challenge from the colonised and subjected peoples of

Africa and Latin America in the three decades to come, they were a voice of freedom to inspire America's own black population in the South and the northern and West Coast cities to their own sustained and determined resistance and claims for their long-denied civil rights.

Significant too was the Gillespie Orchestra rendition of Dizzy's own 'Things to Come' at the Salle Pleyel that same night. Arranged by Fuller, it consists of some hugely forceful ensemble, a searing and soaring Gillespie chorus with power as well as ascendancy, and a finale, which despite the little over three-minute brevity of the performance, breaks into what sounds like an early omen of a free jazz ensemble. In these fortuitously recorded live performances, jazz became truly internationalised, not only as a travelling music which could take its beauty and message anywhere in the world, but also because it could be a music of international support and solidarity, and more so, a music of prophecy and promise. Gillespie truly brought jazz from the restricted space of the US to the open and struggling spaces of the whole world.

Pianos of Fire

But for black jazz musicians locked into US urban ghettos who were held fast within the racist circumscription of their real lives, there was no such apparent access to the wider world and its adulation. Thelonious Monk may have travelled and toured later in his career, but early on, as he struggled to sustain his life in a slum quarter of New York, life was hard and oppressive. His mother Barbara had arrived in New York from Rocky Mount, North Carolina, and became a cleaner, and his father joined them three years later, working as a longshoreman and the caretaker of a theatre boiler. Monk spent his boyhood and most of his subsequent life in the San Juan Hill neighbourhood near the Hudson River, at some distance from Harlem and bordered by the New York Central freight yards. He lived with his mother in a tiny cramped apartment, with a piano squeezed into the kitchen.

Monk was inspired by the early stride pianists (the greatest of whom, James P. Johnson, was a neighbour), but by 1940–43 he was playing regularly with the early bop pioneers at Minton's Playhouse. He joined the Cootie Williams Orchestra in 1944, then became the regular pianist of the tenor saxophone virtuoso, Coleman Hawkins. The Blue Note proprietor Alfred Lion recorded Monk prodigiously in 1947–48, and he was subsequently recognised as a major force in the new music – one of its true geniuses and hierophants.

His true piano soul-mate was Earl Rudolph 'Bud' Powell, born in New York in 1924. Powell, who had also played in the Cootie Williams band between 1942 and 1944, was devoted to Monk and much influenced by his playing. In 1945, in Philadelphia, Powell was badly beaten about the head by the police, apparently while trying to protect Monk from police harassment. Six years on, Monk took the blame for Powell's possession of drugs when New York police raided them while they were in a car parked outside the Monk apartment. His mother was sick inside the apartment and Monk did not want to disturb her by bringing Powell in. Powell was soon transferred to a psychiatric hospital where he was subjected to repeated blows of electroconvulsive 'therapy' and Monk lost his cabaret card which permitted him to play live in New York clubs. His main livelihood was cut from under him on the spot, as he was sentenced to ninety days' imprisonment. Monk was to endure more terrifying police treatment – particularly in Baltimore in 1958, when a racist motel bar attendant refused to give him a glass of water. The barman called the police when Monk protested. He went back to the Bentley car in which he was travelling with a white society friend Pannonica De Koenigswater and saxophonist Charlie Rouse, and when the police arrived they battered his brilliant and creative hands against the driving wheel with their nightsticks.

Such incidents were not uncommon in the lives of urban-based jazz musicians. It was as if the 'southernisation' of the northern cities had also brought much of the southern repressive and racist violence too. Monk and Powell knew this in their consciousnesses and also on their bodies, and understood how important loyalty and solidarity to each other were, being necessary to themselves and an example to other musicians and whole communities. When Monk first recorded 'In Walked Bud' in November 1947 he crystallised that comradeship of jazz and the mutual loyalty of two of the greatest pianists of the music. Monk's playfulness slides down the keys before the ensemble takes up the theme. Then Monk's solo is jaunty, full of humour and wry optimism above Art Blakey's pounding drums, at complete ease with Monk's own piano percussiveness. Trumpeter George Taitt saunters in with a strong burnished solo and Sahib Shihab's buoyant alto keeps up the momentum. The ensemble takes the track home with Blakey's huge drums, full of both the city and the earth.

Monk recorded 'In Walked Bud' many times, with many great confreres. The live recording at the Five Spot venue in New York of late Summer 1957 (which only came to light and was released on CD in 1993) has the pianist partnered by John Coltrane on tenor, with Roy Haynes on drums and bassist Ahmed Abdul-Malik. The recording was made with a portable tape recorder and single microphone, but is still powerfully authentic and full of Monk's invention, angularity and swing, with Coltrane exploring the future pathways which were to send him directly into the vanguard of the music over the next decade.

The same drummer and bassman were on hand for another Five Spot rendition of 'In Walked Bud' in August 1958, but this time with Chicagoan Johnny Griffin on tenor. Griffin was much more obviously a bopper than Coltrane, with an astonishingly rapid-fire technique and, as he runs and hoots through his choruses, with his frequent prodigious spurts and sprints and low, guttural grunts, he is absolutely at one with Monk, who obligingly lays out when Griffin's virtuosity takes over the performance. When Monk returns he is as inspired and resourceful as ever, prefacing moments of solo fire from Abdul-Malik and Haynes. Ironically, this track precedes a short solo by Monk of 'Just a Gigolo', full of tripping irony and unsuspecting corners, bringing back to mind Armstrong's coded 1930 recording.

Finally the last track on Monk's 1967–68 *Underground* album, with the renowned sleeve photograph of Monk as guerrilla-pianist with a machine gun strapped to his side, surrounded with grenades, field telephone, pistols, dynamite and detonator and a tied-up Nazi officer behind him, is a quartet version of 'In Walked Bud'. Monk's band for this recording consisted of saxophonist Charlie Rouse, vocalist Jon Hendricks, Ben Riley on drums and bassist Larry Gales. Bud had died in July 1966, more than a year and a half before this recording and so Jon Hendricks' vocal, made up on the spot, partly with lyrics, part-ly scat, had a special significance as it evoked some of bop's essential originators, including Gillespie, ex-Ellingtonian bassist Oscar Pettiford and Blakey:

> Dizzy he was screaming,
> Next to O. P. who was beaming
> Art was thumping,
> Suddenly, then in walked Bud
> And then they got into something!

Monk's appreciation for Powell's piano genius was anything but one-sided. In 1961 while in Paris, Bud cut an album totally devoted to his old mentor's compositions: *A Portrait of Thelonious*, with French bassist Pierre Michelot, and bop drum-mer Kenny Clarke, who had settled in Paris. The trio's per-formance of 'Thelonious' rings like a musical comrade's riposte to 'In Walked Bud'. The crisp rhythm forged by Clarke and the empathetic Michelot underpin Powell's spinning, inventive phrases, and give new meaning to the question–answer theme of the melody: two pianists in colloquy.

Powell's bop urbanism is all through his music – take for example, 'Jump City', recorded in New York in 1956. Its clipped creative lines and hustle suggest city streets and metropolitan movement, with Art Taylor's drums and George Duvivier's bass striding next to him. Yet the very next track of the session (on the Bluebird album *Time Was*) is an emotive evocation of the memory of Bessie Smith, 'Blues for Bessie'. It is a reminder of the previous generation and their rural struggles, but it is much more. Powell's keyboard statements seem to bring the Empress of the Blues into the bop repertoire, acknowledging her pain as his pain too, making a consciousness of the southern past an essential motif of the urban present in every American city.

Max Insists

The greatest early bop drummer was Max Roach, born in Newland, North Carolina in 1924. With drums contemporary Kenny Clarke, he transformed the sound and meaning of jazz drums, changing the base rhythm from the bass drum to the ride cymbal, offering the drummer much more freedom of sound and intervention. Starting with the drums in gospel bands, he studied at the Manhattan School of Music, and by 1942 he was playing at Minton's Playhouse as the house drummer with Gillespie, Monk and Parker. He had intervals with the big bands of Ellington and Benny Carter before he joined Gillespie in 1943 and began to drum regularly for Parker. He toured with Norman Granz' Jazz at the Philharmonic, drummed at the legendary Toronto Massey Hall concert in 1953 with Powell, Gillespie, Parker and Mingus and formed his quintet, co-led with trumpeter Clifford Brown and with pianist Richie Powell (brother of Bud) and tenorists Harold

Land and, later, Sonny Rollins. Following the terrible loss of Brown and Powell in 1956 through a car accident, Roach, in collaboration with the prodigious bassman Charles Mingus, started a record label which they called Debut Records. But it was for another small and radical label, the jazz journalist Nat Hentoff's Candid label, that Roach and a group of prestigious colleagues recorded *We Insist! The Freedom Now Suite*, in August and September 1960.

By this time, the Civil Rights struggle in the South was reaching its apogee. The Montgomery Bus Boycott of 1955–56 and the formation of the Southern Christian Leadership Conference (SCLC) in 1960 had given strong impetus to the movement, and the album's sleevenotes make pointed references to the sit-ins being organised by black students in Greensboro, North Carolina, in February 1960. The sleeve photograph shows a group of black customers in the process of desegregating a Jim Crow luncheon counter. The spirit of the album is epitomised by the quotation from A. Philip Randolph, the leader of the Sleeping Car Porters Union, which precedes Hentoff's sleeve essay:

> A revolution is unfurling – America's unfinished revolution. It is unfurling in lunch counters, buses, libraries and schools – wherever the dignity and potential of men are denied. Youth and idealism are unfurling. Masses of negroes are marching onto the stage of history and demanding their freedom now!

Now was the time, the moment – and Roach's album caught that moment with a group of musicians, both young and veteran, who combined virtually the entire history of jazz in their sounds.

The first two tracks are 'Driva' Man' and 'Freedom Day', collaborations between Roach and the lyricist Oscar Brown Jr., who in his life had combined acting, writing musicals, newscasting and working for the Packinghouse Workers Union in Chicago. The protagonist in 'Driva' Man' is an overseer of slaves, drawn from the poor white communities of the southern states, the daily scourge of the black fieldworkers. After a brief rattle of tambourine, Abbey Lincoln, the Chicago-born vocalist, grimaces her voice through Brown's words:

> Driva man he made a life
> But the mammy ain't his wife,
> Choppin' cotton, don't be slow
> Better finish out your row,
> Keep a movin' with that plough
> Driva man'll show you how!
> Git to work and root that stump
> Driva man'll make you jump,
> Better make your hammer ring
> Driva man will start to swing.
> Driva man a cannibal
> Ride a man and lead a horse,
> When his cat-o-nine-tail flies
> You'd be happy just to die,
> Run away and you'll be found
> By his big old red-boned hound,
> Paddy-roller bring you back
> Make you sorry that you're black,
> Ain't but two things on your mind –
> Driva Man and quittin' time.

Then with an ensemble of horns and drums behind him, Coleman Hawkins enters – the great virtuoso of the tenor saxophone, fifty-six years old from St. Joseph, Missouri, with his huge rumbling engine of sound. As he powers out his chorus, he falters on a note. 'No, don't splice it!' he protested to Roach when the drummer offered to cut it out. 'When it's all perfect, especially in a piece like this, there's something very wrong.' And this was how the acknowledged nonpareil of the tenor saxophone – whose performing and recording career stretched back to the twenties and sessions with Louis Armstrong, Spencer Williams, Bessie and Clara Smith and Clarence Williams, wanted real sounds over artifice, truth over cosmetics, the authentic voice, mistakes and all. And in a New York metropolitan penthouse recording studio he plays a long solo of the earth, stretching back to the southern land covered in the blood of slaves, while Roach, the prophet of bop drums, hits the rimshots behind his notes, simulating a hammer. The words, the sounds mesh. There were no coded lyrics here, no merely implicit or hinted messages. The music is controlled by its makers, and its defiance is not only formidable and supremely audible; its jazz medium is solid and palpable, forging a challenge in every sense.

'Freedom Day' brings on the more youthful musical brains and imaginations of second generation boppers, like the twenty-two-year-old Memphis-born trumpeter Booker Little – a member of Roach's permanent group, the undersung tenorist Walter Benton and Chicagoan trombonist Julian Priester, only twenty-five at the time, part of a musical generation that would soon move on to break the boundaries of all the jazz that came before, as the movement they were proclaiming was breaking the moulds of centuries of pain and injustice.

'Freedom Day' begins with a tinkling Roach cymbal, then fanfare-like the ensemble introduces lyrics which reprise the elation and spirit of 'Jump for Joy' of two decades before but now brought to 1960, Civil Rights and the heat and struggle of the voter registration campaign in the South. Lincoln sprints into the vocal:

> Whispers listen! Whispers listen!
> Whispers say we're free
> Rumours flying, must be lying
> Can it really be?
> Can't conceive it, can't believe it
> But that's what they say.
> They no longer say no longer

This is Freedom Day!
Freedom Day, it's Freedom Day
Throw those shackling chains away,
Everybody that I see
Says it's really true we're free.
Freedom Day, it's Freedom Day,
Free to vote and earn my pay . . .
But we've made it, Freedom Day.

Immediately, there is a superb dancing solo by Little, with a speeding Roach beside him, crashing into his snares. Benton flies too with Little and Priester riffing behind him before the agile trombonist's quicksilver slides glide him through a rampaging solo, and then Roach takes over before Lincoln repeats the lyrics, even faster.

In *We Insist!* Roach, Lincoln and their confreres moved beyond the USA in their praise songs to freedom. Hentoff described 'Prayer', a duet between Roach's drums and Lincoln's lyric-less voice as a 'cry of an oppressed people, any and all oppressed peoples of whatever color or combination of colors', and it led directly onto the final two tracks which embraced the struggles of African people. For these, Roach featured the Nigerian drummer, Michael (Babatunde) Olatunji who, in 'All Africa', responds to Lincoln's calling of the names of African nations. He answers by his national Apesi drumming and by shouting back proverbial sayings involving freedom in his own Yoruba language. 'Tears for Johannesburg' puts the focus on the South African people and their struggle against the Apartheid system, gradually institutionalised by the Nationalist government after its empowerment by an all-white, minority electorate in 1948. 'The native in our urban areas,' declared an election document, 'must be regarded as a "visitor" who will never be entitled to any political rights or to equal social rights with the white.' Roach was laying bare the proximity of the struggle of his own people and those in South

Africa, particularly in the year of the massacre at the 'model' township of Sharpeville, when the 700 police opened fire on a peaceful demonstration of Africans protesting against the Pass Laws. Sixty-nine people were killed and 180 injured, with the majority of casualties shot in the back. James Schenk's bass accompanies Lincoln's opening lamentation. Roach and the ensemble of horns enter, followed by Little, playing in his burnished tone with Olatunji, Roach and Afro-Cuban percussionists Ray Mantilla and Thomas Du Vall throbbing behind him. Then Benton's solo, probing and serpentine. Priester's contribution seems sage, like a griot's story told alongside the drum commentary and solidarity of two connected continents.

The achievement of *We Insist!* was extended over a number of subsequent albums. In August 1961 came Roach's first Impulse recording, *Percussion Bitter Sweet*, which included Little and Priester again, but with tenorist Clifford Jordan and Eric Dolphy on flute, alto and bass clarinet. Mal Waldron was on piano and the virtuoso bassist Art Davis did much more than keep time. Two more Afro-Cuban drummers, Carlos 'Potato' Valdez and Carlos 'Totico' Eugenio expanded the rhythmic foundation. The first selection, 'Garvey's Ghost', saluted the man who organised 'hundreds of thousands of black people all over the world' – the scope of the percussion emphasises his role among black Americans, those in Latin America and his 'dreams and ambitions currently reaching fruition in the new independent nations of Africa'. The second track, 'Mama', 'is dedicated to the women who work, fight and suffer along with men,' and thematically connects with the blues anthems of Bessie and Clara Smith. But 'Mama' is more like a fast campaigning march than a blues and, in his sleeve comments, Roach makes it clear – as do the powerful, forwarding solos of Priester, Jordan and Little, that 'this piece does not look at women in the romantic sense, but rather as strong, self-sufficient human beings who take an active part in world problems'. The spirits of Rosa Parks and thousands of other struggling women in the Americas and Africa are strongly evoked.

Dolphy's solo flute dominates 'Tender Warriors', a tribute to the Civil Rights youth, those demonstrators, sit-in campaigners, bus boycotters and freedom riders at the heart of the movement, resisting the bullets, power-hoses and nightsticks of the southern police. Mal Waldron's own percussive piano strikes a parallel road with Roach's own drumming before Little enters with a memorable cadence of ringing notes. Dolphy breaks the idealism with his gurgling bass clarinet before Roach lets loose and Dolphy brings back the theme on his flute, completing a moving musical essay of hope and commitment.

Abbey Lincoln returns for 'Mendacity', after an opening statement by Little, bending his notes as in an omen:

> Mendacity, mendacity
> It makes the world go round,
> A politician makes a speech
> And never hears the sound.
> The campaign trail winds on and on
> In towns from coast to coast,
> The winner ain't the one who's straight
> But he who lies the most.
> Now voting rights in this fair land
> We know are not denied,
> But if I tried in certain states
> From tree tops I'd be tied.
> Mendacity, mendacity
> It seems is everywhere,
> But try to tell the truth
> And most folks scream 'Not Fair!'

Dolphy's thematic alto solo suggests lying and falsehood as it winds up, down, beyond and above Davis' plunging bass with some of the astonishing reed phraseology he was to develop in free jazz contexts in the decade to come. Then Roach solos, his drum statements close to emphases and spaces in the lyrics, his inventive strikes and unsuspecting blows finding connections to Lincoln's theme. This is jazz delivering a vibrant and telling critique of the political system of its birthplace. Daring and unambiguous, it resounded with its listeners, and others all over the world. In connection with South Africa again, for example, for the finale of his album *Percussion Bitter Sweet* is Roach's own 'Man from South Africa', written, as the sleevenote explains, to 'express the anxiety, frustration and conflict involved in the struggle for independence by the indigenous South African man.' Waldron, Davis and Roach keep up a lively forward beat while the horns come in, devising their own sound pictures of the life of this South African, with Dolphy in particular stretching and empathising his alto and his imagination across an ocean.

1962 brought *Speak, Brother, Speak!*, a quartet live album recorded at the Jazz Workshop in San Francisco with just two long tracks – and Roach, Jordan, Waldron and bassist Eddie Khan. In his sleevenotes Roach declared that

> the music in this album was created to mirror the street rallies and meetings that exist today in the ghetto areas of the large cities in the USA, such as the Fillmore district in San Francisco, the South Side of Chicago, and Harlem in New York, to mention a few. At these street rallies, or meetings, the people of all walks of life have an opportunity to express themselves vocally, on their impressions of the state of the nation as related to themselves, culturally, socially, economically and politically.

In the twenty-five-minute title performance, the members of the quartet all express themselves with brilliance and at considerable length, replacing the previous theme of government mendacity with one of people's democracy – epitomised in the close jazz comradeship and dialogue of 'Speak, Brother, Speak!'

Roach's predilection for combining jazz musicians with choirs was evident in 1962 on his second Impulse album, *It's Time*, and also to moving social and political effect on his 1971 recording with the J. C. White singers, *Lift Every Voice and Sing*. In adopting the name of the 'black national anthem' for his album, Roach dived deep into his people's cultural history. The dedication of each of the six spirituals that compose it to his own personal heroes of black struggle, gave a message of jazz as integral to the black American narrative. 'Motherless Child', with a searing Billy Harper tenor solo against a full choir, is dedicated to Garvey. 'Garden of Prayer' is a brief but moving salutation to his own parents, with White taking a solo vocal and George Cables accompanying him on electric piano. Roach's drums sound huge against the choir in 'Troubled Waters', dedicated to Paul Robeson. It is continually amazing how often Robeson's massive influence arises within the history of jazz, despite him not being a jazz musician. Roach himself remembered a 1952 benefit concert for the imprisoned black communist militant Benjamin Davis, in which Robeson gave a solo performance in the presence of hundreds of people, including Charlie Parker. As he told Geoffrey Haydon:

> The government had put a gag on him. And he said, 'You know I'm not supposed to talk to you folks tonight.' Then he sung workers' and freedom songs in every language you can imagine: Chinese, French, Russian. When he sang an old spiritual called 'Water Boy', Charlie Parker walked on the stage with a pitcher of water and a glass! These are the things you remember.

Trumpeter Cecil Bridgewater's piercing notes are at the centre of 'Let My People Go', in tribute to the Congolese patriot and president, and founder of the Movement National Congolais, Patrice Lumumba, murdered in Katanga with Belgian connivance in January 1961. Roach's recording looks back to Rex Stewart's 'Menelik' and forward to Africanist

Randy Weston and to the huge African contributions to jazz of Abdullah Ibrahim, Johnny Dyani, Chris McGregor and Louis Moholo in the decades to come. And the performance of 'Were You There When They Crucified My Lord' is a homage to three martyrs of the black American struggle – Malcolm X, Medgar Evers, Martin Luther King 'and many more', sung as another solo by White accompanied by Cables.

Uhuru Africa

Roach continued through a burning jazz lifetime to suffuse all his music with resistance and radicalism, and his preoccupation with African freedom – and African musicianship, was mirrored in the piano and orchestral gifts of Randy Weston, born in Brooklyn in 1926. Weston was a devotee of Thelonious Monk, learned from him, befriended him and sought to fuse Monk's angularities and stride foundations with his own concepts of African music mixed up with bop, gospel, the blues and Caribbean themes. He made a series of quartet and trio albums, before turning to his *Uhuru Africa* project in 1960, which was among the first sustained journeys into the authentic sounds of African music. The illuminating liner notes of the album by one of the great black poets of America, Langston Hughes, clarify the transoceanic relationship, in this way: 'To the African drum beat have been added Birmingham breaks, Harlem riffs, and Birdland trimmings. The basic beat of jazz which began in Africa, thence transplanted to the New World, has now come back home bringing with it most of the contemporary American additions – from blues to post-bop.'

Like Roach's *We Insist!*, Weston's *Uhuru Africa* was issued in 1960, a time when anti-colonialism in the continent was at a zenith. Ghana had achieved independence from Britain with Kwame Nkrumah in 1957, Nigeria followed in 1960 with a large group of ex-French-controlled nations and Zaire. Many more British and French colonies were to gain their independence in the ensuing years. The majority of the new regimes pursued neo-colonial policies, but the urge for freedom had been awakened. Thus *Uhuru Africa* came during an epoch when Africa was rousing and redolent with ideas of freedom and different versions of socialism. In the introduction to the opening movement, Antonio Candido opens the drumming with a Kiswahili call for Uhuru (Freedom) and Tuntemeke Sanga of Tanganyika, chants:

> Africa, where the great Congo flows
> Africa, where the whole jungle knows
> A new dawning breaks, Africa.
> The freedom wind blows!
> Out of yesterday's night Uhuru –
> Freedom! Uhuru! Freedom!

As Hughes emphasises, 'always in African music is that basic beat stemming from percussion, that highly syncopated beat that gives jazz its distinct quality.' And providing it in Weston's big band are not only Roach, Olatunji and two more jazz drummers, G. T. Hogan and the big band specialist Charlie Persip, but also Cuban drummers – Candido and Armando Peraza on congas and bongos respectively. Weston had assembled a band of stellar soloists and ensemble players, whereby every name was an outstanding jazz voice. But it is the huge sound of the aggregated drummers which carries the music. Weston enters, pounding his own piano like a drum as the ensemble blows strong behind him in whirling riffs. Two basses, played by Ron Carter and George Duvivier, add to the rhythmic undertow, as the roar of four great trumpeters – Clark Terry, Freddie Hubbard, Benny Bailey and Richard Williams heaps on the sound until it recedes, leaving the basses still plucking and sawing. The next movement, 'Sunrise at Dawn', features the song 'African Lady', while two flutes played by Yusef Lateef and Les Spann flutter around the lyrics. Cecil Payne's rocking baritone enters, swinging insurgently.

The third movement, entitled 'Bantu', features Julius Watkins' French horn in a short opening statement, then some solo Weston before the rhythm and percussion erupt. Olatunji plays the indigenous thumb piano, then the Nigerian gourd-drum, the shekere. Williams blasts out on open horn, conversing with some typical witty and flamboyant Clark Terry flugel-horn. The huge ensemble sound comes back in a colloquy with the unified drum explosion, then gradually fades out.

The final movement is called 'Kucheza Blues', but Hughes opines: 'Had I been in charge of naming these sequences, I would have called the final movement "The Birmingham-Bamako Blues" for in this section there are overtones of both Alabama and Africa, Dixie and the Negro Motherland.' A sequence of outstanding solos are played out over the seething percussion. Veteran Budd Johnson's tenor, Bailey's trumpet, Jimmy Cleveland's thrusting trombone, Gigi Gryce's bop-based alto, a muted Hubbard, a throbbing Kenny Burrell guitar solo before the theme returns with Weston finding the spaces to chink in his notes. A remarkable Afro-American – American-Afro musical statement is *Uhuru Africa*, which would be expanded even further in 1963 by Weston's next album *Highlife*, based around the popular Nigerian musical form that he imbibed during a concert tour in 1961. Weston proved himself to be a true American musical pioneer, exploring African authenticity with his own Afro-American perspective at truly crucial moments in both continents' histories, making his musical statement of solidarity with *Uhuru Africa*, when it really mattered.

Mingus' Meditations

In September 1957 Governor Orval Faubus of Arkansas stood in the doorway of Central High School in Little Rock with members of the National Guard to prevent the entry of nine black children. This was his histrionic method of preventing the desegregation of schools in the state to which he had been elected, predominantly by an exclusive white electorate, to govern. The national government, still presided over by war hero Dwight D. Eisenhower, did nothing while Faubus' racist populism was newsreeled worldwide. His blatant action, while the federal government prevaricated, provoked national and world indignation. Louis Armstrong, about to perform in North Dakota, was livid as the television pictures showed frightened black children outside the school, and a white man spitting directly into the face of a black girl student: 'The way they are treating my people in the South,' he exclaimed, 'the government can go to hell! It's getting so bad, a colored man hasn't got any country.' He fulminated against Eisenhower: he had 'no guts', he was 'two faced'; Faubus was 'an uneducated ploughboy', and Armstrong cancelled an international good-will tour. He also declared that he would not perform again in Arkansas, or his home state of Louisiana. He would rather play in Africa (the year before he had toured Ghana, playing to a concert of 100 thousand people in Accra, and befriending Prime Minister Kwame Nkrumah), in the Soviet Union and Europe, he affirmed.

Thus the accursed Faubus symbolised everything vicious, criminal and backward about the South, and one of Armstrong's old bassists, Charles Mingus, used the brilliance of his musical brain to express it. By 1957 Mingus had become the pre-eminent jazz bass virtuoso, as well as a fiercely individ-ualist composer and bandleader. His own lineage, having been born in Nogales, Arizona in 1922 with a mixed-race father and a mother who was half-Chinese and half-black, made him both a frequent target and perennial opponent of American racism, and Faubus' criminal behaviour would never have passed him by. Thus in May 1959 he recorded 'Fables of Faubus' on his *Mingus Ah Um* album, with John Handy, Booker Ervin and Shafi Hadi on saxophones, pianist Horace Parlan, Jimmy Knepper on trombone and his regular drummer, Dannie

Richmond. Mingus had some scathing, lampooning lyrics too, but Columbia Record Company would not countenance them, similar to the way they had refused to record Billie Holiday singing 'Strange Fruit' two decades earlier.

Mingus' composition was a burlesque in sound. The tune suggests a bumbling, clumsy chauvinist, a racist buffoon, with the saxophones in ascendant, veering off each other, then Handy suddenly breaking out into a felicitous solo and introducing the bluesy Parlan to offer some stuttering choruses; then in comes Booker Ervin, swinging hard. Mingus' bass is like a huge hollow tree, resounding with deep, twangy notes until the ungainly caricature of the theme reappears. The sense of mockery and derision attached to the Governor becomes even more apparent in the waxing of the 'Original Faubus Fables', which is a part of Mingus' November 1960 album, *Charles Mingus Presents Charles Mingus*. This was issued on Hentoff's small and radical Candid label, so there was no problem about censoring or excluding the lyrics. Mingus used his Jazz Workshop band, a quartet including himself and Richmond, but also Philadelphia trumpeter Ted Curson, and Dolphy playing alto and bass clarinet. It sounds like a live club recording, but in fact the album was cut in Tommy Nola's Penthouse in New York's Steinway building, with Mingus simulating club announcements and the studio lights turned right down. 'No applause ladies and gentlemen,' he declares, 'keep it down and don't rattle ice in your glasses. And don't ring the cash registers.' Then he reveals that the next composition is dedicated to 'the first, or second or third all-American hero – Faubus!', and begins with a call-and-response shouting duo with Richmond. It is a fictional recreation of Café Society, but the music as well as the parody has moved on:

Oh Lord, don't let them stab us!
Oh Lord, don't them tar and feather us!
Oh Lord, no more swastikas!
Oh Lord, no more Ku Klux Klan!

> *Mingus*: Name me someone who's ridiculous, Dannie
> *Richmond*: Governor Faubus
> *Mingus*: Why is he sick and ridiculous?
> *Richmond*: He won't permit us in the schools.
> *Mingus*: Then he's a fool!

Dolphy bursts in, wailing; Curson soars down the scales, the vocal exchanges are repeated, then Curson, powerful and full of muscle, soaring high, comes in again, quoting from 'Wade in the Water'. Dolphy solos again, in short, howling bursts, his alto pulsating as the pace quickens, slows down, quickens again and 'When Johnny Comes Marching Home' again is discernible through his improvisations. Mingus sounds enormous with Richmond's snares behind. 'Original Faubus Fables' only makes the listener marvel at how jazz would have had a very different, much more explicitly political content if its musicians had not been so continually subject to scrutiny and censorship as well as the excluding pressures of commercialism. The political messages by subtle codings and all the ambiguity of the implicit, could well have become much more open and defiant.

As they were strangely, in Mingus' next Columbia album *Oh Yeah* of November 1961, with his adaptation of the same call-and-response technique of 'Original Faubus Fables' in 'Oh, Lord Don't Let Them Drop that Atomic Bomb on Me'. This is Mingus' commentary about a critical period of Cold War politics beginning from the election of John Kennedy to the White House in November 1960, leading up to the so-called 'Cuban Missile Crisis' of October 1962, which included the destruction of the Cuban arms ship 'Coubre'; the abortive Bay of Pigs assault by Cuban exiles bankrolled by the US government, the sabotage and assassination plots of the CIA and the massive Cuba invasion rehearsal that took place in Vieques Island, adjacent to Puerto Rico in April 1962, personally attended by Kennedy and the Shah of Iran. 'Cuba is the key to all Latin America. If Cuba succeeds, we can expect all of Latin America to fall,' declared the CIA director, John McCone, and the threat of all-out atomic war to prevent the influence of the Cuban Revolution spreading was real and palpable. So Mingus' anti-war anthem touched the spirit and fear of the epoch. Mingus plays piano only on 'Oh Yeah' and he begins 'Oh Lord!' with a bluesy chorus before launching into his spoof, but still passionate, prayer:

> Oh Lord! Don't let them drop that
> atomic bomb on me!
> Oh Lord! Don't let them drop it!
> stop it!
> bebop it!

The main soloist is Mingus' latest tenor saxophone recruit to the Jazz Workshop, Rahsaan Roland Kirk, born in 1936 in Columbus, Ohio, who also played flute, plus manzello and stritch – his own patented reed instruments, frequently blowing three horns at the same time. In 'Oh Lord!' It is only his manzello that we hear in a soulful, sharp-edged solo, full of notes of lamentation and a powerful sadness, before Mingus returns with his eternal plea, 'Don't let them drop it on me!'

Mingus began a residency at Monk's old Greenwich Village haunt, the Five Spot, in January 1964, and this gave him an opportunity to prepare a long piece, which his Jazz Workshop group finally performed at an NAACP (National Association for the Advancement of Colored People) benefit at New York Town Hall. On the recording the piece is called 'Praying with Eric', since Dolphy was shortly to leave the band for Europe, but the true name of the nearly twenty-eight-minute piece is 'Meditation for a Pair of Wire Cutters'. In his introduction to the piece to the Town Hall audience, Mingus said:

> Eric Dolphy explained to me that there was something similar to the concentration camps once in Germany now down

South . . . and the only difference between the electric
barbed wire is that they don't have gas chambers and hot
stoves to cook us in yet. So I wrote a piece called
'Meditations' – as to how to get some wire cutters, before
someone else gets some guns to us.

Mingus had a band of outstanding musicians to play his
composition. The pianist is Jackie Byard from Worcester,
Massachussetts, scholar and virtuoso of virtually every keyboard style from stride to post-bop. Richmond, Jordan and
Dolphy are present along with Johnny Coles, born in 1926 in
Trenton, New Jersey, a bop trumpeter who made a superb Blue
Note album (*Little Johnny C.*) in 1963, played in Duke
Ellington's last orchestra on his final European tour of 1974,
but was tragically under-recorded. Dolphy's flute flutters
above the ensemble theme before he switches to bass clarinet,
his vibrato making the sound shiver. Byard plays a serene,
unaccompanied solo before Mingus enters with bowed bass
and an emotionally-wrought statement of beauty and sadness.
Dolphy returns on flute with his birdsong cutting through the
Town Hall walls, until Byard strikes the piano like a drum, and
the entire group storms in, with sudden changes in time and
speed until Dolphy solos, his bass clarinet bending then level-
ling and Richmond swinging furiously. Byard is reflective until
the pace quickens again and Coles dances his notes, then slows
down with only Mingus behind him. A press roll from
Richmond, and the bass is away again, the notes stinging the
Town Hall air and a few bars of 'Dixie' so as not to veer away
from the theme, and Jordan's tenor enters with Richmond
crashing his snares and the tenorist picking up pace and power
until the theme is re-constituted and Dolphy flies above it
again on flute, his breathy notes gradually settling into peace.

Whether or not it was the insultingly short offer of a mere
twenty-minute slot, or the rampantly political nature of
Mingus' chosen performance numbers, but the bassist and his

octet never played his prepared set in front of the deck chairs at the September 1965 Monterey Jazz Festival in California. Instead, he waited a week until the prospect of a far less conservative venue materialised at the University of Los Angeles and, with the same group of powerful and committed musicians, performed a series of vibrant and topical compositions for an eager, responsive and much younger audience. Perhaps he was remembering the enthusiastic reaction of the students of Cornell University at Ithaca, New York State, in March the previous year, when his sextet, including Dolphy, Byard, Richmond, Johnny Coles and Clifford Jordan, had performed a triumphant set, with the recording only unearthed by Sue Mingus decades later, and finally released by Blue Note in 2007.

Mingus' introductions and occasional commentary on the UCLA recording are full of wit, insistence and turbulence. The opener, 'Meditation on Inner Peace', begins with a haunting bowed bass chorus before the entry of the brass trio of trumpeters Lonnie Hillyer, Hobart Dotson and Jimmy Owens, followed by the wailing alto of Charles McPherson, who, unable to make any rehearsals, had listened to Mingus singing his parts over the telephone. An intriguing duet between Mingus, still with bow in hand, and Julius Watkins' French horn ensues, while Howard Johnson's deep tuba heartbeat thumps relentlessly. Dannie Richmond's drums crash out and Mingus strikes his final chords on piano.

Two abortive attempts to begin 'Once Upon a Time There Was a Holding Corporation Called Old America' result in Mingus dismissing several brassmen in the band, retaining only Hillyer to accompany McPherson in 'Ode to Bird and Dizzy' in a quartet with Mingus and Richmond. Charlie Parker's ghost arises through McPherson's soaring and anguished phrases and Richmond's crackling drums, before Hillyer's deft horn dances into sound.

This concert was taking place eight years before the two

hundred Sioux of the American Indian Movement began their occupation of the village of Wounded Knee in South Dakota where, in 1890, some 146 of their ancestors had been mown down by the Hotchkiss guns of the US 7th Cavalry. So Mingus' composition, 'They Trespass the Land of the Sacred Sioux', was as much prophecy of rebellion as vital jazz. The complete band reassembles, with Jimmy Owens taking the lead and Watkins' horn emulating the signal for the cavalry's brutal advance. The ensemble creates a pained, funereal tableau of sound, full of the history of struggling and bleeding America.

The third time of trying finally achieves 'Once Upon a Time. . .', which is in fact an early version of Mingus' 'The Shoes of the Fisherman's Wife are Some Jive-ass Slippers' included in his 1971 album *Let My Children Hear Music*. The finesse and searing intensity of Hillyer's trumpet are at the tune's centre, together with Mingus' pounding piano. As the heat rises, so does Mingus' voice too, urging on his long-time confrere Richmond and galvanising the full blast of Hillyer's brass power.

> One day they came and they took the communists,
> And I said nothing because I was not a communist . . .

For the final track is Mingus' musical adaptation of Pastor Martin Niemöller's universal anti-fascist poem, which he introduces as 'Don't Let it Happen Here . . . . Please!' He speaks out the uncompromising words stridently, and as Owens blows an intense and climactic solo on his flugelhorn, Mingus calls out to his bandmates, pledging his union with those in 'any land . . . to share the same equal freedoms together'.

Mingus and Prison Narrative

A subject that Mingus was to explore continually in his music, right up until the end of his life, was that of confinement, of prisons, of the manacles and chains of the body and the mind. The sixties, seventies and eighties signalled the degenerate truth of 'Lockdown America'. The growth in repressive government legislation which followed the urban rebellions of the sixties and early seventies, with many black prisoners in US jails taking on a heroic and inspirational status – activists, revolutionaries and Panthers like George Jackson, Bobby Seale, Eldridge Cleaver or those who empathised with them like Angela Davis, was signalled and narrated in Mingus' music. The administrations of Johnson and Nixon had their eyes malignantly set on the urban US communities. 'President Nixon emphasised that you have to face the fact that the whole problem is really the blacks,' wrote the disgraced Watergate presidential aide, H. R. Haldeman. 'The key is to devise a system that recognises this while not appearing to.' So there were to be no more Civil Rights movements, no more Watts or Bedford-Stuyvesants, no more Black Panthers – and a new fusion of police power and surveillance, new laws and their brutal and unequivocal enforcement with massive new resources of incarceration were to be developed over the next three decades. Pioneered by William Bratton, the former commissioner of the New York Police Department and an ex-military policeman in Vietnam, 'zero tolerance' practices became an institutional assault on black communities, the youth and the poor, while the huge increase in prison accommodation and the rapid privatisation of the 'corrections' system meant that, by the end of the twentieth century, there were 1,800,000 people in US prisons and wildly disproportionate numbers of these were black and Latino. The prisons which provoked Mingus' indignation were the direct forerunners of the present mould, there to terrorise the poor and the black, to suspend in the midst of their lives the unambiguous symbols of punishment and retribution for the resistance and disobedience of the dispossessed.

On October 1 1975 Mingus waxed two albums, *Changes One*

and *Changes Two* and on each album there was a track which dug deep into the theme of incarceration. 'Remember Rockefeller at Attica' is a churning performance on the first album that revisits the 1971 Attica Prison rebellion and its merciless suppression ordered by the Governor of New York State, Nelson Rockefeller, one-time Republican presidential contender and one of America's richest men. One thousand three hundred convicts took control of the prison, and for four days they held twelve hostages. To Rockefeller this was deemed as a 'step in an ominous world trend' and he decided that an example must be made. The result was a massacre in which thirty-nine prisoners and nine hostages were killed as prison guards opened fire through the tear gas. For Mingus, who conceived the title in the wake of this slaughter,

> I think I ought to give titles to my music that may make people think. We ought to remember that here was a man who could have cut off the water supply and the food supply and ended the prisoners' rebellion that way. Instead he sent in the army and shot his own men as well as the prisoners. That's the part to remember – that Rockefeller is a very dangerous man.

Mingus had a superb group to perform the *Changes* albums, including Richmond and three younger post-bop prodigies who were to achieve much that was daring and innovative over the next two decades: pianist Don Pullen from Roanoke, Virginia; the growling tenorist, George Adams from Covington, Georgia; and Jack Walrath, a white trumpeter from Montana with a vocalistic tone and edgy crackling sound. 'Remember Rockefeller' is a fast-paced, strongly tuneful composition where firstly Adams – leaping between registers with his liquid notes – then Pullen – pounding through his phrases and ending with some Cecil Taylor-like runs – and Mingus, booming and inventive as ever, chase each other relentlessly until the final note.

There is little that is solemn too about 'Free Cell Block F, 'tis Nazi USA', recorded at the same session with the same musicians. The title was linked by Mingus to an article he had read in *Ebony* magazine about executions of prisoners in southern prisons, but you would never have guessed this from the buoyancy, almost joyousness of the tune. The title contradicts the music and vice-versa, but this was a key factor in pressuring his listeners to think and imagine: nothing is as it seems to be, or as its sounds suggest it is. Adams' solo is a tour de force, full of invention with gurgling, skittering notes, but with a sense of freedom and optimism that belies the title. Pullen rocks, with Mingus giving him full rhythmic licence and Richmond behind him crashing his snares. Freedom sounds like a dream that will be realised.

And as a tailpiece, on October 13 1971, more than a year after the Attica slaughter, a group of eminent jazz musicians played a stirring concert to the prisoners of Cook County Jail, Chicago. Organist Jimmy McGriff, a potent blues performer, called his two part composition *Freedom Suite*, and gave powerful stimulus to his two guitarists, George Freeman and O'Donel Levy, to play some riveting blues passages. Also present was the tenor and soprano saxophone veteran, Eli 'Lucky' Thompson (born in Columbia, South Carolina in 1924), who had played with Charlie Parker in the beginnings of the bop explosion in the forties. Playing in a quartet setting with Cedar Walton on electric piano, and the celebrated Cannonball Adderley rhythm section of bassist Sam Jones and drummer Louis Hayes, Thompson blows with real empathy for his listeners, who applaud spontaneously as they begin to recognise the melody of his soprano playing 'Everything Happens to Me'. It is a moving jazz moment, and one when the music digs deep to tell the thousand human stories of those who are listening.

4

freedom suite

In February 1958 the tenor saxophonist Sonny Rollins recorded an unusually lengthy nineteen and a half minute long and
meaning-laden original work, *The Freedom Suite*. With no piano
present, only Max Roach's drums and ex-Ellingtonian-become-
bopper Oscar Pettiford on bass, Rollins gave himself a lot of
time and space to explore and pattern his notes. As a prelude
to the extended composition, Rollins wrote in the liner notes:

> America is deeply rooted in negro culture: its colloquialisms,
> its humour, its music. How ironic that the negro, who more
> than any other people can claim America's culture as his
> own, is being persecuted and repressed, that the negro who
> has exemplified the humanities in his very existence, is being
> rewarded with inhumanity.

It could have been Paul Robeson speaking: in fact it was a
twenty-eight-year-old New Yorker, now developing his own
unique perspective on bop, after vital developmental periods
with Miles Davis, Fats Navarro, Thelonious Monk and the
Clifford Brown/Max Roach Quintet. 1958 was two years after
the Montgomery Bus Boycott, which Martin Luther King had
seen as not only an awakening of the resistance of southern
black Americans: it was not an isolated movement, he stressed.
The struggle against segregation in Montgomery was much

more: 'The oppressed people of the world are rising up. They are revolting against colonialism, imperialism and other systems of oppression,' he declared. And those stories of international struggle resonate and tell of the moments all the way through *The Freedom Suite*, even now.

Roach, characteristically, is right inside Rollins' intentions throughout the performance, as is the virtuoso Pettiford, successor to Blanton in the Ellington orchestra and, alongside Mingus, one of bop's major architects on the bass. Rollins' astonishing skills and melodic invention in sustained improvisation and the power and innovation of the trio's interplay create a compelling essay of black musicianship and jazz genius. The three sections which compose the suite have moments of gospel intensity, waltz-like grace and a discursive power which seem to be an almost vocalised expression of argument and reason. It is a unique and highly significant configuration of sounds and their interpretation in the epicentre of an epoch of social and political struggle.

That era, between 1955 and 1968, the Montgomery Bus Boycott and the Poor People's Campaign, and the years just before and just after, were not only the years of the burgeoning and full force of the Civil Rights movement. They were also the years of the sublime output of one of the greatest jazz phenomena in the music's history: the artistic glory of Blue Note records. There were other outstanding jazz labels during that time: Prestige, Riverside, Verve, Atlantic, Impulse, Bluebird, Mercury, Candid, Vee Jay, Roulette and Contemporary to name only a few, but Blue Note emblematised the musical epoch. Every album they waxed during those crucial years, from the sounds engineered by Rudy Van Gelder to the sleeve designs by Reid Miles and the evocative photographs taken by Francis Wolff, was redolent with the spirit of black artistry and rebellion. Occasionally these messages were open and explicit, but more often they burst out of the music in full voice in the unity of the ensembles and the fire and brilliance of the soloists – in the audacity of their notes, the sometimes rage and protest of their musical phraseology, in the dignity and sense of history of their blues passages, and in the complexity of their sound patterns. If ever a label exposed and reverberated in its utterance and cry the spirit of its age, it was Blue Note records.

'If Your Heart Can't Beat'

And no figure in the music symbolised the sheer strength of that sound than the Pittsburgh-born drummer Art Blakey, whose most eventful years of his musical lifetime lasted right though the greatest decade of Blue Note, from his first albums *A Night at Birdland*, Volumes 1, 2 and 3 in 1954, to his Blue Note swansong, *Indestructible* in 1964. Blakey's politics were in his drums, and they beat on relentlessly through that decade, and before and beyond: 'The drum is an instrument with feeling,' he asserted: 'it is so human. The instrument that is close to the human soul is the drum, because if your heart can't beat, you are dead.' Elsewhere he exclaimed: 'I'm telling my whole life when I play. I ain't hidin' nothin'.' And yet, coming from a steel city like Pittsburgh, he recognised music was as much an escape from working class life as a commentary upon it. This was a jazzman, who as a boy was expelled from school and plunged directly into a steelworks at the age of fourteen. He saw two drunken workers fall into the molten metal and that was the message to escape the circumscription of steel. No wonder he always said through an ever-moving jazz lifetime, that music 'washes away the dust of everyday life'.

But Blakey was a deeply mindful musician who also had an intellectual curiosity about his own roots. His forced departure from school was caused by his audacity in writing an essay in his History class which proudly asserted that the world's first university was in Africa. As he told Wayne Enstice and Paul Rubin in a 1976 interview:

You hear a teacher talking down to you, and you know better. So I rebelled, and I went to the Principal about it and he says, 'Well . . .' I didn't like his attitude either, you know, the way he talked to me. I didn't think it was fair. So I was thrown out of school for doing a report – what messed me up, really. I had to do a report in History class on Africa. They told me that Africans go around in grass skirts and they eat people and they're cannibals. So I went and got a thing on Africa and found out that the first university in the world was in Africa, found out that – ohhhhh I found out so many things, you know, so many lies have been told.

And for Blakey those lies about Africa were repelled by experience. In 1948 he became a seaman and travelled to Nigeria and surrounding countries in West Africa, where he converted to Islam and took the Muslim name of Abdullah Ibn Buhaina.

Yet although Blakey had a profound respect and love for Africa and African music, he saw it and jazz as two entirely different cultural phenomena. He told Herb Nolan:

I went to Africa because there wasn't anything else for me to do. I didn't go over there to study drums. I went over there to study religion and philosophy. I didn't bother with drums. When I was growing up, I had no choice. I was just thrown into a church and told this is what I was going to be. I didn't want to be their Christian, I didn't like it. You could study politics in this country but I didn't have access to the religions of the world. That's why I went to Africa. When I got back, people got the idea I went to learn about music. Africa doesn't have anything to do with American jazz . . . This music came out of American society. You can't mix what comes out of the African cultures with what came out of our culture. I play a western-made drum. People try to put Africa and jazz together. Well, that's the biggest lie ever told. This thing happened over here; it happened in this society. It's about Americans and every American has a share in it. No America, no jazz.

Such a repudiation from a master-drummer who grew up in a race-torn American city and who came from the heart of its working class gives a special meaning to Blakey's musicianship. He saw it as powerfully and aggressively American and hearing his drums you hear America and the America that was his provenance. Two of his great drumming contemporaries, Max Roach and Kenny Clarke, disagreed with him and saw a close bond between African and American jazz drum artistry and message-making. Yet if you listen to some of Blakey's greatest Jazz Messengers recordings, he is telling an American story. Take his tempestuous drum solo, 'The Freedom Rider', from the May 1961 album of that same name. According to the sleevenotes by Nat Hentoff, the piece

> illustrates how Blakey's intensity reaches out to absorb cli-
> mactic present history; because 'The Freedom Rider',
> recorded as was the rest of this date on May 27 1961, repre-
> sents Art's immediate reaction to the explosive growth of
> the Civil Rights movement at that time and since.

For on May 4 1961, thirteen Civil Rights activists had begun the first 'freedom ride', a bus journey from Washington D.C. to New Orleans to challenge racism and segregation on interstate transport in the South. This was the first of more than sixty such rides made by black and white, men and women, young college students and seasoned veterans of the movement, trav-elling together. They were beaten and arrested as they rode through South Carolina, Alabama and Mississippi, gaoled, stoned and firebombed by local police, Ku Klux Klan groups and angry white mobs.

There is no nostalgia or romanticism in Blakey's ferocious yet sophisticated sound; no pretence at Africa or simulation of

African drum patterns. It is America speaking to its own: proud and freedom-loving, showing solidarity with its youth, risking their lives and futures to ride buses, to desegregate transport in the most backward and racist states of their nation. And the title track is only one part of an album expressing potent jazz unity in its ensembles and statements of proud determination in its solos. The subliminal echoes of struggle and freedom ring out from all of the album's tracks. In 'Tell It Like It Is', the forward-stepping and jaunty ensemble theme is soon developed by Lee Morgan's muscled and striving trumpet solo with his bandmates urging him on with their muffled voices. Then Wayne Shorter enters, his tenor sure yet exploratory, serpentine yet straight-ahead, playing hard as if he's in the midst of a road march. A press roll from Blakey and in comes Bobby Timmons' piano, gospellizing and full of spiritual fervour. These are the voices of the rebellion to the south translated to jazz performance at Rudy Van Gelder's Englewood Cliffs, New Jersey Studio.

The same is true of Shorter's composition 'United' on the *Roots and Herbs* album of February 1961. A simple theme like a slogan played as an ensemble, then Shorter and Morgan, the latter stretching skywards for his sounds until pianist Walter Davis Jr. enters with his clipped notes, urged on by Blakey's rolls and rimshots, until it is all Blakey, crashing his drums, calling the volunteers into the unity of the struggle through the percussion of sheer resistance and power, with Jymie Merritt's plunging bass urging him on. Or take 'Free for All', the title track of the explosive February 1964 album. Cedar Walton's stirring piano starts off, there is a thematic ensemble passage, and then Shorter digs in, his phrases full of the earth and those marching upon it, his long notes howling solidarity and rage simultaneously, his sound straining for freedom. Then in with Curtis Fuller's stirring slides, adding thickness and strength, repeated short phrases, emphatic like a man booming at a mass public meeting. Freddie Hubbard, boiling with brass power, searching and finding summit notes as if he could blast anything that prevented him, with Blakey provoking him relentlessly with rolls, crashes and splintering phrases which continue through the drum solo, a commentary upon the freedom and true social emancipation that must come sometime, everywhere. That was the meaning of Blue Note Records, forged by two German emigrants, Alfred Lion and Francis Wolff, two Berliners – the latter a Jew who arrived in New York in 1939 on what was the final escape boat from Nazi Germany. Through their labours they created an enterprise which gave northern voice to a vital southern struggle, a day-by-day crucial and beautiful sound narration of human hope and black persistence.

Right Now!

Another musician who had an effect parallel to that of Blakey was New Yorker Jackie McLean, born in 1932, the son of a jazz guitarist father. And like Blakey he became a staunch and regular Blue Note voice on his Parker-inspired but highly personalised alto saxophone. His album *Jackie's Bag*, recorded in 1959–60, has two tracks of internationalist dedication that show his jazz was breaking across frontiers. By New Year's Day 1959, the Cuban Revolution had triumphed with the American-backed dictator, Fulgencio Batista, fleeing Havana and leaving Cuba forever. Then, in April 1959, the leader of the revolution, Fidel Castro, visited the United States. McLean took a composition which he had written and recorded with Blakey's Jazz Messengers in 1957 called 'Couldn't It Be You?', and renamed it 'Fidel'. Drummer Philly Joe Jones storms into the theme, trumpeter Donald Byrd offers a slightly hesitant solo before McLean's joyous alto takes over, spinning out melodic phrases in front of Philly Joe's ever-surprising drum effects. Sonny Clark takes over, his Bud Powell-inspired keyboard-runs, dramatic pauses and swinging cadences leading back to the theme. Byrd and McLean break, and Fidel returns to Cuba, eventually to face the Bay of Pigs invasion attempt in April 1960, initially described by Kennedy as 'an unspectacular landing at night in an area where there was a minimum likelihood of opposition'. Little did he know.

Directly following 'Fidel', the next track was McLean's 'Appointment in Ghana', played with an almost entirely different personnel. Ghana's 1957 independence signalled the beginning of the decolonisation of Africa, and McLean's 'Appointment' was a heady musical celebration. A stately ensemble beginning with drummer Art Taylor tapping formal time introduces a call-and-response theme, with trumpeter Blue Mitchell being answered by McLean and tenorist Tina Brooks from North Carolina. McLean plays a beautifully fluent solo before Mitchell enters, dancing on his notes and reaching for Ghana's black star. Brooks' blues-soaked tenor seems to be talking history like a Ghanaian griot before pianist Kenny Drew stomps out his choruses. The theme returns and the proud appointment is over, but well-remembered and stamped into African anti-colonial history. And remembered too by Byrd, in one of his albums for Blue Note, *Byrd in Flight*. The opening track, another musical dedication simply called 'Ghana', also features Hank Mobley's 'middle-weight' tenor, pianist Duke Pearson, Lex Humphries on drums and Doug Watkins' bass. Humphries is ascendant through the piece, while Byrd's solo is fast-flowing, lyrical and buoyant. Pearson's tapping choruses have a raindrop-like percussive effect, and the sure-winded, ever-stepping Mobley keeps the emphatic forward pulse of the music moving until Humphries drives on with an emphatic solo before the resumption of the theme.

The evocation of the new African nations in the titles of Blue Note tracks kept pace with those which urged forward the Civil Rights struggles in the South. It was a repeated device used during the first half of the sixties, when literally scores of decolonised African peoples found their national independence from Britain and France. Sometimes this was cause for elation and rejoicing. Lee Morgan, for example, told a sleevenote story of how he met a group of Zambian students during one of his cross-America tours, and he was prompted to name one of his own compositions, featured on his 1966 album *Delightfulee*, after their newly-forged nation which became independent in 1964, thus ending the colonial deformity of Northern Rhodesia. 'Zambia' has Morgan with a group of young jazz eminences – Joe Henderson, the tenorist from Lima, Ohio; Ornette Coleman's drum alumnus – Billy Higgins from Los Angeles; Rollins' favoured bassist Bob Cranshaw; and the pianist of the most acclaimed John Coltrane Quartet, McCoy Tyner from Philadelphia. It's a jaunty, self-confident theme and Henderson comes in strutting, blowing his chorus like a man who knows where he's going and is proudly setting out his direction. Morgan continues this sense of assurance in his choruses, crackling boisterously above the swinging Higgins. And Tyner continues the mood, sauntering home. Morgan blisters a phrase, then dialogues with Higgins, the theme returns and the ambiance is entirely optimistic, ringing with a sense of free and forward movement.

But a very different wind prevails through trombonist Bennie Green's 'Congo Lament', a part of, yet at severe odds with the title of the 1962 Ike Quebec album, *Easy Living*. Quebec was a Hawkins-inspired, full-toned tenorist who also acted as a talent scout for Blue Note, and on this occasion he brought together the Pittsburgh-born, rasping, hooting tenor man Stanley Turrentine with a rhythm section that included Sonny Clark, the veteran bassist Milt Hinton and the enormous drum presence of Blakey. Congo's first Prime Minister, Patrice Lumumba had been murdered in the February of the year before, and the Congo was dismembering. Such events wind through this musical narration. Green's mournful slides open the piece, with the two tenors answering his call. Turrentine's distinctive blues-tinged voice continues before

Green comes in for his eloquent choruses, charged with sadness but emphatic with defiance too. Quebec's proud and compassionate sound preludes a more rooted Clark, who forgoes his habitual storming forward patterns for a much more contemplative and quiescent solo. As the theme fades out, there is a sense of deep empathy of these musicians for the agony of Africa, their own lost continent too.

In January 1962 a resolution in the Geneva Assembly of the United Nations affirmed the right of the Portuguese colony of Angola's right to self-determination. This had followed a turbulent period in the history of the huge central-west African nation's history, including a revolt by the peasantry in the northern province of Malanje in 1961, provoked by the low prices for their cotton, forced upon them by the monopolistic concessionary company that controlled the local economy. This outbreak was compounded by an attempt organised by the main liberation movement, the MPLA, in the capital Luanda, by several hundred Angolans to set free political prisoners in the central prison. A further revolt in the north was suppressed with a terrible ferocity, with twenty thousand Angolans being killed in its first six months. By 1966, the MPLA were strong enough to open a front in the Moxico province in Eastern Angola and pursue a war of national liberation. Such events were the background to Wayne Shorter's composition, 'Angola', the second track on the 1965 album, *The Soothsayer*. Shorter, born in 1933 in Newark, New Jersey, had the year before vacated the tenor saxophone place in Blakey's Jazz Messengers and had led three previous Blue Note sessions – *Night Dreamer*, *Juju*, and *Speak No Evil*. For *The Soothsayer*, he had with him the Indianapolis-born altoist James Spaulding together with Hubbard, Tyner and two members of the new Miles Davis quintet – drummer Tony Williams and Ron Carter on bass. Tyner's introduction is fast and ominous, the subsequent repetitive theme simple and brief before Shorter begins his solo, buoyed up by the nineteen-year-old Williams' springing drums. He tears into his opening chorus, low and liquid, spinning off his pacy notes as if time is now and time is short. Hubbard hurtles in, soon soaring upwards to an African sky while Williams crashes on behind him. Spaulding bursts in, his excitation even more intense, as he gives way to a rampant Williams solo, a repeat of the theme, and out. A message from black American jazzmen is 'Angola', to the very heart of Africa and its people.

As for McLean, always a musical radical, his large number of sixties' Blue Note albums frequently revealed that his jazz was also apace with the dramatic events in the South and the northwards-moving Civil Rights struggle, which by 1965 would begin to focus on urban areas such as the 'War on Slums' in the predominantly black neighbourhoods of Chicago. The power of titles was used in his 1962 session *Let Freedom Ring!* – a phrase redolent with defiance which would echo and re-echo through Martin Luther King's speech after the march on Washington a year later. A quartet album, its four tunes resound with a sense of striving and breaking free – listen to McLean's straining notes at the beginning of his solo on 'Melody for Melonae', dedicated to his daughter, for example, or his sudden squealing pitch later on in the same solo, with Higgins' drums and Herbie Lewis' bass surging forward, and Walter Davis' piano streaming in to make its own pulsating notes. Or the last track 'Omega' – this time dedicated to McLean's mother, where Lewis' powerful bass line undertows everything and pushes McLean to make a beautifully insurgent and freewheeling sound. Or there was the altoist's 1965 album, with its ghosts of Parker–McLean's huge inspiration, *Right Now!*, another quartet session with drummer Clifford Jarvis, Cranshaw on bass and fellow New Yorker Larry Willis on piano. Parallel events in the South included the march on Selma, Alabama and the relentless and brave campaigning in obscure and dangerous rural areas and small towns for black voter registration and the eventual passage of the Voting

Rights Act of 1965. The excitation around the album's slogan-
istic title told of more impending struggles and more step-by-
step successes to come. There are two takes of the title tune,
written by McLean's sometime trumpet partner, Charles
Tolliver, and both start with McLean in the lower register,
establishing a theme while also blowing fanfare-like into faster
time and a higher timbre. There is a dramatic build-up of
momentum and passion, largely due to Jarvis' punctuating and
forward-pushing drums and the repetitive pounding of the
rhythm. Right now, indeed, and you can believe it.

In November 2007, when he brought his big band to the
London Jazz Festival, I asked Tolliver, then sixty-five, how
much such music had been a reflection and message of the
Civil Rights activists and masses of the sixties. Tolliver had
been the trumpeter of the Jackie McLean Quintet alongside
McLean on other signal Blue Note albums with evocative titles
like *Action* and *It's Time* of 1964, and he had played eloquently
and passionately on the Max Roach Quintet album *Members,
Don't Git Weary*, cut shortly after Martin Luther King's assassination in 1968 as a defiant reminder that the campaigning,
despite its tragic setbacks, must continue. Indeed, on the
album's title tune, Andy Bey sang, accompanied by Roach,
Tolliver, Gary Bartz on alto, pianist Stanley Cowell and Jymie
Merritt on electric bass:

> Members, don't git weary
> Members, don't git weary
> Members, don't git weary
> For the work almost done!

I asked him whether that struggle against US racism during
that era, so overwhelming, so momentous, had taken hold of
jazz musicians and led their artistry. 'Yes and no,' he said. 'Yes,
because while we played we expressed the excitement, the danger, the passion of the times. It was with us all the time, it was

always there. But we would have gone crazy if we had let it totally dominate us, if we had constantly thought about it all of the time. But it was with us constantly. We were a part of it and that moment was a part of us. It still is.'

Search for a New Land

In the sleeve photograph of the prodigious Lee Morgan's first Blue Note album, *Lee Morgan Indeed!*, his trumpet bell veers upward like that of his mentor, Dizzy Gillespie. It was 1956, Morgan was eighteen and he had been playing in the great Dizzy's big band since the beginning of the year. Now it was his turn, and all the assurance and cockiness of ascendant and aspirant youth were there indeed in his fierce blowing, with a rhythm section of new jazz eminences: pianist Horace Silver, Chicago bassist Wilbur Ware and Philly Joe Jones on drums. The recording was cut in the Van Gelder studio in November 1956, the same month that the Israeli army, using the British and French Suez invasion of Nasser's Egypt as a pretext, attacked and occupied Gaza, provoking the foundation of Al-Fatah and the Palestine Liberation Organisation. 'Gaza Strip' is the album's fifth track and the young Morgan's soaring response is beckoned by a rampant Philly Joe, Clarence Sharpe's effervescent alto chorus and Silver's ominous soundings. It is a presage of the committed power of Gilad Atzmon's intense albums, four decades to come.

Morgan's 1964 album, *Search for the New Land* was the trumpeter's ninth Blue Note album, in addition to the string of sessions he cut as a member of Blakey's Jazz Messengers and as a sideman on albums made by other Blue Note regulars like Mobley, Shorter and Henderson. The Philadelphia hornman blew with an inspired strength and beauty on the title selection, the meaning of which could not be separated from the urge to find a new life that was the unifying passion of the Civil Rights movement. 'Search for the New Land', the album's

opener written by Morgan, was neither in the usual genre of
his compositions nor an exposition of his customary mode of
playing. Herbie Hancock's tinkling piano cuts into a grandiose-
sounding theme, rustled by Higgins' cymbals. Reggie
Workman's emphatic bass notes introduce a solo by Morgan's
long-time Messengers' partner, tenorist Wayne Shorter, who
reprises the theme above Workman's bowed bass. Morgan's
first notes are high and searching, and as his solo choruses
progress, he begins to bend his notes, while the rhythm section
slows down and shimmers. Hancock's interval preludes a solo
from St. Louis-born guitarist Grant Green, whose first phraseology recalls Greig's 'Anitra's Dance' from the *Peer Gynt Suite*,
before his more characteristic blues cries can be heard within
his notes. Then Hancock comes to the fore above Higgins'
clipping rimshots, the light touch of his sound and his more
impressionistic note patterns leading to the final ensemble
chorus. Nearly sixteen minutes, this track is trailing with hope
and dreams.

Also included on *Search for the New Land* was another evocation of a 'new land' in Africa, in Morgan's tribute to Jomo
Kenyatta, who became president of the Kenya African Union
nearly two decades before in 1947, but was not designated as
independent Kenya's first president until 1963, after the
Kenyan people had endured a decade of struggle against the
British colonial government, armed and unarmed, and after
many of their nationalist leaders, including Kenyatta, had been
detained and imprisoned. It was black America holding up the
mirror of its own struggle to Africa again in 'Mr Kenyatta',
which radiates a keen sense of optimism and movement
throughout the unity of its ensembles and the virtuosity of its
soloists. Morgan begins, bristling with audacious leaps, as if
like his subject, he were facing Mount Kenya, and Shorter
comes in running, spinning some ecstatic phrases and making
way for a fast-moving Green, creating sparkling lines with the
horns riffing behind him. As Morgan closes the piece with

some typical hard-blasting notes, Africa and black America clasp hands and share destinies.

In December 1962 Green recorded his seventh Blue Note album, *Feelin' the Spirit*. Most of his previous work with the label had shown him to be an exceptional blues guitarist, particularly adept in an organ trio context or side by side with strong horns – he always claimed to model his technique on brass or reed players, rather than other guitarists. But *Feelin' the Spirit* represents a prime moment in his canon. It is devoted to spirituals and includes a young Herbie Hancock free of all electric contrivances, one of Monk's later bassists – Butch Warren – and the ubiquitous Higgins on drums. Garvin Masseaux came in as tamborinist. The album proved to be something of an apogee for Green and is certainly his most rootsy recorded session. He ploughs through these six ancestral themes like a man inspired. For these were traditional folk tunes with deep resonances for the Civil Rights movement at work and in struggle in southern towns and cities, and the musicians give them a powerful contemporary meaning as the walls of racism and segregation were, one by one, coming down. And 'Joshua Fit de Battle of Jericho' is at the centre of the album, along with 'Go Down Moses', two decades-old songs of resistance with massive overtones of protest and defiance. Such anthems were not usually associated with the sounds streaming from bop musicians, but it is clear that they watered their musical roots and pricked the consciousness of the deep pain and struggle of their people's history. In 'Just a Closer Walk with Thee', a tune with strong jazz connections – primarily with New Orleans marching bands – Hancock discards his impressionism and delivers a rocking church-like chorus full of down-home phrases. But this is very much Green's album and is full of his sense of pain, joy and immense guitar artistry. In 'Jericho', he seems to be marching alongside the Montgomery bus boycotters; and in a blues-laden 'Nobody Knows the Troubles I've Seen', perhaps he was thinking of the little girls in Birmingham, Alabama, murdered in church by racist bombers. As for 'Deep River', it seems to drive into the bottomless waters of his people's lives and struggle. Throughout it makes the listener marvel: music and life, never to be divided.

Selma and Ole Miss

By early 1965, the Civil Rights movement had fixed its determination to challenge the Alabama voter registration law which excluded so many black voters from their right to a ballot. From a gaol cell in the city of Selma, Martin Luther King, a recent recipient of the Nobel Peace Prize, had written a letter, in an advertisement paid for by the Southern Christian Leadership Conference and published in the *New York Times* on February 4 1965, exposing the 'abstruse' and bureaucratic barriers black citizens faced in their efforts to become legally registered. His letter ended with the indignant declaration: 'This is Selma, Alabama. There are more negroes in jail with me than there are on the voting rolls.'

As part of the brave march on Selma on March 7, six hundred protesters gathered and prepared themselves at the Edmund Pettus Bridge, which spanned the Alabama River on Selma's eastern flank. As the ranks of state troopers and mounted possemen advanced over the bridge towards the campaigners, attacking them with nightsticks and tear gas, King gave out his message: 'In the vicious maltreatment of defenceless citizens of Selma, where old women and young children were gassed and clubbed at random, we have witnessed an eruption of the disease of racism which seeks to destroy all America.'

No wonder, then, that the Blue Mitchell Quintet album waxed in July 1965, which included the exuberant and impassioned track 'March on Selma', was entitled *Down With It!* Not that it was a profoundly or fully politicised jazz album – it began with a pounding, funky version of 'Hi-Heel Sneakers', with tenorist Junior Cook and Mitchell himself digging into a hugely popular dance and juke box tune. And in the way that many white jazz commentators or liner notes writers would systematically sidestep or ignore the sound of resistance that burst from black jazz musicianship, the writer of the sleeve essay of *Down With It!*, one Phyl Garland, asserts that 'March on Selma': 'bears no actual tie to the civil rights movement, but can simply be dug because it's such a catchy lick.' Which is just about the equivalent of declaring that 'Strange Fruit' is only a song about peach trees intended for fruit farmers. Now Pensacola-born Cook and Blue Mitchell of Miami, both Florida-born, long-time musical confreres in the Horace Silver Quintet, knew all about the South and its Jim Crow systems. And how they could play, too! 'March on Selma' is stirred up by Chick Corea's opening piano chorus before Cook churns out a juicy tenor solo beside drummer Al Foster and bassman Gene Taylor's relentless forward rhythm. Mitchell enters, blowing in his direct, full-brassed tone, bristling with defiance. Corea's rolling solo continues the impetus until the ensemble fades out into the distance. A track without doubt of its times, bursting with the energy of resistance.

John Handy, who had been the featured altoist in Charles Mingus' Jazz Workshop in the 1959 Columbia version of 'Fables of Faubus' continued to make superb music into the sixties and by 1967 had assembled a quintet, with an unusual grouping of instrumentalists. There was no piano, but Bobby Hutcherson's vibes and Pat Martino's guitar more than filled the space, with the astonishing young bassist Albert Stinson and Doug Sides on drums. On a June night in 1967, the quintet was recorded live at New York's Village Gate, including a thirty-one minute version of Handy's composition, 'Tears of Ole Miss', subtitled 'Anatomy of a Riot'. This was another story of racism of segregation in education, this time at the university level, provoked by black student James Meredith's attempt to register and attend classes at the University of Mississippi in September 1962. Here a virtual racist twin of Faubus, Alabama Governor Ross Barnett, stood bodily between Meredith and his right to a university education in his own state university. As Taylor Branch described the confrontation in his epic account of the Civil Rights movement, *Parting the Waters*:

> Barnett, bathed in television lights, blocked the threshold of Room 1007. Legislators inside climbed atop chairs and tables to obtain a better view. Barnett 'interposed' Mississippi's sovereignty, as embodied in his own person, between Meredith and the University officials, who maintained an outward willingness to obey the orders.

'Tears of Ole Miss' was four years in gestation, first conceived in 1963, the year after Meredith's ordeal, when Handy was playing with the Freedom Band that he organised in San Francisco after he returned from attending the march on Washington. It was a ten-piece band, referred to as a 'protest' band, but a 'protest band' that did not play strictly 'protest' music. 'We just played music in general,' Handy writes in the sleevenotes to the album *New View*, which includes 'Tears': 'my kind of music, things I'd been writing for the past ten years. Our purpose was to raise money for civil rights by playing at concerts, theaters and in parades. Lots of people who didn't give a damn about civil rights came to hear us because they liked our music.'

'Tears of Ole Miss' was the one exception, and it is full of the spirit of Mingus, redolent with the irony of sounds. Handy begins his long musical narrative with a skipping alto solo, with Sides' snares rattling beside him. He reaches for high notes and squeals and his improvisation gives an impression of carefree movement. Hutcherson takes over with a similar sound picture of freedom and mobility – much more like hope than oppression, his notes falling on the ears like drops of southern rain, much too fast for tears. Martino's guitar virtuosity is stunning, his solo leaps – until he turns to a series of braking chords. Handy returns, more complexed and convoluted, his sounds are longer, more brash and pained. Then whistles are blown, sirens are simulated, the theme of 'Dixie' comes to dispel the freedom of sounds and Handy's notes become more introverted, his phrases more terse and agonised. Stinson walks his solo bass, Hutcherson urging him on with gradually lengthening phrases until it is his solo time again, his direction suddenly seeming more purposeful, more strategic. Martino runs up and down his strings, his speed astonishing. A drum solo flanking more whistles, some screams, then the final return of Handy and Hutcherson, the former blowing the full range of his alto, a cry of the blues and back to the theme. It is a story being told, a key moment in American history, by five griots of jazz.

Eric's View

And that same history sprang out of the notes of another great altoist and ex-Mingus sideman, Eric Dolphy, in January 1964 in a New York studio when, as part of a group called the 'Sextet of Orchestra USA', he played in a session dedicated to the music of the German composer and Bertolt Brecht collaborator, Kurt Weill. The musicians played arrangements from the Brecht/Weill opera called *The Rise and Fall of the City of Mahagonny*, a story of the mythical Florida city sunk into a degenerate and self-destructive pattern of life, which falls from boom to bust. One of the tracks, 'Alabama Song', had little to do with the real life of black Alabama people, but instead reflected on the lives of the seven lost Mahagonny prostitutes who have wandered over the state line. The director of the sextet, trumpeter and jazz critic Michael Zwerin, reported in his sleevenotes on what he suggested Dolphy might do with the Weill song:

In 'Alabama Song' I asked soloist Eric Dolphy to express
on this piece how he felt about Alabama, as the background would be an updated version of how Weill and
Brecht had felt about it. In the last chorus the piano and
bass parts are actual extracts from the original score, but the
harmonic changes in Eric's part are a variation. By keeping
to these changes Eric automatically played what musicians
call 'outside' – that is, polytonally.

This is how it was prescribed but the actual happening is
staggering and reflects Dolphy's words quoted in his biography
by Vladimir Simosko and Barry Tepperman: 'To me, jazz is like
part of living, like walking down the street and reacting to
what you see and hear, and whatever I do react to, I can say
immediately in my music.' Or, again: 'This human thing in
instrumental playing has to do with trying to get as much
human warmth and feeling into my work as I can. I want to say
more on my horn than I ever could in ordinary speech.'

The sextet's 'Alabama Song' begins as an arrangement, a
cleverly and carefully reconstructed version of Weill's original
theme. Zwerin plays the melody on bass trumpet with Richard
Davis' bass and Connie Kay's drums giving an uplift which
almost makes it levitate, become unworldly, with all verisimili-
tude gone. Then pianist John Lewis' piano causes the tune to
weave and bobble during his chorus. But nothing can prepare
the listener for Dolphy's derailing contribution. 'Tell of
Alabama how it is,' said Zwerin, and what spurts out is
an astonishing musical narrative. His bass clarinet gurgles,
splutters, chokes, shouts, screams and demands in short staccato phrases, ending in high-pitched squeal. The rest of the
sextet play on behind him, almost like musical automatons
simply repeating the theme orthodoxly, unexcitedly, as a
sound palimpsest for Dolphy's impassioned testimony. I first
heard this recorded performance in 1967, when I bought the
album in Western Canada, a few months before I went to

Washington D.C. to join the Poor People's March in July 1968. It seemed to me then, as it still does now, as resonant an artistic statement about American racism as anything I have ever read, seen or heard since and a fulfilment of Dolphy's own aspirations:

> There's so much to learn and so much to try and get out. I keep hearing something else beyond what I've done. There's always been something else to strive for. The more I grow in my music, the more possibilities of new things I hear. It's like I'll never stop finding sounds I never thought existed.

Bobby Hutcherson's 1968 Blue Note album, *Spiral*, included a track called simply 'Poor People's March', as a tribute to what was one of the final formal campaigns of the Civil Rights movement, and the first mass national protest after the death of Martin Luther King in April 1968. I remember well the excitement at the Washington climax of the campaign, the dozens of shanties, tents and trailers pitched and parked in the mud next to the pool in front of the steps of the Lincoln memorial, the carts and horses, the thousands of people from all over the USA arriving to pledge their support and solidarity and to promise that the struggle would continue. I remember in particular the beautiful singing of 'Come by Here, O Lord' by King's widow, Coretta, from the memorial steps, and the huge emotive response. Hutcherson's group, including the tune's composer, tenorist Harold Land, pianist Stanley Cowell, with Reggie Johnson on bass and drummer Joe Chambers, play the theme at a sprightly pace until Land launches a beautifully poised solo, staying with the low register, before Hutcherson continues – jubilant, optimistic, bursting with life. Cowell rocks his piano for a chorus before Johnson steps in to solo, thudding and vibrating, shaking the studio with his depth and power. As the theme returns you know that the mood of the musicians is entirely positive, that what has gone before will continue, and that the sacrifices, however costly and tragic, have promised a different, freer and more vibrant future.

Hughes' Jazz Tribute

A month after Rollins recorded his epochal *Freedom Suite*, the black bard of Harlem, Langston Hughes, recorded his *Weary Blues* – a jazz and poetry album which featured jazzmen of two generations and traditions. March 1958 found Hughes in a New York studio with the English composer and critic Leonard Feather, plus New Orleans trumpeter second only to Armstrong – Henry 'Red' Allen, Basie-ite trombonist Vic Dickenson, reedman Sam 'The Man' Taylor, Milt Hinton on bass and swing drummer Osie Johnson. As they waxed their music, Martin Luther King was stabbed while he signed autographs at Blumstein's Department Store in Harlem, mere whistling distance from the musicians. The letter knife used by his attacker missed his aorta by a millimetre, and almost miraculously his death was averted by the surgical team at the local Harlem hospital. Thus Hughes' poem, recorded on the *Weary Blues* album with the title 'Could Be', was never more apt.

Hughes' informalities, often like blues doodles in words, amble through a number of related poems on Harlem themes, while the musicians match his mood, making a colloquy – with pianist Al Williams rolling through 'Morning After', or Sam 'The Man' and Henry Red adding caustic instrumental comments to 'Blues Montage', and

> You've done taken my blues and gone
> You've also took my spirituals and gone

As Hughes affirms that it is only the black man and the black woman who will write:

> about me, black and beautiful
> and sing about me
> and put on plays about me
> I reckon it'll be me myself,
> Yes, it'll be me.

We are introduced to a very different set of confreres from the track 'Consider Me' onwards. This is Mingus' Jazz Workshop, on this day nominally led by pianist Horace Parlan for 'contractual reasons'. Mingus is credited as having 'arranged' and 'conducted' the music as well as being the bass player, and it is definitely his musical conception that we hear, and the experience is suddenly more incisive; the sense of congeniality of the previous session has gone. First there is his bowed bass, and then

> When you turn the corner
> and run into yourself,
> then you know you have turned
> all the corners that are left.

Through Hughes' 'boogie woogie rumble of a dream deferred' we hear Parlan's blue notes, trombonist Jimmy Knepper's growls and Shafi Hadi's ironic saxophone melodism as Mingus' bass power vibrates to the words:

> What happens to a dream deferred?

> Does it dry up
> like a raisin in the sun?
> Or fester like a sore –
> And then run?
> Does it stink like rotten meat
> Or crust and sugar over –
> Like a syrupy sweet?

Maybe it just sags
like a heavy load.

Or does it explode?

And the intensity continues as Hughes simmers in his
phrases, and the jazzmen are emphatic with him, right through
to the closing track, 'Jump Monk', with all members performing at full pelt and with full commitment:

Democracy will not come today
through compromise and fear
I do not need my freedom while
I'm dead
I can't live on tomorrow's bread
Freedom is a strong seed
Planted on a great need
I live here too
I want freedom just as you!

5

not in our name

The New Orleans-born blues pianist and singer, Champion Jack Dupree, had his own long comment on the US war in Vietnam in his 'Vietnam Blues' of 1970. His lyrics, put so starkly and movingly, articulated the feelings of many a jazz musician too:

> I feel so sorry for the people
> over in Vietnam,
> There's a whole lot of things
> Uncle Sam don't understand.
>
> Why don't they leave Vietnam,
> leave those poor people alone?
> They just got a whole lot of problems
> just like I have here.
>
> I know every mother be glad
> to see their son come home,
> Yes, Uncle Sam might as well pack up,
> pull out and go back home.
>
> Lord, the war in Vietnam, that's one war
> that will never end,
> And the Vietnam people, they got
> a whole lot of friends.

They got the Japanese
They got the Chinese
They got the Melanese
They got the North Koreans
the Russians
They got the Africans too –
and they got me too!

When the lights come on
all over the world again,
Well the people of Vietnam will have
a whole lot of friends again!

This was not facile protest; it involved a deep empathy with the Vietnamese people, and an understanding that they faced problems of poverty and divided families that were similar to working people in the USA. The lyrics were also conscious of the support that the Vietnamese people had from poor and struggling communities all over the world, including, so Dupree says, in America.

A Song of Songmy

In January 1971, Freddie Hubbard, who was one of the Blue Note stars of the previous decade featuring on dozens of his own and his confreres' albums, cut what was possibly the most audacious jazz album ever made. He called it 'Sing Me a Song of Songmy' and recorded it for Atlantic, a major, commercial-ly-oriented record company, which in itself was astonishing. But the album combined musical protest about the worst US atrocity of the Vietnam conflict – the March 16 1968 massacre at the Vietnamese village of My Lai – with an outcry against the deaths of protesting students at Kent State University in Ohio in 1970, and ends with the words of Che Guevara, maker of the Cuban Revolution, Argentinian guerrilla and former number one enemy of the US government who had been killed in Bolivia in October 1967. For a jazz tradition that spoke of political realities through implication, code and ambivalence, there had been nothing like this before. Here was an album that was dedicated to absolute cultural resistance and fully explicit anti-government protest, being put into the heart of the market by a major record company, featuring the work of an already established jazz virtuoso who had been given full licence to follow his theme through Vietnamese and Turkish poetry, Brahms' *Ein Deutsches Requiem*, Scriabin's 'Etude in B flat minor', Hubbard's own lyrics and an essay by Soren Kierkegaard. All within forty-three minutes.

The official Peers Commission Report of 1970 had this to say about the Massacre of Songmy:

> During the period 16 to 19 March 1968, US Army troops of Task Force Barker 11th Brigade, America Division, massacred a large number of non-combatants in two hamlets of Son My Lai Village, Quang Ngai Province, Republic of Vietnam. The precise number of Vietnamese killed cannot be determined but was at least 175 and may exceed 400.

The young commander of the 'Charlie Company' platoon which carried out the slaughter, the Miami-born William Laws Calley, asserted:

> We weren't in My Lai to kill human beings really. We were there to kill ideology that is carried by – I don't know. Pawns. Blobs. Pieces of flesh. To destroy Communism. I looked at Communism as a Southern looks at a negro, supposedly. It's evil. It's bad.

That My Lai was an extended, transnational lynch party composed of 'boys next door' like Calley himself, puts Hubbard's extraordinary album within the tradition of the anti-lynching campaigns of the Popular Front and the songs and music that left so much in art about iconic figures like the

Scottsboro' Boys and Emmett Till. The old people, mothers and children who made up the majority of victims of Song My shared their family. The theme of kinship radiates all through Hubbard's musical and declamatory essay, probably among the bravest jazz albums ever made.

A threnody to the memory of Sharon Tate, the film 'starlet' murdered by the merciless Charles Manson, begins the album, suggesting that the US slaughter and despoliation in My Lai and Vietnam generally, was born of the same demonic and anti-human impulse. Hubbard's quintet, composed of tenorist Junior Cook, pianist Kenny Barron, Louis Hayes on drums and bassist Art Booth, take several choruses, with Hubbard soaring through a high-note sequence and processed sounds directed by the album's composer, Ilhan Mimaroglu. 'This Is Combat, I Know' begins with solo tenor from Cook, some dark notes from Hubbard, and then the Vietnamese poet, Nha-khe, reads in English a translation of Fazil Husnu Daglarca's Turkish words:

This is combat, from land to sky
Burn me
Burn me, if you like,
But don't burn the forest that shelters me!

This is combat
Or whatever you want,
Burn my sky
Burn my knives if you like
But don't burn my prize cows!

This is combat, I know.
Burn my heart
Burn my loaves if you like
But don't burn my rice paddies!

Some powerful, high pitched and burnished Hubbard against synthesiser chords and mournful string orchestra begins 'Monodrama', the second section of *Songmy*. Then Hubbard sets down his horn and begins to recite more of Daglarca's words, this time the poem 'Black Soldier':

> You black man
> US Army, Private First Class,
> For freedom you shoot down
> your own freedom.
> Your body lies crucified
> on a steel cross.
> The cross is profit and loss
> at each end . . .
> You are the night
> Which has locked itself into darkness.

The quintet bursts in. Barron rocks the piano as Hayes crashes the cymbals behind him; Hubbard rises to the skies; Cook cheeps and gurgles on a vibrating tenor chorus; bassist Art Booth delivers a twanging, deep-rooted solo. Then Nha-khe reads his poem, 'Lullabye for a Child in War' in Vietnamese, before the electronic percussive effects of explosions, screeches, sirens, whistles and screams tell the story of the war's agony.

> And yet there could be
> love and kisses
> As the purple grass
> embraces the pink grass.
> And yet there could be
> love and kisses
> As the crimson branch and
> the green branch caress.
> And yet there could be
> love and kisses

As a black tiger
fondles the white tiger.
I hope love will never,
Never forsake me.

declaims Nha-khe from Daglarca again, followed by Hubbard's breathy, elegaic trumpet.

Hannibal's Testimony

Another brassman with a fiery, passionate surge of sound is the trumpeter Hannibal Marvin Peterson, born in Smithville, Texas in 1948. He came north, to New York in 1970, and played with Rahsaan Roland Kirk, Pharoah Sanders and Gil Evans, as well as forming avant-garde bands under his own name. By 1974, his indignation against the war in Vietnam, in particular against the cruelty and suffering inflicted upon Vietnamese children, prompted him to compose and record a unique and momentous album called *Children of the Fire* released by the tiny Sunrise label. The sixteen-piece Sunrise Orchestra, including violins and violas, was conducted by David Amram, a French horn virtuoso, composer and bandleader who had played with figures as diverse as Lionel Hampton and Mingus and composed for the New York Shakespeare Festival and the New York Philharmonic. The orchestra included some notable jazz musicians, with cogent contributions from bassist Richard Davis, pianist Michael Cochrane and drummer Billy Hart. Peterson split *Children of the Fire* into five movements, and vocalists Alpha Johnson and Waheeda Massey sang its powerful lyrics. The first movement, 'Forest Sunrise', of children's lives of discovery and sensation in a peaceful Vietnam before the US invasion, soon contrasted with the horror of the second, simply called 'Bombing'. Johnson cries out from the vortex of 'this fire that has no end' and asks:

What is this rain that falls from the sky
This rain that burns me until I die?

At the centre of the fourth movement, 'Aftermath', is
Hannibal's fierce trumpet chorus, harsh, full-voiced, blazing
with sudden, fearsome phrases that express the terrible betrayal of Vietnamese children, as they accuse their killers and
torturers:

Where are you now you men of war
Men that kill yet pray.
How can you feel that it will save you
From the death you have brought
Unto my day?

From Davis' deep crater of a bass is plucked a message of
agony and loss, and three decades on the same message spills
from the mouths of the children of invaded Iraq:

Please take these eyes
So that I might not see how my mother cries
And where is my father who stood by my side
And where is my sister and my brother?

And what too of the slain children of Atlanta? For from
Vietnam to Atlanta was not so far. In that city, known as the
'Black Mecca of the South', between 1979 and 1982 forty black
children were mysteriously murdered, their bodies found
strangled, beaten and sexually assaulted. Hannibal's over-
whelming empathy with children that had created *Children of
the Fire* in 1974 for the children of Vietnam, created *The Angels
of Atlanta* in 1981. Within a crazed culture of pornography and
religious zeal, of psychotic Vietnam veterans doped with violence, of the Ku Klux Klan and extremist race-hate groupings
like the Defenders of the White Seed and the John Birch
Society, these children were slaughtered. A picture of such a

society was set down with brilliance and awesome realism by Toni Cade Bambara in her novel *Those Bones Are Not My Child*, published posthumously after years of the author's research in 1999. But Hannibal had put this horror into jazz formation eighteen years earlier with *The Angels of Atlanta*, and it was a domestic extension of his Vietnam essay: the same savagery, the same betrayal of children. With the help of the Harlem Boys' Choir (in the manner of Max Roach and his *Lift Every Voice and Sing!* and *It's Time!* albums), and a group of premier jazz artistes including Kenny Barron, Dannie Richmond, bassist Cecil McBee and tenorist George Adams, Hannibal told the terrifying story. It was Vietnam transposed to Georgia and its great city.

It is the trumpeter accompanied solely by the boys' choir who begin the album's title track. As Richmond, Barron and McBee enter and the frantic up-tempo blowing of Adams takes over, followed by an astonishing high-speed solo from Barron and a dramatic re-entry from the choir, Hannibal delivers a rapid-pace chorus of scorching artistry, full of harnessed rage, proclaiming that Songmy has come home, has always been a part of home, that a desecrated Vietnamese village is also a neighbourhood in a huge city of the American South. Barron's lone piano begins 'The Story Teller', eventually joined by Dierdre Murray's mournful cello and Adams at his most quivering and spouting with testimony. When Hannibal begins his chorus, the parents' story of loss and tragedy has only just begun. He continues it, and you hear in his notes too the voices of bereaved British mothers like Doreen Lawrence or Sukhdev Reel, searching for the killers of their murdered London children, as well as the still weeping mothers of Songmy. The final tune is 'Sometimes I Feel Like a Motherless Child', a moving summative performance with the horns of Adams and Hannibal pealing above McBee's heartsounding bass. As the pace quickens, a feeling of optimism stirs through the notes, particularly through Adams' stomping solo, Murray's buoyant cello chorus and Hannibal's final anthemic trumpet-song, sounding out the last words in explosive breath, that:

There is no
Death
In
Spirit

Deadly Mean War

There were many jazz musicians who played out their opposition to the US war in Vietnam, but few with the boldness of form and content unified by Hubbard and Hannibal. Stanley Cowell's album of 1969, *Blues for the Vietcong*, released by Freedom Records, had a striking sleeve design by the artist Andrea Klein, built around the motif of a flag of Vietnam peppered by bulletholes in one corner. When the record was reissued as a Black Lion CD, the design had disappeared, as had the title, which was now the much less contentious *Travellin' Man*. But on the title tune of the original album, Cowell, born in Lima, Ohio, in 1941 and much influenced by the mighty Art Tatum, plays electric piano, for which he had a particular empathy and technique. Drummer Jimmy Hopps begins the piece with some orientalist-sounding cymbals, and Cowell explores his theme with both agility and creative cultural tension, drawing a pained yet resiliently reactive sound from his wired keyboard.

In January 1969 Richard Milhous Nixon took office as President of the United States of America. On February 14 some $32 million was allocated as expenditure for the war in Vietnam. The day after, the United States Air Force reported the loss of the eight hundredth military aircraft over Vietnam. On January 22 the Pentagon announced the highest weekly number of combat deaths since the war began: 543. The following day the Secretary of Defense revealed that to provide more soldiers for Vietnam (a figure of 206 thousand was quoted by the Pentagon), the National Guard would be needed to be called out. In March 1969 Nixon ordered the bombing of Cambodia through the 'secret' Operation Menu, and in April 1970 fifteen thousand American military personnel crossed into Cambodian territory.

By November 1969 widespread indignation and protest against the war was growing: a quarter of a million people gathered in Washington to register their opposition. In October, at Rudy Van Gelder's legendary Englewood Cliffs studio in New Jersey, the St. Louis-born guitarist Grant Green had recorded his twelfth Blue Note album, *Carryin' On*. One of the tracks, prominent amongst material aimed primarily towards the R and B and pop markets, was called 'Cease the Bombing', almost a pre-reposte to Nixon's later exclamation during the the Vietnamese offensive of Easter 1972: 'The bastards have never been bombed like they're going to be bombed this time.' Green, vibist Willie Bivens and the tenor saxophone of Claude Bartee achieve an almost imploring tone in their ensemble to the tune written by the pianist on the date, Neal Creque, and Green's own blues-tinged solo is picked out with a stark melodic clarity.

On April 30, Nixon formally announced the US escalation of the war in South-East Asia and the invasion of Cambodia during a national television address. On May 4, students at Kent State University in Ohio protested, and four of their number were killed, shot down by the Ohio National Guard who fired into the mass demonstration. The national outrage at these deaths registered deeply within the consciousness of jazz. Nine years after this atrocity on US soil, the baritone saxophonist Hamiet Bluiett performed his 'Requiem for Kent State' during a performance with the Sam Rivers Big Band at Kent State University itself. The grounding power and depth of Bluiett's lone saxophone voice brings back the sound of Robeson. Part dirge, part defiance, planted in the blues and moulded in post-bop, beyond-category licks, Bluiett's notes range upwards and downwards from the bottom of the earth to the summit of the Ohio sky.

Another theme fused to the war in Vietnam was draft resistance. Some of the great songs of the epoch were anthems of protest against the war and its compulsory service – Dylan's 'Masters of War' and Phil Ochs' 'I Ain't Marching any More' were key to the youth consciousness of the times, and Leon Thomas' 'Damn Nam (Ain't Going to Vietnam)' was their jazz sibling, born out of a similar anger and indignation at a Fillmore East concert in New York City, organised by the Student National Coordinating Committee in March 1970. Lonnie Liston Smith's pumping blues piano and Harold Alexander's piping flute choruses, with Alvin Queen on drums and Jimmy Phillips' bass accompany Thomas as he sings and scats his own words:

> You can throw me in jail
> I won't be going to Vietnam,
> It's a deadly mean war
> And nobody gives a damn.
> They got boys upon the frontline
> They got boys upon the backline too,
> They got so many weapons
> What do they want with me and you?
>
> Won't somebody tell me
> How is a man supposed to get a thrill?
> If he's got to drop a napalm bomb
> And not see the thing he's gonna kill?
> How much does it cost
> To fly a man up to the moon,
> When I think of the hungry children
> That I see everywhere every afternoon.
> So you can throw me in jail –
> forget about the bail

I won't be going to Vietnam.
It's a dirty mean war
And nobody gives a d-a-m-n damn.

Bien-Hoa Blues

Such was the defiance of the thousands of draft resisters and
those who went on countless marches throughout the USA,
Canada and much farther afield. But what about those who
were there? The jazz musicians who spent harrowing months
and years fighting in a war that was never of their choosing? In
March 1988 the violinist Billy Bang, who had been Sgt. William
Walker (US 51613087) in Vietnam, recorded his own composition 'Bien-Hoa Blues', in a Milan studio, as part of his album
on the Soul Note label, *Valve No. 10*. Bien-Hoa was the name
of the US Army base camp where Bang was stationed in
Vietnam. Born in Mobile, Alabama, in 1947, he was sent to the
war as a teenager, being drafted directly from high school,
finally returning to the US in 1967. After two days in Vietnam
he was dropped by helicopter into a fire fight, subsequently
became a 'tunnel rat' and a sergeant. 'I became a squad leader,'
he writes in the sleevenotes of his 2003 album, *Vietnam
Reflections*. 'I used to take out ambushes, sweeps and set up military offences. I lived in the jungles, in the rice paddies, in the
rubber plantations, in the fields. Some guys were stationed in
places where they could have instruments, or play records, but
I had no music. The rhythm of machine guns is what I heard.
The only instruments I had were an M79 an M14 and a 45.'
Bang idolised Coltrane and dreamed of meeting him when he
returned to the US. But 'Trane died before he was discharged.
And his frontline partner on *Valve No. 10*, Memphis-born
tenorist Frank Lowe, thought of Coltrane and listened to him
too in Vietnam, whenever he could:

John Coltrane helped keep me alive when I was in Vietnam. I heard him everywhere I travelled before I was shipped out, and I bought some Coltrane records with me to Vietnam and listened to them constantly. His music was like life to me, and death was just down the road a few hundred yards away.

'Bien-Hoa Blues' also has Dennis Charles on drums and bassist Sirone who had recorded his own jazz essay on the horror of the war in 1971, as part of the Revolutionary Ensemble trio with violinist Leroy Jenkins and drummer Jerome Cooper. After some military-style drumming from Charles, the theme moves at a brisk march with Lowe's tenor soloing. Sirone takes a thudding chorus, still in martial mood then Bang breaks it up with a spiky and iconoclastic entrance, sawing hard at his strings and forcing some sharp and uncomfortable sounds. He recaptures the theme, trading breaks with Charles, who finishes with an oriental cymbal clash.

It wasn't until 2001 that Bang was to relive Vietnam again through his music. *Vietnam: The Aftermath* was a sustained effort by Bang to confront 'my personal demons, my experiences in Vietnam'. Since his return, all his days had been 'a continuous struggle for him', as they had for many thousands of veterans all over the USA. Writing in the album's sleevenotes, he lays bare all the truth of his Vietnam.

> For decades I've lived constantly with my unwillingness to deliberately conjure up the pain of these experiences. At night, I would experience severe nightmares of death and destruction, and during the day, I lived a kind of undefined ambiguous daydream. By allowing these awkward and unfathomable feelings to lie dormant in some deep, dark place, I was able to tolerate my frankly vegetative way of living. It was preferable somehow – and safer – to let these

monstrous thoughts imbedded in my unconscious to remain in that state – inactive.

This was the sad state of my life, which made it easy for me to seek an artificial comfort in drinking and drugs.

Vietnam: The Aftermath is much more than a deep therapeutic experience for a musician to uncover and unleash all the suppressed pain and anguish of a 'God-forsaken war'. It is also a message of a people unburdening themselves – and not through introvertion but by reaching out in friendship and solidarity – as other jazz veterans do too, including tenorist Frank Lowe (Spec. 4th Class US 53395173), trumpeter Ted Daniel (Spec. 4th Class US 51619091), drummer Michael Carvin (Spec. 4th Class US 64104864), percussionist Ron Brown (Spec. 4th Class R.A. 11826198) and conductor Butch Morris (Spec. 4th Class R.A. 18835698), together with other confreres, pianist John Hicks, bassist Curtis Lundy and Sonny Fortune on flute. These Americans, borrowing many of the tonal and harmonic elements of South-East Asian music, play their jazz for an entire wounded and misled generation.

'Yo! Ho Chi Minh Is in the House' opens the album. Daniel respires into his horn for a breathy, almost wheezy introduction, before Lundy's bass, Hicks' piano notes and Carvin's cymbals map out oriental effects for Bang's thematic centre, his strings springing with surprise and acknowledgement. Daniel enters again, his sound pure and unflurried before the poised Hicks adds his solo. 'KIAMIA' (an acronym for 'killed in action/missing in action') is a quartet performance with Bang as the sole horn. It is a gentle, moving melody, and one of passionate remembrance. Carvin punctuates the violin's tender bowed and plucked notes with sudden cymbal slashes. And as you listen, you read on the sleeve that part of the proceeds of the album 'will be donated to the Veterans' Quality of Life Access Network Inc. (VOLAN)'. The sounds of 'Tunnel Rat (Flashlight and a 45)' are definitely autobiographical sounds.

Bang plucks out his theme to Carvin's striking cymbals, then changes key and the performance takes on a fast, stomping movement with, first, Bang seething forward, then Daniel taking a sharp-edged solo, crawling fast abreast of him. Hicks solos with his customary expressive eloquence, and Carvin is definitely as much in a New York Subway with his drums as he is in a Vietnamese tunnel. 'TET Offensive' is the jazz story of a Vietcong mass attack, conducted by Butch Morris, with Daniel's and Lowe's horns adding the discomforting sounds of fear. The 1968 TET offensive cost the US 2500 lives, and was a political disaster because immediately before it was waged, American generals were boasting that they were winning the war. 'We are definitely winning!' declared General Harold K. Johnson, while General Westmoreland assured the National Press Club in Washington on November 21 1967: 'We have reached an important point where the end begins to come into view. The enemy's hopes are bankrupt.' Their bombastic and absurdly unprophetic announcements are put into desperate historical irony by Bang's music – his violin whinnying with pain.

The 2001 reprise of 'Bien Hoa Blues' contrasts Bang's strident strings, Daniel's cutting brass and Lowe's more rooted tenor, all thrusting forward on the force of Carvin's drum licks. 'Mystery of the Mekong' is built upon Lundy's phantom bass sounds, rising up from the depths of the flow, and Sonny Fortune's rhapsodic and misty flute; while 'Fire in the Hole' is a cooker, with Bang and Fortune both hot and spinning off phrases of a common language, and Hicks in-between meshing their messages. And finally there is the astonishing 'Saigon Phunk', the backbeat entry to Vietnam for the young, black, cigar-smoking recruit with the automatic weapon over his shoulder pictured on the sleeve cover. When you look elsewhere and see the middle aged man, his weapon exchanged for a violin, and you listen to him and his bunkmates – Daniel's soaring power, Lowe's rumbling beauty and then a climbing, bursting passion on his choruses climaxed by Bang's own apogee of a solo, you know this is a thirty-year-aftermath, by people who knew brutal history as well as jazz on their very breath and pulses.

Montreal, October 2004, and Bang was back in the studio, this time for the recording of *Vietnam Reflections*. Bang felt different, unburdened after *Vietnam: The Aftermath*. As he said, 'after creating the music, rehearsing it and recording it – I felt a lot lighter. I was able to talk more about my situation in Vietnam, I was able to watch some films about it. I sort of resolved some contradictions I had about it within myself.' And *Vietnam Reflections* goes beyond the previous album in its spirit of reconciliation – bringing together black US veterans with two Vietnamese musicians, Co Boi Nguyen and Nhan Thanh Ngo. And the album is dedicated to Lowe, 'our brother, friend and compatriot', who had died in the interim in September 2003.

The first track, 'Reflections', has the trio of Hicks, Lundy and Carvin in strong and swinging fettle, laying down the rhythmic foundation for a Vietnamese-sounding theme which flautist Henry Threadgill embellishes with strong melodic lines. Bang saws in, assured and authoritative and Daniel too is back, his solo full of space and freedom. The lullaby 'Ru Con' sung in Vietnamese by Co Boi Nguyen also features the traditional Vietnamese dulcimer – the dan tranh. It is the first of three tracks where Bang seeks to give the people's music of Vietnam a jazz character. In 'Ly Ngua O' (Black Horse), there is a sound picture of a Vietnamese wedding, with the bride and groom in a horse-drawn carriage and a strong improvisional passage from Bang, and 'Trong Com' (Rice Drum) celebrates the rice harvest in the northern regions of Vietnam. The slow, reflective melody of 'Don Moi' is an ideal vehicle for Bang's elegaic beauty and Hicks' lucid elegance, and the vibrating thud of Lundy's bass gives the surest of foundations. In 'Lock and Load', post-bop veteran James Spaulding soars into the music with a compelling solo, preceding some fast-shifting choruses from Bang. In 'Reconciliation 1' and 'Reconciliation 2', two musical traditions strive for unity – not easy, given the barriers of history and culture, but the plucking of both violin and dan tranh seek to find a courageous way. For Howard Mandel, author of the sleevenotes, key questions are provoked: 'Can jazz and Vietnamese folk forms find commonality?' and 'Can US and Vietnamese people, once foes, redefine themselves?' Perhaps some of the answer too, is to be found in Bang's exquisite 'Waltz of the Water Puppets' with Spaulding's flute in beautiful ascendancy.

Jazz as a catalyst of post-war reconciliation – made by black jazzmen who were drafted into the apex of the battle, without preparation, without agreement, without choice. It is a part of the music's stature that it can achieve this union, a part of its depth, its emotive passion, its empathetic understanding, its capacity for human growth and love. All this was expressed by Bang after he recorded *Vietnam: Reflections*:

> I learned to respect and love the Asians after Vietnam. I came to this general feeling that these people never really did anything to me. It was my own government that sent me way over there to kind of pick a fight. I regretted that. I felt perhaps guilty about it. Because of that I have become more open to allow relationships and friendships with people of Asian descent.
>
> But that's only me, and the music has different things in it that touch different people in different ways. I'll tell you, I've been approached by a lot of people who lived through that period, telling me, 'Thanks, your music has helped me heal as well.' To hear that is fantastic – I've finally done something valuable through music.

Transformations, and jazz the agency. Words like 'healing', 'reconciliation', 'respect' and even 'love' – and all after the most brutal of interventionist wars – and while others are still being pursued in other nations of the same continent in 2008 as I write. And Billy Bang – squad leader, tunneller, armed combatant now ensures a peace symbol photograph adorns the sleeve of *Vietnam Reflections* and Coltrane still breathes through him.

Cascais Declaration

On November 20 1971, the Ornette Coleman Quartet, consisting of Coleman on alto, Dewey Redman on tenor, Charlie Haden on bass and drummer Ed Blackwell, performed before twenty thousand listeners at the Cascais Jazz Festival, near Lisbon. In the Portuguese colonies of Africa – Mozambique, Angola and Guinea-Bissau – the liberation movements of these future nations were fighting the Portuguese colonial armies, and making significant headway. While touring, Coleman's quartet had pointedly played Haden's composition 'Song for Che' at every concert; and at Cascais the tune was directly dedicated to 'the black liberation movements in Mozambique, Angola and Guinea-Bissau', right in the face of the Portuguese fascist government of Marcello Caetano. The audience, which included many Portuguese students and others who were to play prominent roles in the 1974 Portuguese Revolution, was ecstatic. Haden remembered how 'the cheering continued through most of the song. It was incredible.' As their set finished, Redman, Haden and Blackwell gave a clenched-fist salute, to the frenzied appreciation of the crowd.

Haden later averred that 'the guys who were recruited in Portugal to go fight the black liberation armies in Africa, refused to fight, like the guys who go to Canada here. If they refused to fight they weren't put in jail. They were put on the front lines to be killed.' For his own solidarity and sentiments, Haden – the sole white member of the quartet – was arrested the day after the Cascais concert, as he arrived at Lisbon

Airport to leave the country. The police detained him, interrogated him, and showed him various brochures and propaganda advertising all the good things that the Portuguese were doing for 'their Africans' in 'their colonies'. Haden remembers how their belligerence changed to pleasantries upon the arrival of a US embassy official. He was allowed to leave Portugal the following day.

The incident was high-profile and caused a strong flurry in the world of jazz. Haden was a white jazzman but he was entering, directly and unambiguously, into the international political arena of African solidarity and exposure of the last vestiges of direct European colonialism and virtually defunct Portuguese imperialism – and publicly shattering the myth of popular support among the Portuguese people for these brutal and costly colonial wars. Suddenly, jazz was at the centre of world politics and the future of Africa. And Haden made sure the jazz world fully understood the import of the incident when, in 1976, he released a duet performance (with the drummer Paul Motian) of 'For a Free Portugal' on the album *'Closeness' Duets*. In it he superimposed a recording of his Cascais dedication and the subsequent ovation, together with another recording of the national anthem of the Movimento Popular de Libertação de Angola (MPLA), the liberation movement of Angola – with the voice of the Angolan military leader Hoji ia Henda prominent. By the time that 'For a Free Portugal' was released, not only had the Portuguese people swept away the old fascist regime through their own revolution in 1974, Angola itself had declared its own national sovereignty in November 1975: jazz had shown its propensity for political prophecy.

'Song for Che' had been recorded in 1969 by the Liberation Music Orchestra, a Haden initiative with Carla Bley (born in 1938 in Oakland, California) the main arranger. Haden had written the song in 1967, when he had read of Che's death in Bolivia. As he wrote in the notes of the LMO's first eponymous album, it was 'written for Che, for his people, and for the struggle which immortalised him'. It begins with Haden's solo bass, the huge wooden sound springing at the listener, contrasting with the treble twang of Sam Brown's Tanganyikan guitar and the tingling bells. Dewey Redman comes in with an agonized solo, screeching at the topmost register of his tenor and falling in an expressive cadence. This first Liberation Music Orchestra album, issued by Impulse was unprecedented. Here was a big band, multiracial in composition and playing tunes and songs from the international struggle of labour. Haden first conceived of the orchestra when he heard and was inspired by the republican songs of the Spanish Civil War, and the participation of partisans from fifty-seven different nations to defend the Republic. There are four of these songs in the album, as well as others which point to the liberation struggles in Latin America and the Civil Rights campaign in the USA. The war in Vietnam is remembered by 'Circus '68 '69'. Haden explains the genesis of this in the sleevenotes:

> The idea for 'Circus '68 '69' came to me one night while watching the Democratic National Convention on television in the Summer of 1968. After the minority plank on Vietnam was defeated in a vote taken on the convention floor, the California and New York delegations spontaneously began to sing 'We Shall Overcome' in protest. Unable to gain control of the floor, the rostrum instructed the convention orchestra to drown out the singing. 'You're a Grand Old Flag' and 'Happy Days Are Here Again' could then be heard trying to stifle 'We Shall Overcome'. To me, this told the story, in music, of what was happening to our country politically. Thus in 'Circus' we divided the orchestra into two separate bands in an attempt to recreate what happened on the convention floor.

Music replicating and lampooning the battle of ideas, the battle of classes – and jazz was picking this up. 'Circus' has some of the parodying qualities of 'Fables of Faubus', with Haden's bass aping some Convention buffoonery and Andrew Cyrille's drums providing a clashing sound-drop with the affected cacophony blocking out the strains of the great freedom anthem. It is not until the next, and final, track of the album that we hear 'We Shall Overcome' in all its huge glory, played with massive and unblockable power by Roswell Rudd's trombone, telling of eventual victory – of both the Civil Rights campaigners in the heart of America, and the Viet Cong, continents and oceans away.

The Liberation Music Orchestra reconvened on record in 1982 for the Munich-based ECM label. *The Ballad of the Fallen* took as its thematic centre the US government's support for the conservative and brutal regime in El Salvador, and its provision of arms against the FMLN, the rebel army of the Salvadorean people. On the back of the sleeve is a painting by a young Salvadorean refugee, with prominent inscriptions such as: 'No to US intervention; Yankee invader out of El Salvador', or 'Our only crime is that we are poor. We are tired of so many bullets sent by Ronald Reagan.' The album begins with 'Els Segadors' ('The Reapers') a song of Catalan farmers from the Spanish Civil War, followed by the title song from El Salvador. Haden's approach was to revive the Popular Front ambiance within the sounds of jazz by straddling history and the present. He also included 'Grandola Vila Moreno', the José Afonso song which was played on Portuguese radio as the signal to army officers to begin the insurgency against the Portuguese fascist government in 1974. The orchestra included Bley, Don Cherry, Motian and Redman again, but some impressive newer voices too such as Native American Jim Pepper's tenor and Sharon Freeman's French horn. Bley also arranged the Chilean anthem, 'The People United Will Never Be Defeated', for the LMO, a brief rousing praise-song of popular struggle, and 'La

Pasionaria', dedicated to the Communist leader Dolores Ibarruri, who inspired the republican resistance during the Spanish Civil War. No poet ever got closer to the cry of the blues than Langston Hughes, and the album leans on his words of the title song, unsung but beautifully phrased in the crafted and guttural solos of trombonist Gary Valente, Pepper's tenor and Mick Goodrick's acoustic guitar:

> Don't ask me who I am
> Or if you knew me.
> The dreams that I had
> Will grow even though I'm no longer here.
> I'm not alive but my life continues
> In that which goes dreaming.
> Others who continue the fight
> Will grow new roses
> In the name of all these things
> You'll find my name.

The periodic albums of the LMO – usually separated from each other by about a decade, appeared again in 1989–90. This time, a brace of recorded sessions – the first a live gig at the Montreal Jazz Festival in July 1989, the second an album cut for the Japanese label DIW, and called after a 1962 collection of poems by Langston Hughes, *Dream Keeper*. The two most memorable tracks of the latter album make jazz solidarity with two huge struggles on two continents. The first is an adaptation of the South African freedom anthem, 'Nkosi Sikelel'I Afrika', played at an advancing pace and featuring consecutive saxophone solos by altoist Ken McIntyre and then by Redman. Its sauntering speed and the sheer optimism of its sound bring a message of the doomsday of Apartheid and the impending freedom of South Africa's long-abused people. The second is a Haden composition simply named 'Sandino'. The Nicaraguan nation-builder was, of course, the icon of the

Sandinista revolution, and by the time of this recording – April 1990 – that revolutionary opportunity had passed. In February 1990 the Sandinistas were defeated in the national elections after a decade of government which saw unlimited US interference, destabilisation and continuous support for the murderous 'contras' and their forays over the frontier with visitations of death and mayhem. 'Sandino' begins with a duet between Haden's bass and Mick Goodrick's guitar. Pure and unified, it introduces Tom Harrell's gentle-toned trumpet, with Motian's acrobatic percussion behind him. Sharon Freeman's French horn bounces with Motian's drums and Goodrick's guitar has a serene Spanish tinge, outlining the nobility of the theme melody. The final ensemble chorus has a buoyancy and optimism, finally carried by Haden's huge bass.

The finale, 'Spiritual', is dedicated to Martin Luther King, Medgar Evers and Malcolm X and includes the voices of the Oakland Youth Chorus. Ray Anderson's muscled trombone slides provide its opening strength before Branford Marsalis' tenor, with a gospellised intensity, pays its tribute. The great American trunk of Haden's bass picks up the theme, alongside Bley's passionate chords. *Dream Keeper* managed to imbue its jazz soul with the experience and blood not only of the great struggle of the musicians' own nation, but with those of the people of El Salvador, Venezuela, Cuba, Nicaragua, Spain and South Africa – which by 1990 was an indication that jazz was everywhere, and freely lived in the dreams and aspirations of just about every nation on earth. And this was Haden's achievement, for it took his committed musicianship and that of his LMO colleagues, to expose that to the world of jazz and beyond.

As for the live concert recording cut in Montreal, there is another serene version of 'Sandino', with Harrell's trumpet particularly euphoric and an assured and rhapsodic piano chorus from Geri Allen. And then there follows, almost like a long and proud remembrance, a thirty-seven minute rendering of

'We Shall Overcome', making you recall the first LMO recording of 1969, which lasted precisely one minute and nineteen
seconds. Anderson makes some extraordinary sounds on the
trombone, vocalising, bending, growling and snorting his notes
while Motian rocks and crashes behind him. Ernie Watts
swings out his tenor as if he were playing at a latter-day Jazz at
the Philharmonic – for suddenly the freedom anthem has
become a sacred riff on which every jazzman and jazzwoman
fully expresses their virtuosity and pride in their singular
music. Allen is soulful and racked with gospel, trumpeter
Stanton Davis walks on clouds, Haden tunnels down deep into
the theme – the resonance of his notes is enormous. The tune
is reprised, the epoch has been re-lived and its story re-told in
a country to which the enslaved fled as on a subterranean railway, and but a century and a half before.

And sixteen years later the orchestra formed again, in 2005,
and on the sleeve cover Haden and Bley take a pole each of the
original banner under which the 1969 members assembled and
stood. Now their album bears the name of the current anti-war
slogan – *Not in Our Name*. And these are reflections of America
in the new millennium, its wars, its crimes – but also its beau-
ties and huge potential – for this is also a deeply patriotic
album. Haden writes:

> We were hoping sanity and justice would prevail. They lost
> out to greed, cruelty and injustice. The machine won the
> election again by hook and by crook. The way it won in
> 2000.
>
> We want the world to know, however, that the devasta-
> tion that this administration is wreaking is not in our name.
> It's not in the name of many people in this country.
>
> This CD brings Carla and me together full circle – thirty-
> six years after we made the first Liberation Music Orchestra
> recording in 1968 when the Vietnam War was raging. The

issues remain. And our opposition to the inhumane treatment of this universe remains.

The title tune is about war, the war in Iraq, as thirty years earlier other jazz musicians played their music in the notes of Vietnam, Birmingham, Selma and Little Rock. Steve Cardenas' guitar delicately opens the song, Miguel Zenon's dancing alto takes over as the ensemble hums behind him. The tune is flowing like Bley's piano notes and those of the trombone, trumpet and French horn that follow. It is the truth, the testimony of jazz talking.

And making music about an end to war too, this time in England, were the British jazz musicians of the Paul Dunmall Moksha Big Band on March 29 2003, very soon after the joint US/British invasion of Iraq. Dunmall, a powerful British free tenor saxophonist, had been invited by a BBC radio programme, *Jazz on 3*, to celebrate his fiftieth birthday on air. He gathered together an impressive fifteen-piece big band, including such free jazz stalwarts as trombonist Paul Rutherford, bassist Paul Rogers and pianist Keith Tippett. He wrote in his sleevenotes to the eventual album: 'At the time of writing this piece the war in Iraq was in full flow, consequently the idea of the performance as a birthday celebration seemed trivial, even perverse, so I respectfully inscribed the music *I Wish You Peace.*'

The recording is a summative session, with the orchestra exuding an anthemic power and the soloists radiating a jazz commitment and artistry of an inspired order. In 'Part One', Dunmall's tenor sounds throughout, successively soft and gentle, rasping and rampant, angry and restrained over an ominous ensemble, Rogers' pungent bass-lines and Tippett's darkly rippling chords, all building to a climax and musical replication of shock and awe. 'Part Two' exposes the brass, initially with Rutherford's worrisome trombone in the foreground and Tippett's dazzling keyboard runs. Rogers' resonating, almost whistling bowed bass begins 'Part Three', followed by

Dunmall's haunting soprano chorus and a mounting ensemble crescendo led by a blistering tenor with sudden intimations of the World War Two ballad 'We'll Meet Again', which bursts and explodes over what could be the Somme, Guernica, Stalingrad, Hiroshima, Songmy or Soweto, but it is Baghdad and it is 2003.

Two afternotes, both from 1975, both about America and Africa – Mozambique to be precise. In June 1975 this former colony of Portugal achieved independence from Portugal after a long, hard and sacrificial armed struggle, waged by the Frente de Libertação de Mozambique (FRELIMO). In the same year Archie Shepp recorded his album *A Sea of Faces*, which included 'Song for Mozambique' with these lines

> Later!
> They tell us
> But we know
> The time is now
> Sow your crop
> Mother
> Weep no more
> Reap thy bitter crop
> Father,
> Hard times will soon
> Be over

Familiar enough as a theme – it is 'Jump for Joy' springing in Africa with Shepp's vibrant soprano, flowing in the Zambesi delta as well as that of the Mississippi. But in the same year Dizzy Gillespie came forward too: the great teacher, performer and disseminator of bop and its disciple in Cuba, now, in 1975, takes his horn to Mozambique. On his album *Dizzy's Big 4*, the virtuoso of the trumpet played his own tune, 'Frelimo', in the year that liberation movement won its country's freedom after four hundred years. Blowing alongside Ray Brown's ever agile bass, Joe Pass' fleet guitar and Mickey Roker's drums, the master plays with such facility, lightness and brilliance that it sounds as easy as blowing a feather. But Gillespie is blowing with supreme artistry for Africa and Africans, for forebears, dead and living combatants, and contemporaries; he is blowing out of the jazz tradition for the world's future, for a world that is real and was never a fantasy.

Westbrook's Affirmation

The child's picture of war on the sleeve of the 1969 recording of the Mike Westbrook Concert Band, *Marching Song*, with its images of a rampaging tank below a jet fighter spewing bombs, is in a harrowing concord with the music inside the cover, probably the undersung British bandleader's most powerful achievement amongst many.

Well-esteemed throughout Europe, but hardly known in the USA, Westbrook, from the West England city of Plymouth, combined with fellow Devonian, saxophonist John Surman, and some of the cream of the young British free jazz musicians of the era to create what the double album's sleeve commentary called 'an anti-Vietnam jazz symphony', although we assume that what the writer meant was 'an anti-Vietnam War jazz symphony'. Yet its first performance at the Camden Jazz Festival in London, with the recent commemorations of the fiftieth anniversary of the end of the First World War still in the consciousness of many of the musicians, may well have struck many as a sardonic note too. The military disasters and mass murder from the Somme in 1917 to Songmy in 1968 were shown not to be so far apart in Westbrook's epic musical vision, and close to the conception of three of his heroes; Blake, Weill and Ellington.

Volume One of the 'symphony' begins with 'Hooray', punctuated by mass jingoistic applause, drums, brass and a huge martial ensemble sound of braying horns. Westbrook's solo piano introduces the contrasting reflections of 'Landscapes', with emphatic sounds of doubt and foreboding from growling trombones, menacing trumpets and worried flutesong. The paired bowed basses of Harry Miller and Barre Phillips stir the sense of trepidation before the entry of reedmen Mike Osborne on alto and Surman's soprano, which continues into the 'Waltz' theme with some Coltranish choruses before the ensemble aggregates, as if these soldiers were being compelled to the front by the stylistic dances of those who controlled them. Trombonist Paul Rutherford scatters the national-chauvinist illusions with some ominously rasping slides throughout the sinister 'Other World' of the nightmarish trenches, while in 'Marching Song' itself the two drummers, John Marshall and Alan Jackson, lead the foray in mock-military style before tenorist Alan Skidmore bursts through with a ferociously sustained solo that seems to call out a terrible warning – a cautionary sound of immense power and authority, messaging to the consciousness of the young combatants, and climaxing in a volcanic riffing ensemble chorus.

The dark, sonorous opening of bowed bass to 'Transition', the first section of *Volume Two*, presages sombre, possibly calamitous days ahead, expressed by Malcolm Griffiths' solo trombone. The momentum of war builds up on the home front and towards the field of battle until the reality of the catastrophe is at first portended in Surman's 'Prelude', where the clarinet and flutes suggest the fleeing of birds, and 'Tension' where the build-up of drums, Skidmore's plunging tenor saxophone and the rising and descending tumult of the ensemble prepares the advance 'up the line to death', aided by the frightening wails, the scraped basses and percussive discord of 'Introduction'. 'Ballad', immediately before the storm, played by Osborne's alto, is as a final melodic relief before the monstrous artillery passage of 'Conflict', nearly eleven minutes of agonising ensemble sound, unremitting sonic violence and pain that is unique in the canon of jazz. As the orchestral fury begins to abate, the tuba of George Smith creates a long succession of pounding notes that portray the inhuman essence of war perhaps as no other musical expression could. The mock-anthemic ensemble finale, with the hinting echoes of 'God Save the Queen', point to the 'masters of war' in both London and Washington, and the powers which unleash their savagery on all continents.

6

flowers for Emmett Till

In the summer of 1955, in Money, a town in Mississippi, a four-teen-year-old black boy called Emmett Till who had come down from Chicago to visit his relatives, allegedly had the temerity to whistle at a white storekeeper's wife. Three local white men kidnapped him and threw him into the Tallahatchie River with a seventy-pound cotton gin fan to weigh him down, tied to his neck with a collar of barbed wire. It was a racist out-rage which shocked the world. As far away as Mozambique, José Craveirinha, a poet in the colony's capital Laurenço Marques, wrote in his poem, 'Hymn to a God of Tar':

> Moon hid the heart
> Out came gold
> Out came the polished stones
> Out came the ship, with hold
> full of machines
> Out came news of Emmett Till doll of coal
> Out came the boss' Cadillac . . .

In 1957, the Philadelphian composer and trumpeter, Cal Massey, wrote a tune called 'Bakai' for a Prestige recording session featuring John Coltrane on tenor, Johnnie Splawn on trumpet, baritonist Sahib Shihab, and a rhythm section of pianist Mal Waldron, Al Heath on drums and Paul Chambers on bass. Coltrane was born in Hamlet, North Carolina, in 1926, but moved to Philadelphia in 1943. He played alto in a navy band while in the military, switched to tenor when he joined Eddie 'Cleanhead' Vinson's band in 1947, then played in the Dizzy Gillespie Big Band (1948–49). More experience followed with stints with Earl Bostic, Johnny Hodges and Jimmy Smith before he joined the Miles Davis Quintet in 1955. Fired by Davis because of his heroin addiction, he began to recover under the influence of Thelonious Monk and then began to cut a number of key albums as leader. *Blue Train*, his only Blue Note album as leader, came out in September 1957, but before that came the May recordings (issued in an album called *More Lasting Than Bronze*), which included 'Bakai'.

The title word 'bakai' was an anglicisation of an Arabic word meaning 'cry', for Massey had written the tune in memory of Emmett Till and his agony, although its coded message still suggested the difficulties that jazz musicians faced in 'going public' with tunes that spoke directly of southern racism. The track begins with some emphatic Heath cymbals and Shihab playing a deep, rhythmic riff answered by the other horns, before Waldron steps in, playing in characteristic percussive style with punching, repetitive phrases. Coltrane enters decisively, surging with energy and with a subliminal blues sound, anything but mournful or passive. Shihab continues the defiant mood, digging out his notes from the earth before the cymbals strike out again and the theme is repeated, gradually fading out. This, of course, is the relatively early Coltrane, the spiritual intensity yet inchoate and emergent, but 'Bakai' is still a moving and memorable tribute. Massey's own version of the tune on his own Candid album of 1961, *Blues to Coltrane*, suffers from an out-of-tune piano (played by Patti Bown), but there is a powerful bass solo by Jimmy Garrison, a regular member of Coltrane's greatest quartet, along with tenorist Hugh Brodie playing with intense fire. Massey himself has a slightly cloudy sound, and sharp-edged too, but only restricts himself to playing the theme. An obscure and legendary figure, more illuminating information is given about his life and achievement in the liner notes to his son Zane's album of 1993, *Brass Knuckles*:

> Cal Massey was also a man of strong moral and political convictions, and his staunch devotion to civil rights issues cost him a lot of work in the sixties. Avoiding specifics, Zane explains: 'Because of an incident with a very well-known producer at the time, he was told he would have a very hard time finding work, so he created his own work. In order to provide for his family he had to do it for himself.' Massey's solution to being blackballed by the mainstream New York jazz community was to present concerts independently. Aged and wrinkled hand bills from that time announce all night sessions with Tyner, Morgan, McLean, Shepp, the Heath Brothers, Curtis Fuller, Hank Mobley, Jimmy Garrison and many more that Massey organised in Brooklyn, away from the stifling status quo of Manhattan.
>
> Also organised by Cal Massey were various benefit concerts. A fundraising event to construct a playground for St. Gregory's Church, the Masseys' house of worship, is recalled vividly by Zane. Among the talent assembled was 'Coltrane, Roland Kirk, Wynton Kelly, John Ore, and they did all this for free. It was a beautiful concert, and they achieved their goals and built the playground.'

The narrative leaves you guessing how many other musicians had the same community consciousness and activism as Massey, and how many suffered and were victimised or excluded because of it. 'Bakai' tells his story as well as the tragedy of Emmett Till and, implicitly, many more like them both.

And jazz musicians keep telling the story through their commitment and musicianship, even into this new millennium. In 2004, and on the duet album *Bluebird*, featuring the joint brilliance of white New York pianist Benny Green and black Georgia-born guitarist Russell Malone, there is the track

'Flowers for Emmett Till', a staggeringly beautiful guitar solo, where, quite contradictorily, Malone's quiescent runs and softly lyrical improvisation make the horror of Emmett's torture and agony as cruel as history tells, even half a century later.

Alabama and Africa

Dolphy's fiery and history-filled solo on 'Alabama Song' told one story of the repugnant ruling culture of that state: Coltrane's 'Alabama', on his 1963 Impulse album, *Coltrane Live at Birdland*, tells another. Langston Hughes gave this horrific story words within his sleevenotes of the *Joan Baez/5* album, which included the Richard Farina song, 'Birmingham Sunday':

> It was September 15th 1963, when four little girls went to Sunday School one Sabbath morning and never came back home. Instead they left their blood upon the church wall, with splattered flesh and bloodied Sunday dresses torn to shreds by dynamite, victims of the race war in the American South.

And as Baez sang the chorus:

> On Birmingham Sunday the blood ran like wine
> And the choir kept singing of freedom.

It was just two months after this outrage that Coltrane recorded his live 'Alabama', with Tyner, Garrison and drummer Elvin Jones. Within just five minutes they express the sense of extreme shock, rage and tragic sadness of a people. As Tyner caresses his keys, Coltrane blows a haunting opening threnody. The bass and drums enter, Coltrane continues, the pace quickens, Jones' bass drum propels the quartet forward until a sudden ceasing. Coltrane blows the lamentation again against Garrison's mournful bass and Jones' tinkling cymbals, until the climaxing conclusion, with a surge of notes, a crashing of drums, and silence. 'Alabama' is perhaps the most moving jazz performance to emerge as a direct message of the civil rights movement, and an incisive commentary on the huge crimes of its epoch. It is the essence of jazz: real music telling of real times, the people's story told by four of the people's brilliant musical bards.

Coltrane's attachment to the idea of Africa was profound. It began through the expression of a stream of exoticism with his 1958 Savoy releases of a series of his tunes with African-sounding names, including the colonial name places of 'Gold Coast' and 'Tanganyika Strut', both written by the trombonist Curtis Fuller, and the titles 'Oomba' and 'Dial Africa', the former suggesting something of a vaudeville perspective of the continent. 'Dial Africa' has a tom-tom beginning from drummer Art Taylor which sets a sound close to caricature, and Wilbur Harden's hazy, somewhat leaden trumpet solo reflecting early Miles Davis, makes way for Coltrane, who sparks and vocalises on his tenor before trombonist Curtis Fuller continues the sombre tone. 'Oomba' has some strident Coltrane at its beginning, but seems hesitant and changeable in its rhythm as if it is unsure of exactly the kind of perspective of Africa it is trying to transmit. 'Gold Coast' seems more 'Africanist' than African, with more effects than authenticity. Fourteen and a half minutes in length, it offers much opportunity for solo work. Harden begins with some skilfully lyrical moves and Coltrane plays some luscious scooping phrases, recognisably those he developed more fully in later Atlantic and Impulse albums in his so-called 'sheets of sound' improvisations, and Fuller is more audacious, leaping upward in his choruses, exploring and searching. 'Tanganyika Strut' is certainly a strut, but sounds more Harlem than Dar-es-Salaam. Harden takes off into a beautifully fluent middle-range solo, and the rhythm section, devoid of any effects, just plays with a swinging, straight-ahead bebop momentum. Coltrane loves it and rides it superbly, the phrases pelting from his horn. Detroit-born pianist Tommy

Flanagan enters, completely at home and laid back, finding as many spaces as patterns as he improvises. Taylor offers a boppish drum solo without the pseudo-Africanisms, the theme returns and the music seems to stop exactly in the place that it should. Late new generation bebop at its lively and swinging best is 'Tanganyika Strut', the only message of Africa is in its title.

But what changes by 1961 and Coltrane's epochal *Africa/Brass* double album. Coltrane had handed the responsibility for arranging to Dolphy, and brought together a stellar group of musicians to play a series of Coltrane originals. Even the sleeve told an African story, and the Meade tribal masks from Sierra Leone and photographs of West African instruments, an Attye Drum from the Ivory Coast, a Cameroonian finger piano, a Bankongo hunting horn from Zaire and a Liberian Grebo Guitar, suggested much more of real Africa was to be inside this music, although there were also two versions of an old and very English ballad: 'Greensleeves', and a potent evocation of the struggle against slavery in the USA: 'Song of the Underground Railway'. The opening track, simply called 'Africa', shows how different this Coltrane/Dolphy conception of the continent is from that in the *Dial Africa* session. There are two master-bassists at work in Reggie Workman and Paul Chambers, and the phenomenal drumming of Elvin Jones alongside, and McCoy Tyner's orchestral piano. It is but three years since 'Tanganyika Strut' and Coltrane too, like the people of the new Tanzania, seems as if he has found his own independence and new musical confidence as he soars in front of a multi-horn section. Tyner continues with the two basses and drums, sounding very large. Then the horn ensemble enters in call-and-response mode, two trumpets, four French horns, alto, baritone, two euphoniums, two trombones, and then it is the piano and twanging bassline. 'I wanted the band to have a drone,' Coltrane declares in the sleevenotes. 'We used two basses. The main line carries all the way through the tune. One bass plays almost all the way through. The other has rhythmic lines around it. Reggie and Art have worked together and they know how to give and take.'

It seems that Coltrane had listened to many records of African music for 'rhythmic inspiration', and the bassline emerged as a fundamental undertow to the conception of *Africa/Brass*. As Jones begins his drum solo the basses drop out, one returning with bow, buzzing like insects, before Coltrane returns with his fanfare-like phrases and the other horns wailing in unison behind him. It is an enormous continental sound which gradually fades, the bowed and plucked basses still emphatic until the end.

A second take of 'Africa', recorded two weeks after the first, on June 7 1961, closes the *Africa/Brass Sessions Vol. 2* album. There are two bassists here too, but Art Davis replaces Chambers. Coltrane is titanic above them, his notes surging out. As Tyner begins his solo, the basses leap into the listeners' ears: it is the sound of Africa beginning to free itself, but without effects and attitudinising. There is simply huge, heartfelt and virtuoso jazz in all its complexity: the sound of solidarity in the massive and compelling rhythms of the two basses and drums. As Coltrane recognised, and strove to emulate: 'There has been an influence of African rhythms in American jazz. It seems there are some things jazz can borrow harmonically, but I've been knocking myself out seeking something rhythmic.' He and his confreres certainly found it in 'Africa'.

It may at first seem strange that two versions of 'Greensleeves' should find their way onto *Africa/Brass*, enfolded between the two readings of 'Africa'. Yet this was a song written at a time of Britain's commencement of colonization of both Africa and the Americas – pitched together in unity on the *Africa/Brass* album. And the same imperial outrages created the hellish energies and enterprises which resulted in the slavery of indigenous Africans and the eventual near-genocide of indigenous Americans. 'Greensleeves' is, of course, a melody of sumptuous beauty associated with the British royal Tudors and their court: a song of the same aristocracy which commissioned the imperial voyages which resulted in the first colonial depredations and cruelties. How ironic that it should sound on this album, layered between two variants of an anthem of the continent which suffered most. The first take begins with a thudding bass: the ensemble horns enter, and then it is Coltrane on soprano saxophone – one of his first outings on the instrument with which his art and virtuosity were to become iconic. That this instrument's power should be devoted to a tune originally played on more genteel sixteenth century woodwind horn, now changed to an instrument so profoundly of the twentieth century is also a historic contrast of extreme vitality. It is as if a courtly ballad has been transformed into an African praise song, so powerful is Coltrane's soprano, the mass of backing horns, the grandeur of Tyner's piano and Jones' thunderous drums. On the second take the bass is even more mighty and Jones' percussive undertow has even greater suction. Coltrane begins his solo with the same marathon passion and tenacity that was to take him through all those hundreds of performances of 'My Favourite Things' over the coming six years until his death. Tyner sounds like a minstrel – but a minstrel of the people reprising the melody, then veering away from it in a joyous chorus, and finally returning to it as Coltrane soars back in a last felicitous improvised excursion, with the brass echoing behind him and Jones as much in Africa as he is in urban America. 'Greensleeves' re-made, re-contextualised, becoming the theme of a new post-colonial epoch.

There are two more tracks on *Africa/Brass*. One is 'Blues Minor', a 'head' arrangement, with Coltrane back on tenor, swinging rumbustiously with the combined horns riffing behind him. Tyner carves out a rapid solo, then Coltrane is back, digging earthwards, then soaring up again as the theme returns. But one of the golden performances of the early Impulses on this album is 'Song of the Underground Railroad'. Escape to Canada was often a slow and gradual process for the slave whose mind was fixed on freedom, but Coltrane's piece is fast and furious – this is the fleeing of pursuit, the ever present danger of capture always threatening. Coltrane hurtles through his solo with Jones crashing his snares behind him, the drums the constant inspiration for the fugitives to find their destination beyond the boundary. Jones said of the *Africa/Brass* album, that he 'was trying to think in terms of the African interpretation, as much as I was capable': and in 'Song of the Underground Railway' it is the African dash for freedom in a strange and captive land that he interprets on his drums, forever the sound of the lost continent found again an ocean away.

In 1961, in a town called Albany in the state of Georgia, the local police arrested 267 protesting black students and held them in jail, provoking widescale store and bus boycotts, black sit-ins at lunch counters and public parks. Martin Luther King announced that the movement must 'keep on marching until victory is completely ours' and, soon after, met the leader of the Algerian Revolution, Ahmed Ben Bela, in New York. By December, King was publicly comparing the US Government's neglectful and hostile attitude to the Civil Rights Movement in the USA with its lack of action in ignoring the plight of black people in South Africa. The Kennedy administration had made its 'choice between advantageous economic aid and military alliances' on one hand and 'the establishment of racial and political justice' on the other. The Civil Rights Movement and the black South African freedom struggle was recognising a common enemy. And all this was happening while Coltrane and his confreres were recording *Africa/Brass* and Coltrane was launching his saxophone freedom cry along the length of this twentieth century Underground Railway.

Archie's Message

No jazz musician has spoken more openly and directly about the unity of jazz and human liberation than Archie Shepp – saxophonist, vocalist, dramatist and poet. Jazz is, he once declared, 'one of the most meaningful, social, aesthetic contributions to America. It is antiwar; it is opposed to [the war in] Vietnam; it is for Cuba; it is for liberation of all people . . . Why is that so? Because jazz is a music born out of oppression, born out of the enslavement of my people.' No ambiguous, concealed or codified words here; the message of the words is clear, as is the message of the music. Born in 1937 in Fort Lauderdale, Florida, Shepp migrated north to Philadelphia when he was seven. As a youth he was exposed to some of the great jazz figures of the post-war age, a generation of new musicians from Lee Morgan and McCoy Tyner to Ted Curson, Bobby Timmons and Jimmy Garrison. He went away to pursue a scholarship in Vermont, majoring in drama and literature, before returning to Philly to begin a professional life of music. By 1963 he had organised the New York Contemporary Five, and in 1965 his friend John Coltrane helped him gain a recording contract with Impulse – his first Impulse album, *Four for Trane* celebrated the cultural union he had with Coltrane.

In June 1963, the Mississippi leader of the National Association for the Advancement of Colored People (NAACP) and long-time Civil Rights activist Medgar Evers, was shot, murdered, by a local Klansman outside his home in Jackson. In November the influential New York Contemporary Five, composed of cornetist Don Cherry, tenorist Archie Shepp, Danish/Congolese altoist John Tchicai, with Don Moore on bass and J. C. Moses on drums, were touring in Scandinavia. The live performance at the Jazzhus Montmartre in Copenhagen on November 15 was recorded, and among the tunes is Shepp's composition, 'The Funeral', dedicated to Evers. Its origin is a cogent example of the power of titles in coincidental form, since it was written, and it seems titled, two months before Evers' death, but was first performed the very night that he died. The Contemporary Five was a powerfully innovative group. Cherry had been a part of Ornette Coleman's revolutionary quartet, and played on albums like *The Shape of Jazz to Come*, *Change of the Century* and *Free Jazz*, and both Tchicai and Shepp were to play on Coltrane's double album *Ascension* in 1965. Shepp had made several pathmaking albums with iconoclastic pianist Cecil Taylor in 1960–61, including *Air* and *The World of Cecil Taylor*. So the Contemporary Five, although short-lived and with only a single recording, was a key band of its times. And 'The Funeral' is not as one played by a marching band in New Orleans. It is performed with a shocked solemnity, jagged and full of pain. Cherry's cornet cries against Moses' angry drums; Tchicai's alto enters wailing and before the closing ensemble Moore plucks some barren and agonised notes and Shepp blows mournfully. Like Coltrane's 'Alabama' the Five's 'Funeral' is a direct jazz response to a real act of murderous racism, and the music expresses the moment in all its cruelty and loss.

So different then, to another tune for Evers, by now a revered and distant historical figure, recorded by young musicians of at least two generations hence in 1991 at the Newport Jazz Festival, a long way from Jackson, Mississippi, and featuring the young guitarist from Syosset, New York State, Mark Whitfield. He plays 'Medgar Evers Blues', his own composition, as part of an all-star octet, Jazz Futures, including trumpeters Roy Hargrove and Marlon Jordan, pianist Benny Green, bassist Christian McBride, drummer Carl Allen and reedmen Tim Warfield and Antonio Hart – all young lions of the time. Whitfield plays through his tune with mid-tempo optimism, a beautiful narrative clarity and with the four horns riffing behind him – as if Evers' sacrifice and those of many of his contemporaries have provoked vital changes all around him and clearer pathways for the future. Released from the tragic moment of historical reality that defined the Five's performance, Whitfield and his confreres are stomping forward, a new generation with advantages and freedoms won and secured by those who struggled before.

In 1965 came another album, *Fire Music*, and Shepp had some powerful 'new' players on hand – Ted Curson, Reggie Johnson, altoist Marion Brown and drummer Joe Chambers. But perhaps the most compelling track on the album is a trio performance of 'Malcolm, Malcolm – Semper Malcolm' with bassist David Izenzon and J. C. Moses on drums. Malcolm X had been assassinated in 1964, but for Shepp he was being born again in every young black person of the Americas. 'Malcolm knew what it is to be faceless in America and to be sick and tired of that feeling. And he knew the pride of black, the negritude that was bigger than Malcolm himself. There'll be other Malcolms.' For Shepp's tribute was a riposte from a new jazz generation to the shame and alienation of 'Black and Blue'. Nothing could be more different. Originally dedicated to the martyred Medgar Evers, it becomes Malcolm's memorial too. Shepp begins with these lyrics and Izenzon's mournful bow:

> A song is not what it seems,
> a tomb perhaps.
> Bird whistled while
> even America listened.
> We play, but we aren't always dumb.
> We are murdered in amphitheatres
> on the podia of the autobahn.
> Philadelphia, 1945.
> Malcolm, my people,
> Dear God, Malcolm!

Shepp and Izenzon's bass duet against Moses' thudding drums. Shepp's rasping tenor, adenoidal and agonised, wails over the loss. His memorable line, 'we play, but we aren't always dumb' seems to speak of the generation of jazz musicians before his own, and the messages lying deep and implicit in their notes. Now there will be no more dumbness.

Fire Music also includes 'Los Olvidados', a reference to Luis Buñuel's film of 1950, and to Shepp's own work amongst the black urban youth of New York's Lower East Side. Shepp was seeing the despoliation, destruction and incarceration of a new generation of young black people, the forgotten ones of American cities, and 'Los Olvidados' begins to strike their note and become a theme throughout his lifetime of musical utterance. 'Los Olvidados' begins with some leaping ensemble before Chambers hits a long roll, the pace quickens and Curson delivers a skipping solo, audacious and soaring like the young men of the streets. Johnson's bass is carping, as Brown and Shepp weave in and out of each other, with mutual challenges. Shepp grates out his solo, running and dodging, pursued by the other horns. These youths have a pounding energy; they are restless – a sense picked up in Shepp's next recording session for Impulse, both in the three takes of 'The Chased' (included later on the CD version of *On This Night*) and in 'The Pickaninny (Picked Clean – No More – Or Can You Back Back Doodlebug)'. Take one of the former is a churning pursuit played by Shepp, Izenzon and Moses, hurtling forwards, fiery and unnerving with Shepp playing with husky fury like an impassioned Ben Webster at full pelt, choking his notes while Izenzon buzzes beside him and Moses pummels his drums. Izenzon's solo gives no release from the hunt, so relentless is he in emulating Shepp's frantic patterns on his own instrument. On the LP *On This Night* Nat Hentoff's sleevenote of 'The Pickaninny' affirms that 'with unmissable finality . . . the piccaninny of the past is no more. . . Having been picked clean, the pickanniny now knows where he's at – and he's moving,' and the title reference to 'can you back back doodlebug' is southern demotic telling that the old ways of viewing the black child are consigned to the past. He or she is a new person now, and Shepp's sound portrait has much to tell the listener. Playful, jaunty, confident, precocious – this child, as shown by Shepp's frolicsome opening solo, now *must have* a childhood – the premature adulthood of 'starting work at seven' from Basie's 'It's the Same Old South', has got to change. And she must have an education too, with no more Faubuses or Barnetts stopping the way when she reaches her university. All this is immersed within Shepp's assured and dancing notes, Moses' clipping drums and Izenzon's virtuoso bass.

The title track, 'On this Night (If that Great Day Would Come)', a Shepp composition dedicated to the colossal intellectual contribution of W. E. B. Dubois, is described by Shepp in the sleevenotes as 'a synthesis of how I sum up contemporary America as a man of color'. Shepp plays piano behind Christine Spencer's soprano voice as she begins to sing, with Rashied Ali's fluttering cymbals and the chiming of Bobby Hutcherson's vibes. This is not the blues: it is a labour anthem that she is singing, a jazz 'Internationale':

> Now is the time for all men to stand
> Rise up you starved and toiling masses!
> My brothers, sisters all
> We cannot fail, justice is our avenging angel,
> All hail the bird of truth!
>
> Behold the blood from my brother's veins
> How will we remember?
> Come soon that day when slaves break
>   their chains
> And the worker's voice resounds
> Give back the valleys, steppes and plains
> They are mine, they are mine!

'On this Night' is unique in the jazz canon. The words may be closer to a Robeson praise song, yet they mesh with Shepp's astonishing tenor solo after Spencer's passionate, almost operatic vocal and Henry Grimes' sawing bass chorus.

Like the sound of enraged breath, Shepp respires through his
horn rather than blows through it, and he seems to be voicing
the words he spoke during the same year:

> Don't you ever wonder just what my collective rage will . . .
> be like, when it is – as it inevitably must be – unleashed. Our
> vindication will be black as the colour of suffering is black,
> as Fidel is black, as Ho Chi Minh is black. It is thus that I
> offer my right hand across the world of suffering to black
> compatriots everywhere. When they fall victim to war, dis-
> ease, poverty – all systematically enforced – I fall with them,
> and I am a yellow skin and they are black like me or even
> white. For them and me I offer this prayer, that this twenty-
> eighth year of mine will never again find us all so poor, nor
> the rapine forces of the world in such sanguinary circum-
> stances.

A jazzman speaking – unlike any who had spoken before –
speaking like George Jackson, Bobby Seale or Huey Newton.
The music of Louis Armstrong, Duke Ellington and Charlie
Parker had come this far in forty years. An absence of fear and
trepidation, as victories in the accursed South were being
accomplished on a daily basis by the poor and the ordinary.

Shepp's 1972 album, *Attica Blues*, provoked by the Attica
Prison revolt, is one of the most audacious and explicit jazz
albums. It combines big band jazz set within a seventies electric sound; telling, poetical lyrics; tributes to two of the great
jazz inventors, Armstrong and Parker; two compositions by a
neglected jazz genius – Cal Massey; and all contextualised
within a thematic sound essay of doomed and heroic youth.
But more than any other American, the epochal figure of
George Jackson is invoked in this album. Brought up in poor
black neighbourhoods of Chicago, then Los Angeles, Jackson
dropped out of school, became involved in petty crime and by
the age of eighteen he had been convicted for robbery, having
been the driver of a getaway car after a robbery of seventy

dollars from a petrol station. His sentence: 'one year to life' – effectively a life sentence. In May 1961 he was sent to Soledad Prison, in 1962 moved to San Quentin and suffered long spells of isolation and continuous denial of parole, as well as being seriously injured by guards when he went to the aid of another inmate who was being beaten up. In January 1969 he was returned to Soledad, and to isolation. In his first letter of his book, *Soledad Brother*, written on June 10 1970, Jackson wrote:

> Black men born in the US and fortunate enough to live past the age of eighteen are conditioned to accept the inevitability of prison. For most of us, it simply looms as the next phase in a sequence of humiliations. Being born a slave in a captive society and never experiencing any objective basis for expectation had the effect of preparing me for the progressively traumatic misfortunes that lead so many black men to the prison gate. I was prepared for prison. It required only minor psychic adjustments.
>
> I was captured and brought to prison when I was eighteen years old and because I couldn't adjust. The record that the state has compiled on my activities reads like the record of ten men. It labels me brigand, thief, burglar, gambler, hobo, drug addict, gunman, escape artist, Communist revolutionary, and murderer.

'Attica Blues' is a commentary on this passage, the true meaning of these words put to music. And by the time that the album was issued, Jackson was a dead man, shot and killed inside San Quentin on August 21 1971, seeking to save other inmates from an 'official massacre.' He wrote in one of his letters: 'I've been in rebellion all my life,' and Shepp's record takes up his revolt in jazz.

On the sleeve photograph Shepp is at his piano, his saxophone resting on its lid. Behind him are two posters: one the photograph of the three black American Olympians raising their gloved fists at the 1968 Mexico games; the other depicts

African themes – masks, figures and dancers. It is an expression of Jackson's own declaration in his July 4 1970 letter to Angela Davis published in *Soledad Brother*: 'Our problems are historically and strategically tied to the problems of all colonial people.' The title composition, 'Attica Blues', is much less a prison lamentation than an anthem of hope, dominated by Cornell Dupree's funky guitar, Walter Davis Jr.'s electric keyboard and Leroy Jenkins' fiery, sizzling violin – and the earthy, gospelised vocals of Joshie Armistead and Albertine Robinson, reminiscent of Aretha Franklin, singing repeatedly

> If I had the chance to make one decision,
> Every man would walk this earth in an equal position . . .

The next track is the elegy to one of Shepp's young cousins, known as 'Steam', an exemplary black youth, cut down as his adult life was beginning:

> Someone
> Comely as we
> Will be
> Will be
> Summer
> Soft as the rain
> And sweet as
> The end of pain
> A star
> Gleaming
> Bright as fire
> In the night
> A theme
> Whenever I think of 'Steam'

Jenkins' violin is the strident voice, along with Shepp's husky soprano, particularly in the second take, where the tender lyrics are movingly sung by Joe Lee Wilson. 'Steam' is a beautiful and tragic lost youth of the ghetto, like Milton's *Lycidas* a song of lamentation filled with the spirit of hope.

But the climax of the *Attica Blues* album is the 'Blues for Brother George Jackson'. An emphatic bassline, a strong orchestral ensemble and Shepp's tenor weaving between its chorus and Marion Brown's alto, then Shepp again, both low-down, exultant, rousing above Beaver Harris' pounding drums which link directly to the lyrics of the next tune, 'Ballad for a Child'.

> I would rather be a plant
> than a child in this land;
> Not a child, not a man.
> Branches can grow free
> Again and again and again,
> If a man had a choice
> before he was exploited,
> Then his offspring
> would do more than dream.

Jonathan's Struggle

Unissued and lying among the Blue Note stacks until 2008, Todd Cochran's composition 'Jonathan' was recorded by a group led by vibist Bobby Hutcherson in July 1971 in Los Angeles, just eleven months after the death of George Jackson's seventeen-year-old brother, Jonathan. In his dedication to his brother at the front of George's epochal epistolatory text, *Soledad Brother*, he describes him in this way:

> Tall, evil, graceful, bright-eyed, black man-child – Jonathan
> Peter Jackson – who died on August 7 1970, courage in one
> hand, assault rifle in the other; my brother, comrade, friend
> – the true revolutionary, the black communist guerrilla in
> the highest state of development, he died on the trigger,
> scourge of the unrighteous, soldier of the people.

On that day, Jonathan, provoked by his brother's transfer to San Quentin Prison, had entered the San Rafael Courthouse during the trial of a San Quentin prisoner, with a bag full of handguns. He uncovered a carbine from under his jacket and declared to the court: 'All right, everybody, this is it!' He tossed guns to the prisoner and two of his witnesses, took the judge, the District Attorney and three jurors as hostages, and marched them outside, towards a van in the courthouse parking lot where some guards had already arrived. During the subsequent shoot-out, Jonathan, the judge and two of the prisoners were killed – even as the court still echoed with Jonathan's final words as he left the chamber: 'We are the revolutionaries! Free the Soledad Brothers by 12.30!'

In the last epistle of *Soledad Brother*, written two days after these events, George Jackson declared: 'We reckon all time in the future from the day of the man-child's death. Man-child, black man-child with submachine gun in hand, he was free for a while. I guess that's more than most of us can expect.'

And it has taken thirty-seven years for Hutcherson's recording 'Jonathan' to appear, so dangerous to America was its subject and dedicatee – as dangerous and as righteous as Guevara of Argentina and Cuba, as Camillo Torres of Colombia, as Victor Jara of Chile, as the determined Vietcong, as the African guerrillas of the MPLA in Angola, FRELIMO in Mozambique and the PAIGC in Guinea-Bissau – all kindred and contemporaries of the Jackson brothers.

Todd Cochran was a classically-trained pianist and composer, born in San Francisco, who had previously combined with Hutcherson in an experimental project, *Blue Note Meets the L.A. Philharmonic*. Cut during the same sessions that produced the material later issued on Hutcherson's Blue Note album *Head On*, the omitted 'Jonathan' includes a sonorous solo by Hutcherson's long-time confrere, the Houston-born but Los Angeles-based tenorist, Harold Land. There is a reflective keyboard contribution by Cochran and a flickering chorus from trumpeter Oscar Brashear after Hutcherson's etching of the theme and his long, audacious solo, full of sudden pauses and plunging cadences. So now, after four decades of silent concealment we have it, and Jonathan Jackson's moment is at last exposed as a real and essential moment of jazz history too.

Nefertiti

In one of the last letters of *Soledad Brother*, Jackson wrote to Angela Davis: 'I love you like a man, like a brotha, like a father. Every time I've opened my mouth, assumed my battle stance, I was trying in effect to say I love you, African – African woman.' Davis had been arrested in October 1970 in New York, on false charges of murder, kidnapping and conspiracy – from which she was finally acquitted by a Californian jury in June 1972. As a black militant, communist, intellectual, ceaseless campaigner for the black incarcerated and member of the Soledad Defense Committee, she had become a legendary revolutionary figure within US black urban communities. Recorded in September 1971 on Lee Morgan's final Blue Note album, *The Last Session*, and composed by ex-bassist of Blakey's Jazz Messengers, Jymie Merritt, 'Angela' begins with Merritt's plunging bass and bells played by fellow-bassman Reggie Workman. Morgan's simmering modal trumpet blows out over Harold Mabern's electric piano. The trumpeter was to be killed by a disaffected woman friend in Slug's Saloon in New York in 1972 but, with huge historic irony, 'Angela' is a dignified, almost majestic tribute to a heroic young black woman.

It was a view of woman hugely different from the exploited female of the blues universe, or the brutalised woman personified in so many of the Billie Holiday songs – betrayed, beaten, deceived. Jackson's correspondent is idealised into a symbol of resistance, loyalty, dignity and love. Black woman is recast, reconfigured, reconceived by the black male artist, and her blackness is beautiful, ultimately beautiful. Nowhere in jazz is this more lucid than in Miles Davis' album *Nefertiti*, which has other keys to its times too. By 1965 Davis had assembled one his most brilliant and enduring quintets, with Wayne Shorter on tenor, pianist Herbie Hancock, Ron Carter on bass and Tony Williams on drums. *Nefertiti*, of June 1967, was their fourth studio album, and their last that was completely acoustic. The title tune, composed by Shorter and seeming to characterise African womanhood in sublimity and pride, includes a virtuoso drum performance by Williams – still only twenty-two at the time of the recording. Shorter opens with a rhapsodic solo passage, beside Hancock's chordings with Carter diving down the bass strings, and Williams' cymbals tingling. Davis comes in alongside Shorter in an ensemble of stately cadences and already Williams' drums are everywhere. The ensemble rises to a crescendo, then gradually lowers its sound, with Williams pounding and clashing in drum glory. There are no real solo statements beyond Shorter's few commencing bars, some Hancock chords and a sequence of final bass notes, but the performance is one of huge beauty and collective musicianship.

Also a part of *Nefertiti* is Hancock's composition 'Riot', quietly redolent of suppressed rage. On Friday August 13 1965, violent disturbances broke out in the Watts ghetto of Los Angeles, with crowds of the disenfranchised and dispossessed storming blocks of shops with Molotov cocktails. King characterised the uprising as 'a class revolt of the underprivileged against the privileged', and symbolic of the anger seething in millions of urban blacks in communities throughout America. 'Riot' is a short enough piece, only three minutes long; Carter's dancing bass is emphatic, and Shorter's opening solo seems to hold an unleashed level of passion. Davis' solo crackles and below Hancock's keys there seems a mounting fury. It is an astonishing performance, if only for the way in which the musicians seem to be keeping a lid on some potentially irrepressible eruption, any time soon. 'Riot' has a singular and uncanny feeling of jazz prophecy, a feeling which also emanates from other dramatic tracks in this album: listen to 'Madness' or 'Pinocchio'. Perhaps it is the extraordinary ominous fusion of cymbal and snare which Williams concocts and his amalgam with Carter. They are like no other drums/bass duo anywhere in jazz for their creation of trepidation and furious uncertainty. Hancock recorded 'Riot' again under his own leadership in March 1968, as a part of his album *Speak Like a Child*. He and Carter are present again, with Mickey Roker on drums, and an ensemble non-soloing frontline including flugelhornist Thad Jones. Hancock is more impressionistic in his playing, less imbued with threats, and although Carter is still ominous in his bassline, the absence of Williams makes the sound less epochal, less racked with portent, less of a foreboding message.

Many jazz compositions and album titles of the early seventies onwards took on the pride, and sometimes the rhetoric of the black struggle. It was the reversal of everything that Armstrong had sung in 1929 in 'Black and Blue': 'my only sin is in my skin' became an ugly apostasy, completely set aside for the imagery of 'black is beautiful'. This huge change in self-belief, self-esteem and self-confidence became integral to the music – won through the civil rights victories in the South, and in the brave examples of the Black Panthers and prison resisters integral to the black urban neighbourhoods. A whole generation of jazzmen grew within the flowering of a new black aesthetic, and their music fructified within its influence, when Black Power slogans were integral to real changes of confidence and new realms of radical action in politics as well as art. One of these slogans, provocative and self searching, 'If You're Not a Part of the Solution, You're Part of the Problem', frequently seen as a warning to white fellow-travellers, is a track on the Joe Henderson live album of 1970, *Joe Henderson Quintet at the Lighthouse*.

Henderson had the precocious twenty-six-year-old trumpeter from Laurinburg, North Carolina, Woody Shaw, alongside him, as well as George Cables on seventies-style electric piano, the furious drummer Lenny White and Ron McClure playing electric bass. This is Henderson's tune, and its undercurrent of electric timbre and White's backbeats give it a typically epochal message, not without its subliminal menace and Henderson's characteristically squiggling, uneasy sound, with bent, distorted notes and stuttering phrases. Shaw often sounded as if he was playing on the most acute of edges, and he does here too with drama and intensity, as if a disaster were impending. Cables' electric pianism was as piercing and inventive as any of his era, and he too leaves a sense of 'things to come' in the air, as if the tune itself is the harbinger. There is a similar sense to the final track, 'Mind Over Matter', of another Henderson album, *In Pursuit of Blackness*, cut in May 1971. Here Curtis Fuller is on trombone and there is another reedman, Pete Yellen, on alto, bass clarinet and flute. Stanley Clarke comes in on bass. The bass clarinet underlines the sense of portent with White's fervent drums and Cables' amazing piano, and outside all is the sound of Henderson's tenor, chortling and squawking, bawling and hollering, at last calmed by the serenity of Fuller's slides. The sound is worrisome – a nonverbal commentary on an internal struggle of a new jazz generation.

Woody Shaw put the sense of preoccupation in these words in the sleevenote of his album *Blackstone Legacy*, which was cut in 1970:

> We're trying to express what's happening in the world today as we – a new breed of young musicians – feel it. I mean the different tensions in the world, the ridiculous war in Vietnam, the oppression of poor people in this, a country of such wealth. The cats on this date usually discuss these things, but we're also trying to reach a state of spiritual enlightenment in which we're continually aware of what's happening but react in a positive way.

Blackstone Legacy is dedicated to the freedom of black people all over the world. And it's dedicated to the people in the ghettoes here. The 'stone' in the title is the image of strength. I grew up in the ghetto – funky houses, rats and roaches, stinking hallways. I've seen all of that and I've seen people overcoming all of that. The music is meant to be a light of hope, a sound of strength and of coming through. It's one for the ghetto.

The album cover has a powerful, almost silhouetted image of a line of southern Sudanese women walking over the dry land of their Aluma province, and yet the photographs of the musicians inside their sleeve seem as American as it is as possible to be. It is a hard duality, but one that these Americans seem determined to crack with the consciousness of their musicianship and their understanding of the significance of the people's culture they are building – a working out in jazz of Jackson's belief, written in his book *Blood in My Eye* during the final few months of his life and finally published in 1972, that 'conditions are right *now*, for the beginnings, at least, of a revolutionary culture; these conditions have always been present here inside the Black Colony but . . . no leadership until now.'

'They Shot Him Down'

As a preface to his album *Volunteered Slavery* of 1969, Rahsaan Roland Kirk wrote the following adage at the top of the sleevenotes: 'We are all driven by an invisible whip. Some run, some have fun, some are hip, some lip, some dip, but we all must answer to the invisible whip.' The track begins with a lone Kirk on tenor, with tambourines and an entering bass: Then the voices emerge:

Volunteered slavery
you got me on the run,

Volunteered slavery
you got me having fun
Oh, volunteered slavery,
Oh, volunteered slavery,
Oh, volunteered slavery!

Kirk's horns, Charles McGhee's trumpet and Dick Griffin's trombone blow free, and then merge into a chorus of the Beatles' 'Hey Jude', echoing the lines:

If you want to know
how to be free
You got to stay in bed
all day with me!

Kirk was a humourist of jazz, yet he was saying something of deadly seriousness in *Volunteered Slavery*. How was it, while brave black people in the South, and in the ghettoes of western and northern cities, were sacrificing their lives in the pursuit of freedom, others were willingly selling theirs to the old masters, or to new masters of the same ilk, through the processes of new forms of 'blaxploitation'? Two years before the death of George Jackson and the Attica martyrs, Kirk was identifying and lampooning those within his community who cared little and profited much. It was sharp and brave music. Even in his version of the Aretha Franklin hit, 'I Say a Little Prayer', written by the songbook ikons Burt Bacharach and Hal David, Rahsaan adds a foreword which completely changes the meaning of the song from a lovesong of a woman anticipating a meeting with her man. There are some mournful notes of a tenor, and someone shouts like a street crier:

They shot him down!
They shot him down!
They shot him down!
We going to say
a little prayer for him anyway!

and the ensemble bursts out, with cries, whistles, some tail-gate-like trombone and rocking piano. This is beyond mere hokum. A gospellised pop song becomes part-threnody, part parody, but the meaning is clear: another black man in street or prison has been cut down.

Rahsaan made his last album in 1977, *Boogie Woogie String Along for Real*. He had suffered a serious stroke in 1975, and lost musical use of his right hand despite prolonged therapy. But indefatigable and hugely tenacious, he devised a method of using his other hand alone to play reed instruments, and on this final album he plays with his usual prodigiality tenor, flute, harmonica, clarinet and electric kalimba. The last track, 'Watergate Blues', is written by the bass-player of the Modern Jazz Quartet, Percy Heath (it was recorded by the reconstituted MJQ in 1984). Thus Rahsaan in his last record was the first to chronicle in jazz the disastrous break-in of the Democratic Party National Committee HQ in the Watergate Hotel, Washington D.C., in 1972 by members of President Nixon's administration, provoking presidential cover-up, impeachment and Nixon's eventual resignation in August 1974. Heath plays cello on the 1977 Kirk recording and duets with Rahsaan's flute and harmonica, zipping as a featured soloist above Philip Bowler's solid bass all through the performance. Kirk bellows out 'Watergate!' before the music begins and ends with a cry of 'Take him away! Don't give him no break!', his ultimate defiant recorded words.

Spaulding's Tribute

In May 1988 James Spaulding recorded an album for Muse called *Gotstabe a Better Way*. Spaulding was a fiery, spirited horn-man affected by the free playing of fellow altoist Ornette Coleman. He had also recorded with Sun Ra's Arkestra in the late fifties and early sixties, before he moved to New York in 1962. There he formed his own bands, but also recorded frequently as a sideman with Max Roach (*Drums Unlimited*, 1966), Freddie Hubbard (*Hub-Tones*, 1962; *Breaking Point*, 1964); and Randy Weston and Art Blakey (*Blue Spirits*, 1965–66). Spaulding's passionate contribution to Hubbard's 1967 album *Backlash*, includes his boiling, rhapsodic chorus from the title tune, which as Hubbard commented, was 'saying a whole lot about freedom for black folks back in the day.' It was as a prelude to *Gotstabe a Better Way*. Then, in the late seventies he concentrated upon study, gaining a degree from Paul Robeson's old college, Rutgers, before returning full-time to music in the early eighties and beyond. *Gotstabe a Better Way* is really a tribute album to black heroes, and there are tunes dedicated to Garvey ('Ginger Flower Song'), Malcolm ('Remember There's Hope') and 'Blue Hue', which Spaulding composed as he was recovering from the shock of the assassination of Martin Luther King in 1968. The album has these essential words of King on the front of its sleeve, from his opening address to the 1964 Berlin Jazz Festival:

> Jazz speaks of life, the blues tell the stories of life's difficulties, and if you think about it for a moment, you will realise that they take the hardest realities of life and put them into music only to come out with some new hope and sense of triumph.

And within the sleeve, together with the usual photographs of the musicians and introductory commentary, there are extracts from notices posted in the times of slavery of absconded slave-musicians. So we read:

> RUN AWAY. . . a Negro man about forty-six years of age . . . plays on the violin and is a sawyer (*Virginia Gazette*, April 24, 1746)

CAESAR . . . absented himself from my new plantation
. . . plays well on the French Horn (*South Carolina Gazette*,
April 19, 1770)

RUN AWAY . . . Negro named Zack . . . speaks good
English, plays on the fife and German flute, had a fife with
him. (*Poughkeepsie Journal*, 1791)

RUN AWAY . . . a mulatto fellow named John Jones about
twenty-six years old . . . is a mighty singer. (*Maryland
Gazette*, April 14, 1745)

Musicians and ancestral jazzmen all, permeated the sounds
of Spaulding and his confreres – Mississippi-born bassist and
pianist Ron Carter and Mulgrew Miller; Ralph Peterson from
Pleasantville, New Jersey; New York percussionist Ray
Mantilla and the young vibist Monte Croft, all playing in the
spirit of the African drummers depicted on the sleeve with
Marcus, Martin, Malcolm and the runaway rebel and founder
of the 'underground railway' to Canada, Harriet Tubman,
whose portraits also stare from the sleeve cover, alongside
those of Ellington, W. C. Handy and a runaway slave.

And the music does not disappoint or become complexed
by its iconic dedications. The opener, 'Bold Steps', soars into
sound with Spaulding's burning alto and Peterson's fierce
drumming behind him, before Carter, Miller and Mantilla
burst into fire. Peterson, a Blakey disciple, is a profound presence all through the album, knowing and showing how the
drum was the first sound of jazz. 'Blue Hue', remembering
King's death, prompts Spaulding to remember: 'I'll never for-
get that day. People were stunned, crying and running home to
be with their families.' The performance is built upon Carter's
bass heartbeat and Spaulding's weeping notes. The Caribbean
laps all through 'Ginger Flower Song', remembering Garvey's
Jamaican origins. Mantilla's congas create the setting with

Spaulding's flute direct from the formidable Zack of
Poughkeepsie, and some lively vibes from Croft. 'Remember
There's Hope' begins as a threnody to Malcolm, with
Spaulding's praying flute, but Carter and Peterson carry the
theme powerfully with Mantilla's bells and scrapers until
Miller's testifying solo, Croft's proud choruses and Spaulding's
flute begin to fly towards hope itself.

Finally there is the emblematic 'Gotstabe'. Spaulding
describes its genesis in this way:

> My family and I had been evicted from our Harlem apart-
> ment because I refused to buy it. Our stuff was out in the
> streets and I thought 'Gotstabe a Better Way'. This tune is
> the voice of the homeless, the poor and the downtrodden
> crying for help in the richest country on the face of the
> earth. I've always wanted to write and play things that cele-
> brate our humanity and connect heart to heart.

The jazz musician speaks, then he plays, with a history of his
people's struggle in image, word, music and real story inside
him. From the picture of Africa painted in sound of 'In Flight
Out', where Peterson's grounding drums, Spaulding's fluttering
piccolo and Croft's intense vibes colour the vision through
resistance in Virginia and the Carolinas and the courage of
heroes and twentieth century martyrs, to the reedman's own
struggle for shelter in Harlem and his indignant howl of saxophone from its streets, his narrative unfolds with jazz as its
form and its message of defiance and hope.

7

black lightning

In Spring 1962, Duke Ellington was playing a concert in Zurich, Switzerland. He was persuaded to visit a local night-club after his concert – the African Club, and found a twenty-eight-year-old South African pianist with his trio. Ellington was deeply impressed, and later arranged for the pianist to record for his label, at the time the US Reprise label. The pianist was Adolph Johannes Brand (known firstly as 'Dollar' Brand, then later renamed in the Muslim faith as Abdullah Ibrahim), born in Cape Town in 1934 of a mother who was of the Bushman people and a Basuto father. Ibrahim had already established a strong reputation in his home country, through his close musical association with the Johannesburg-born altoist, Kippie Moeketsi (born in 1925) and their band called the Jazz Epistles, which also included trumpeter Hugh Masekela, trombonist Jonas Gwangwa, bassist Johnny Gertze and drummer Makaya Ntshoko. In 1962, disgusted with the privations and divisions of the Apartheid system, Ibrahim left South Africa, firstly for Europe and then, after his meeting with Ellington, for the USA where he played at Carnegie Hall, the Newport Jazz Festival, the Village Vanguard and was embraced within the highest places of jazz achievement. Meanwhile, back in South Africa, Moeketsi, also sickened by the frustration, violence and waste around him, gave up his saxophone, not returning to it until 1971.

And while these events in the jazz world passed, in South Africa the Prime Minister and leader of the Nationalist Party Dr Henrik Verwoerd, announced 'a four stranded vertical development of Apartheid', with 'separate development' for whites, blacks, Indians and 'coloureds', and the first Bantustan, Transkei, received its bogus independence. In May 1963, South Africa's all-white Parliament passed a law legalising torture by the security forces. The Bantu Laws Amendment Act was passed which, according to Liberal MP Helen Suzman, stripped the African in his own country (although white ownership of South African land was eighty-seven per cent) 'of every pretension he has to being a free human being in the country of his birth', reducing him to the level of a chattel. It was racial slavery again, Jim Crow many times worse in Africa, and jazz had its part to play in exposing and destroying it one more time. Then in October 1964 the Rivonia treason trial began of Nelson Mandela, Walter Sisulu and eight other leaders of the African National Congress (ANC). They received life sentences. Mandela had pronounced:

> Above all, we want equal political rights. Our struggle is a truly national one. It is a struggle of the African people, inspired by our own suffering and our own experience. It is a struggle for the right to live.
>
> During my lifetime I dedicated myself to this struggle of the African people. I have fought against white domination and I have fought against black domination. I have cherished the ideal of a democratic and free society in which all persons live together in harmony, and with equal opportunities. It is an ideal which I hope to live for and to achieve. But, if needs be, it is an ideal for which I am prepared to die.

Ibrahim's US debut album, *Duke Ellington Presents the Dollar Brand Trio*, includes his own composition, dedicated to his friend and confrere, 'Kippi'. It is a sad, rolling, somewhat mournful theme, picked out lucidly in Ibrahim's incomparable timbre. 'He was influenced by Bird and taught all of us a lot,' declares Ibrahim in the sleevenotes, in words of salutation. Ibrahim returned to South Africa in 1968 recording several times with Moeketsi. He remembers how, when they played together in Johannesburg's nightclubs in front of white audiences, Moeketsi would always resist being pushed out of sight through the kitchen at the ends of sets, and how he always resisted the racism that surrounded all black jazz musicians in South Africa. But 'Kippie's life was not wasted,' despite his death in 1983 and relatively small recorded legacy: 'How could it be when it was Kippie who gave us everything we know? We have just built on from what he taught us.'

In the 1971 recording of *African Sun*, for example, in the title track we hear Ibrahim and Moeketsi together in a quartet context. Moeketsi had only just returned to playing, Ibrahim had been in the American spotlight. Yet the two play in a brotherly unity with Ibrahim striking the keys with a pounding message of African drums, and Moeketsi gruff, rasping and direct, almost if another drum were inside his horn. Then in 'Bra Joe from Kilimanjaro', Ibrahim rolls out his solo introductory notes, striking a repetitive undertow before Moeketsi grates in, scraping the sky with his jarring notes and terse vocalised sound, then returning towards the end with a more reflective passage of wonderment and marvel. It is an astonishing pairing, all-African, with sound both new and indigenous. 'Rolling' is exactly that, with Victor Ntomo's bass and Nelson Magwaza's drums taking Ibrahim and Moeketsi down another pathway. Kippie skips, trips and saunters, full of life and breeze, as if forward is the only way. And then there is the Eubie Blake/Andy Razaf (from across the Mozambique Channel in Madagascar) American Songbook classic, 'Memories of You'. Heartbreakingly realised, Moeketsi's chorus is as raw and nerve-endingly sensitive as any alto solo that you will ever hear. He cries out from his world of deformed relationships and endless humiliations with a voice of agonised beauty, with Ibrahim striding up and down the keys beside him. One of the great jazz performances is this from a land whose government was offering the majority of its people unlimited pain, changed to the sounds of sublime jazz.

Something similar is found pouring from the tenor horn of Winston 'Mankunku' Ngozi through the length of his performance of his 1968 anthem to John Coltrane, 'Yakhal' Inkomo' (Bellowing Bull). Coltrane had died in 1967, leaving admirers all over the world, and Ngozi's rapturous tones and pained, mournful phrases touched something in the emotions and consciousness of the South African people. *Yakhal' Inkomo* became the all-time best selling jazz album within the country, moving thousands of South Africans who had never previously heard of John Coltrane.

Ibrahim continued to water the roots of South African jazz by employing a concoction of indigenous genres to create something entirely new. In the 'townships' and slums outside the white cities, where millions of Africans had been 'endorsed out' by the Group Areas Act to live in desperate shanty cities and new hellish suburbs, jazz meshed with other musics. In creating his sound portrait of such an urban nightmare, 'Mannenberg – Is Where It's Happening', Ibrahim used aspects of jazz mbaqanga melody, the marabi dance rhythm, Xhosa ragtime, hymn melodies (darkly prominent in his music), kwela and US swing and bop themes – particularly those of Monk. Ibrahim's piano has the timbre of a harpsichord – dry, tingling, grating with sand, dust and wind, while the horns – Basil Coetzee's tenor and Robbie Jansen's alto – blow gurgling choruses over Paul Michaels' spare bass and Monty Weber's rattling snares. It is the sound of desolation and affliction, with Coetzee's smarting notes messaging grief and wretchedness, within a subliminal tenacity. When the end finally comes, the pianist exclaims 'Oh, Mannenberg', and there is the seed of hope, a hope which grows in the seventeen-minute long 'Black Lightning'. There is a peal of thunder, the crack of a storm and the theme begins. Three horns, Moeketsi's alto and the tenors of Coetzee and Duku Makasi exchange phrases with Ibrahim. Then Moeketsi enters, dynamic, powerful, creatively assured, his rasp carrying huge conviction. Coetzee blows a flute chorus, not unlike a rallying call, sweeping over the riff made by the other two horns while Ibrahim drums on his keys. Makasi's solo has staccato phrases, jabbing at his improvisation then lengthening out his notes while the horns play out the theme together, then separately, and vocal interjections spill all around it as Kippie's alto grates and Ibrahim's piano pounds down in the final notes. 'Black Lightning': it carries the sound of resistance, the echoes of 'Umkonto we Sizwe' – the spear of the nation.

In 1976 Ibrahim left South Africa again. It was the year of the massacre of more than 600 schoolchildren as they marched in the streets of Soweto, the giant township outside Johannesburg on June 16 to protest against the teaching of Afrikaans in black schools. This time it was a self-imposed exile, and one which signalled protest and intense opposition to Apartheid. In 1977 Steve Biko, the widely admired and respected black activist, was killed in detention and eighteen black organisations were banned, along with two prominent black newspapers. In 1979 Solomon Mahlangu, ANC combatant, was executed. In 1980 there were nationwide boycotts against Apartheid education, a wave of industrial militancy, rent protests and bus boycotts – and in June, ANC guerrillas sabotaged the SASOL oil-from-coal complex. Over 900 people were detained during the year. In January 1981 the South African army attacked houses in Maputo, Mozambique, killing thirteen ANC members and in November there was a successful boycott of the elections to the government-sponsored South African Indian Council. In 1982 the government streamlined and strengthened its security laws and expanded its armed forces in the face of intensified national resistance – and in Dortmund, Ibrahim, showing strong support for insurgency, recorded his solo piano album, *South African Sunshine*. This was a combination of jazz standards such as Billy Strayhorn's 'Chelsea Bridge' and Paul Mason Howard's 'Shrimp Boats', with radical originals focusing on South African realities like 'Soweto', 'Children of Africa' and 'Hit and Run'. The last of these, through its expressive lyrics, advocated the ANC strategy of armed struggle – hitting, running and seeking freedom, 'through the barrel of a gun', moving guerilla-like and invisibly like ghosts to strike 'where it hurts them most', while coolly serving the white Apartheid-supporting oppressor his breakfast: 'Boss, here's your morning toast.'

But the most telling track was 'Tula Dubula':

> South African Sunshine,
> see how the guns shine,
> hungry lips feed on the sound of freedom.
> Tears in their eyes are not from crying,
> but gas and bullets and the sound of sighing.
> Tula Dubula,
> No need to say much more,
> it's all been said and tried before
> it's all over now but the dying.
>
> Night in the cornfields
> and the town's a-sleeping
> what's this I hear softly a-creeping.
> Soldiers of Africa, fighting for freedom,
> invincible children, inheritors of weeping.
> Tula Dubula
> No need to say much more,
> it's all been said and tried before,
> it's all over now but the dying.

There's a new world a-coming,
falsehood will all be gone,
they'll come a-marching into town at dawn
Singing songs of freedom and laughing in the rain,
Gone will be this old world, things won't be the same
Tula Dubula.
No need to hear much more
we've heard all these lies before
it's all over now with their lying.
In the township afternoon,
songs of their impending doom,
the racists and their puppets are a-dying
Tula Dubula.

By 1985 Ibrahim was performing with a version of his band Ekaya that, apart from himself, was composed completely of seasoned American jazzmen. Carlos Ward was on alto and flute, Ricky Ford on tenor and Charles Davis on baritone. Dick Griffin played trombone, Cecil McBee played bass and on hand was Monk's old drummer, Ben Riley. *The Mountain* was an album composed almost entirely of Ibrahim tunes – including one especially for Apartheid-free South Africa's future first president, 'Nelson Mandela'. Mandela was finally released from prison on Robben Island on February 11 1990, but this track was recorded a full five years before his freedom, when Mandela had turned down a deal allowing his release if he were to renounce the armed struggle, and the ANC was spearheading mass national resistance. It radiates a huge sense of optimism. The rhythm jumps, the ensemble sweeps along. Davis delivers a baritone solo of chuckles and laughter, Griffin's trombone guffaws its message and Ricky Ford's tenor sounds like a griot telling a people's story with only one outcome – a narrative continued gleefully by Ward. And all through the romp Ibrahim's piano is rocking forward, leading the chronicle, taking it towards its end, and the end of Apartheid, and one more time, another jump for joy.

Masekela's Journey

Hugh Masekela, famously, was given his first trumpet by Father Trevor Huddleston in the Johannesburg suburb of Sophiatown, before its people were forcefully relocated and their community was destroyed by the Apartheid government in 1955 to make way for the new all-white suburb, eventually renamed 'Triomf'. From being lead trumpeter in the Huddleston Jazz Band (Huddleston later persuaded Louis Armstrong to send him a trumpet from the USA) Masekela found his way at the age of twenty to the renowned Jazz Epistles with Brand, Kippie Moeketsi and Jonas Gwangwa, and in 1960 to London, and eventually to exile in the USA, where Harry Belafonte arranged a scholarship for him and he was frequently recorded from the mid-sixties onwards. Quite a journey, but one which caused him continually to hearken back to his early years in Johannesburg.

Masekela made a succession of waxings, some with potent political implications, and none more so than 'Stimela', a train story in the tradition of Ellington, provoked in 1972 in the middle of a party in his rented home in Woodstock. As the tune and its words came to him, he left the revelry to find a piano, to set down the notes and lyrics. As he recalls:

> I remembered my grandmother's house in Witbank, where migrant labourers who worked in coal mines came to drink. My sister Barbara and I were still toddlers and the miners would tell us their sad stories about how they came on the coal train from Mozambique to work in the mines. They spoke of the filthy, conditions they were surrounded by in their all-male hostels, their longing for their families, the cruelty of their white employers and foremen, their measly

pay and how much they longed to return home to Delagoa Bay where they could be away from living a stray dog's life, where they would eat real food instead of the slop they were being fed and where they would be safe from the cave-ins which killed so many of their colleagues. This song is about the train.

Masekela recorded the haunting theme of 'Stimela' many times, his horn sounding like a lonely train ploughing through the night, before his earthy vocal, backed by a chorus, churned out the words. I remember a twenty-minute version he performed at Ronnie Scott's in 1999, and the raw, locomotive power of his trumpet sound. It was South African testimony at its most arresting and creative, played with intense and brilliant musicianship, and it told the story of a defiled social and political system through the lives of men who suffered some of its most dire consequences. Its sense of alienated and exploited working life sends its listeners right back to October 1925 and 'Coal Cart Blues', played by the same man who had despatched his trumpet across an ocean, to reach a young contender on the southern tip of the continent of his ancestors.

Masekela's mother, Polina, was the leading social worker of Alexandra township, where Nelson Mandela's wife, Winnie, did her fieldwork. The family connection was strengthened when Masekela's father visited Winnie when she was internally exiled to the distant town of Brandfort. From then on, Masekela's parents were carefully watched by the South African police. Mandela himself was in clandestine contact with the trumpeter from 1985 onwards, when he was developing a school of music in Botswana. Masekela later wrote: 'I was intensely moved by the fact that a man who had been imprisoned for over twenty years could have so much passion and regard for the work that was being done by some musicians in a small town in Botswana. It brought tears to my eyes. His confidence about our imminent liberation was overwhelming.'

Masekela's part-jazz praisesong, part-anthem for Mandela's coming release and South Africa's freedom from Apartheid, 'Bring Him Back Home (Nelson Mandela)' was first recorded in 1986 on the album *Tomorrow*. Masekela and chorus sing out in jubilation:

> Bring back Nelson Mandela,
> Bring him back to Soweto
> I want to see him walking down
> the streets of South Africa
> Tomorrow!

And Masekela's fiery, elated horn strikes out a chorus of joy, hope and prophecy.

Blue Notes from Africa

In 1964 another group of South African musicians, the Blue Notes, travelled to Europe, initially to play at the Antibes Jazz Festival, and found a reluctant exile. Their pianist, Chris McGregor, was a white man born in Umtata, later to become the 'capital' of South Africa's first bantustan, Transkei. His father had been a missionary of the Church of Scotland and his son's understanding of life and music had been transformed by hearing hymns sung in Xhosa by his father's congregation. McGregor's bandmates were all outstanding musicians. Dudu Pukwana, born in 1938 in Port Elizabeth, was a tempestuous altoist who combined township jazz, rhythm and blues with Parkeresque licks and an appetite for free music. He and tenorist Nick Moyake had played together in Port Elizabeth before they joined the Blue Notes. Bassist Johnny 'Mbizo' Dyani was born in 1945 in East London, came to Cape Town as a singer but turned to bass when he heard Johnny Gertze playing with Ibrahim. Drummer Louis Moholo had established a big band in his native city of Cape Town, and played as if a storm were inside him. Queenstown-born trumpeter Mongezi Feza's performances in Europe caused him to be heralded as a true horn-genius, capable of exquisite lyrical sounds imbued with passion and mercurial wit.

The Blue Notes did not stay together in Europe long. But their diaspara across the continent caused dramatic waves within the circles of jazz. Moyake soon returned to South Africa where he was to die of cancer but the other five confreres transformed much of British jazz with their originality, passion and brilliance. McGregor, Pukwana, Feza and Moholo became the nucleus of Brotherhood of Breath and stimulated the development of British jazz musicians such as tenorist Evan Parker, trumpeters Harry Beckett (who been born in Barbados) and Mark Charig, altoist Mike Osborne and trombonist Malcolm Griffiths. Moholo and Johnny Dyani also teamed up with Steve Lacy, and later toured Argentina.

Then the Blue Notes as a unit, plus new partner drummer John Stevens and his Spontaneous Music Ensemble, spent a sojourn in Denmark, playing at Copenhagen's Montmartre club and finding themselves suddenly within exalted jazz circles, performing alongside free jazz spirits from Albert Ayler, Cecil Taylor, Don Cherry and John Tchicai to more seasoned voices like those of Dexter Gordon and Ben Webster. At last, they were in the heart of it, and the influence and inspiration were two-way. In London, Stevens played a major role in connecting local free jazz musicians with the South African exiles, and by the late sixties the Spontaneous Music Ensemble lineup included a combination of Stevens and free altoist Trevor Watts with Dyani and Feza. New musical cultural and human alliances were being made in Britain's jazz scene, as the blows against Apartheid were being stepped up, harder and harder, in the homeland. It could be said that the kind of cooperation and multiracial unity being expressed by the music of black and white jazz musicians in London was exemplary for the struggle in South Africa. Not for Mongezi Feza though. The

British National Health System did little for this brilliant South African. Taken into hospital in 1975 with many symptoms of a nervous breakdown, he found not recovery but pneumonia, and died still young and unfulfilled.

In the Townships was recorded in London in 1973, and features 'Dudu Pukwana and Spear', a quintet of Pukwana, Mongezi, Moholo, the white South African bassist Harry Miller – another talented exile, and tenorist Bizo Muggikana. This is jazz, the like of which London had never heard before, transported with real authenticity from the Apartheid State's urban ghettoes. A fusion of hooting alto and vocal chorus begins 'Baloyi', with Moholo's crashing drums and Miller's thumping bassline. It is a music of huge energy and excitation, full of Africa and its thirst for freedom. On 'Ezilalini' Pukwana switches at first to piano, and Feza's horn soon comes on strong, soloing with spiky eloquence, cutting and mercurial. Then in comes Pukwana in a dangerous-sounding duet with Feza, both horns sounding on the edge. 'Zakude' has a more bluesy sound, with Pukwana wailing over a slow repeated riff, until the time changes and Feza soars above the other two horns. 'Sonia' is Feza's composition (the others on the album are all by Pukwana) and begins with some click scat, and then Dudu's horn begins to howl above the ensemble decibels of Mongezi and Bizo until a premature fadeout. 'Angel Nemali' gives the full sound of Moholo, thundering behind the horns. Pukwana steps forward roaring and then squeezing out his notes in sculpted squeals. 'Nobomvu' has another fiery theme, led by Pukwana gurgling through his solo and 'Sekela Kluluma' has an anthemic spirit, immediately associated with mass action and resistance in those same townships. Hearing this music three decades ago brought with it the understanding that the people's resistance and the huge, mass culture behind it would not be contained; that their freedom and the breaking of Apartheid were irrepressible; and that this astonishing music – original yet forged through the international sense of promise that jazz brought – was a messenger as much from the South of Africa as it had been from the South of the USA.

1973 also brought another recording inspired by the people of South Africa, the *Live at Willisau* album by the Brotherhood of Breath. What was remarkable was that notes and rhythms forged in South African urban shebeens, streets and festivals and the dances and genres they provoked – the Marabi and the Kwela – were now being carried to the heart of European jazz, played not only by their own exiled musical geniuses like Mongezi, Dyani and Pukwana, but being learned and applied within their own musical settings by the most talented and progressive white European jazz musicians. But other partnerships were developing too. White exiles like McGregor and Miller were at last playing freely and without fear with their black compatriots. Miller had arrived in England to play the fusion of pop and blues which characterised the music of his white countryman, Manfred Mann, but soon turned to the much less ephemeral sounds of the Brotherhood of Breath. All within this ensemble was the remarkable trumpet pairing of Harry Beckett and Mongezi Feza. Beckett's ancestry was African, having been brought to Barbados through the British imperial enterprise of slavery centuries before. Feza's alienation from the African continent was of a different epoch and through entirely different imperial circumstances, yet here they were, playing their horns side by side in this extraordinary orchestra in 1973, as Feza's homeland was rocked by a huge wave of black workers' strikes. 'Do It' has a long solo by the British free tenorist Evan Parker; 'Restless' features some rapid-fire, non-stop Miller basswork, a storming Moholo and Pukwana at his most frantic. 'Camel Dance' has a pounding rhythm unleashed by Moholo, some churchy sounds from McGregor and the ensemble and Beckett travelling skywards, and answered by an equally stratospheric Pukwana, chewing on his notes. 'Davanshe's Dream' features the old partners

Pukwana and Feza, goading each other as jazz comrades do, with Miller's bass foundation solidly provocative, while 'Tunji's Song' has an extraordinary trumpet solo from Feza, spinning phrases together from the bottom of his horn and whirling them upwards in vortiginous spirals while the other horns riff behind him.

And just a week before the Willisau concert, the Brotherhood of Breath had played another concert, in Bremen, Germany, which was recorded as the album *Travelling Somewhere*. Trombonist Malcolm Griffiths joined the horns as did the British altoist Mike Osborne, which created an even more fevered sense of ensemble – hear it on 'Ismite is Right', enveloped within a huge gospelised South African sound, not unlike some of the ensembles of the Liberation Music Orchestra, but with Moholo's thunderous drums. 'Kongi's Theme' came from the film *Kongi's Harvest*, with a screenplay written by the Nobel Prize-winning Nigerian author Wole Soyinka. McGregor was invited to write the score, and 'Kongi's Theme' features the trombone of Nick Evans and the howling obbligatos of Osborne. 'Wood Fire' has the sound of a Sun Ra orchestration, with the ensemble never resting, even in the heart of solos. Evans and Griffiths are intersected by Pukwana's strident alto as this fire takes hold and is burning everywhere. Osborne plays with a beautiful fluency through his own 'Think of Something', but the most memorable moments of this throbbing album are with Feza's trumpet in the title tune. Sometimes the introduction, with its piano swing, makes you think you are about to hear a Basie performance, but as soon as Feza begins blowing, bursting his horn with passion and exposing a raw and pained sound which no other trumpeter has ever made with the ensemble ripping behind him, you know that this is the narrative of what Apartheid has done to South Africa, and his story is the strangest amalgam of torture and hope.

Chris McGregor once said of Archie Shepp, 'he became a

pioneer figure for us; he talked so clearly about the black music situation in the States, and naturally we saw quite a few similarities and parallels with the South African situation we had just left.' These similarities became jazz unity in Tokyo in 1978 when Shepp and Ibrahim recorded a duo album for the Japanese label, Denon. The second track was an elegy to Feza, 'Barefoot Boy from Queen's Town', written by Shepp and performed with the reedman on soprano saxophone. Ibrahim begins with a skipping riff, before Shepp enters, playing his soprano in the high register, expressing a sense of playfulness and joy, but all within his breathiness, as if he were indeed a boy out of breath, never stopping, never resting, spanning the unity of two massive popular struggles in two huge continents.

Mbizo's Times

Meanwhile, in Denmark, Dyani was engaged in developing his own jazz testimony and recording it through Steeplechase, the local Copenhagen-based label. *Witchdoctor's Son* of March 1978 pitched him with John Tchicai, the altoist with both Congolese and Danish roots, his old confrere Pukwana and two Brazilians, guitarist Alfredo do Nascimento and drummer Luez 'Chuim' Carlos de Sequeira. Tchicai had been a bandmate of Archie Shepp in the New York Contemporary Five in 1963 and played alongside Coltrane on the master's album *Ascension* of 1965. *Witchdoctor's Son* creates a cosmopolitan amalgam of jazz, bringing together Africa, Europe and South America in an early expression of 'world music'. Pukwana's 'Radebe' gives the South African his own vehicle for a powerful, agitated outing and Dyani's often-recorded 'Ntyilo Ntyilo' is an opportunity for him to sing his melody to the accompaniment of Brazilian guitar and drums. In the traditional song 'Magwaza', Dyani's vocal precedes Tchicai's solo, which sounds as oral as the voice that came before it, racked with voice inflections sounding above Dyani's powerfully resonating bass.

The 1978 album *Song for Biko* commemorated the life and struggle of Steve Biko with a quartet of three South Africans – Dyani, Pukwana and drummer Makaya Ntshoko, together with the Oklahoma-born trumpeter Don Cherry, Ornette Coleman's horn partner on his early, revolutionary recordings. Biko was murdered in custody in September 1976 and very quickly became a martyr of the resistance movement. The title tune contains an elegaic, mournful solo by Pukwana, with Ntshoko's superb drumming behind him – African in spirit, yet with all the jazz skills of a Billy Higgins or Charles Moffett. Cherry sounds much less mercurial than usual, and plays the theme and his solo with a huge sigh of sadness and respect. Dyani bends his huge notes under the horns and Ntshoko's blows, and throughout the performance we hear the Ornette Coleman format transformed to an African praisesong. Yet it happens as if it were entirely and culturally natural, as if the music of a quartet which was condemned and rejected by many in the land of its original forging, should be wholly apt to pay homage to a hero of Africa.

Thus this adaptation of the Ornette Coleman Quartet – a syncretism of America and Africa made in Europe – is created to give inspiration to the struggle of the South African people. Dyani said of 'Wish You Sunshine', the album's opener, that it was 'about my people. I'm trying to keep up my people's spirits at a time when there's been so much unrest.' And this was the period post-Soweto of 1976, as well as post-Biko: a critical time of the struggle. 'Wish You Sunshine' begins with some stark solo notes by Dyani before the horns enter and Cherry plays a dancing, buoyant solo which floats above the bass and drums before Pukwana and Dyani play together in a sequence of beautiful brotherhood and Ntshoko is beside them also, spurring them on.

Dyani and Pukwana are also partners on the album *Mbizo* (Dyani's nickname), recorded live in 1981 at the Third Eye in Glasgow. The drummer is Churchill Jolobe and the second horn is Ed Epstein, playing alto and baritone. On the first track, Pukwana's 'Dorkay House', Dyani's bass sounds huge as Pukwana steams into his solo, blowing irreverent allusions, Mingus-like, to 'The Yellow Rose of Texas' before Epstein blasts in, playing in the lower reaches of a very heavy baritone. 'House Arrest' goes inside the Apartheid state again. It has a sinister, worried theme and Dyani's bass seems to be the organising force, in the same way that the Mingus bass was at the creative centre of all his workshops' most powerful performances. Pukwana's testimony is agonised but he pours out his notes like a man at last released from bondage, telling his loved ones about every chained moment. And it is no surprise to find that the final track on the album is called 'Dedicated to Mingus', since the giant bassman's spirit has been at its centre. Dyani's enormous notes dominate the performance. The theme moves quickly, but with a sense of anxious foreboding, and Pukwana's squeezed notes, together with Epstein's growls are full of the real world and its crimes and sorrows which Mingus certainly never feared to confront directly in his music. And Dyani, from the tip of his own continent, was his brother.

Yet another internationalist element enters Dyani's instrumentation in *Afrika*, recorded in October 1983, when the focus of the world was on the Caribbean – following the implosion of the Grenada Revolution and Ronald Reagan's subsequent US invasion. Immediately in the first track, the South Africa-focused 'Blame It on the Boers', steel drummer Rudy Smith enters with a sharp and bouncing solo, as if the interference in the Caribbean and Africa were a part of the same world reality. Epstein is still present on *Afrika*, with a second bassman – Thomas Østergren from Denmark, and South Africans Gilbert Mathews on drums and Thomas Dyani on Congas. Veteran American baritonist Charles Davis, from Goodman, Mississippi, completes the line up. The most powerful track is also the shortest, just two minutes and twenty-nine seconds. It remembers the sacrifice of three ANC Umkhonto we Sizwe (Spear of the Nation) combatants, Simon Mogoerane, Harry Semano Mosolili and Thabo Motaung, who were convicted of acts of sabotage against police stations and commuter rail lines in Soweto, and power plants in the nation's capital, Pretoria. On August 5 1982 they were sentenced to death. The three martyrs all stated that they had been tortured during their interrogation by the police. Dyani's 'Pretoria Three' memorialises their struggle. His solo bass beginning has the sound of a spiritual, and the theme melody has the beauty of an early Ibrahim composition. His final note rings and lingers in its fullness of depth like an eternity. Two more tracks remember two heroes of South African jazz. The first, 'Kippie-ology', is rapid, started by Dyani in a spirit of plucked strings and joined by some conga fire and Smith's steel drums, pounding a sound that Moeketsi may not have dreamed of joining with his own. The second, 'Dedicated to Abdullah Ibrahim', remembers another pioneer, and steams along in a joyful, repetitive chorus with Matthews' romping drums as its engine.

Between December 1983 and May 1985 Dyani recorded *Born Under the Heat* in Stockholm, which included three tracks where he played piano. The first, 'Wish You Sunshine', is a piano suite, dedicated to three South African pioneer jazz pianists – Gideon Nxumalo (a teacher of Ibrahim), Pat Matshikiza and Shakes Mgudlwa. The brief portrait of Tete Mbambisa celebrates another, and Dyani plays with a percussive solidity, echoing early Ibrahim. 'Lament for Crossroads' is an astonishing aural re-creation of the forced removal of thousands of dwellers of that Cape township to barren faraway 'homelands' by the South African police. The horns combine Swedish trumpeter Ulf Adaker and tenorist Krister Andersson with American veteran alto and baritone saxophonist Charles Davis and South African star tenorist of the 1950s, Peter Shimi Radise. Dyani's bass founds a cacophony of horns, animal effects, children's cries, thudding hoofs and whinneys as Radise's tenor leads the ensemble, in the heart of the coercion of the people. 'The Boys from Somafco' is a track of free movement and hope, identifying with the exiled school students of the ANC's Solomon Mahlangu Freedom College in Mongoro, Tanzania, named after the hanged ANC martyr. 'Namibia' is dedicated to SWAPO, the Namibian liberation movement in armed resistance against the South African army, and features the two Swedish horns. 'Song for the Workers' brings back to the fore trombonist Mosa Gwangwa in a kwela-based tune with Dyani switching back to piano, and Radise blowing a gruffly fluent solo. *Born Under the Heat* is a deeply committed album redolent with the power of titles, none more stirring that its finale, 'Let My People Get Some Freedom', where guitarist Pierre Dorge plays a romping solo and long-time South African drummer Gilbert Matthews is fiery and full of cymbal.

Dyani's last record was *Angolian Cry*, an act of solidarity with a neighbouring, sister people who were facing the final wrath of the Apartheid army. Acts of aggression against the Angolan people by the South African military were escalating, with cross-frontier strikes across the Namibian border becoming regular occurrences from 1977 onwards. These had the objective of clearing the extreme south of Angola and creating a zone of attack for the US-backed UNITA, the renegade Angolan movement headed by Jonas Savimbi. Savimbi was an earnest ally of the South African regime, whose attacks against targets in southern Angola were becoming increasingly bloody.

An important part in the gradual defeat of Apartheid was taken by the Cuban army fighting to defend the MPLA government alongside Angolan soldiers, which prevented the invading South African army overthrowing the Angolan government between 1975 and 1991, an historic moment being at Cuito Cuanavale, when the Cuban troops defeated the South African forces. In 1991, following the overthrow of Apartheid, South Africa's new president, Nelson Mandela, told a rally in

Matanzas, Cuba, that this victory, as part of the Cuban contribution to Angola's defence, was 'a turning point in the struggle
to free the continent and our country from the scourge of
Apartheid.'

'Angolian Cry' represents all these events: a cry of pain, a cry
of struggle, a cry of victory. Dyani's solo bass begins before
Washington, D.C.-born Billy Hart's drums resound to introduce the theme played by Tchicai and Beckett. Tchicai's tenor
sound is one of sorrow and hurt, his notes resonate with
Angola's betrayal and agony. Beckett, as usual poised and pellucid, gives his Caribbean sound to the West African nation,
note-perfect in his searing high-note passages, before Hart
gives his drums back to Africa. It is an all-round brilliantly real
song of love for Africa. Also included in the album is another
Dyani piece, 'U.D.F.'. The United Democratic Front (UDF)
was launched in August 1983 at a twelve-thousand-strong rally
in the ampitheatre of Mitchell's Plain, a sprawling working
class suburb of Cape Town. The Front was an amalgam of six
hundred affiliates, including trade unions, youth and student
groups, sporting clubs and professional bodies, and communi-
ty-based organisations. The UDF was organised regionally, and
sought to bring together the widest possible range of opposition forces to the Apartheid regime, and here was Dyani and
his confreres adding their voices of participation to an alliance
which was to have a critical organisational role during the final
years of Apartheid. And, as with the Civil Rights Movement,
the churches were to have a key role. One of the principal
speakers at the founding event, Dr Allan Boesak, spoke of the
'politics of refusal' that was to unite the movement. Dyani's
'U.D.F.' is, as you would expect, an ensemble piece led by
Dyani's bass chorus, under three minutes long, with a defiant
edge and determined spirit.

Two of the tunes of *Angolian Cry* have children as their
theme and 1985, the year of its recording, was a year when, as
in 1976 in Soweto, South African children across the country

launched themselves into acts of resistance, in particular in Cape Town and its environs. A Cape Town mother told a Social Workers' conference: 'I envy people whose children jump around and play. Our children are no longer children; they have become the adults. My ten-year-old says there's no time for play. The games she acts out are what to do when the police come. She says, 'is this cupboard big enough for me to hide in? No, I'll rather hide in the laundry basket. I must remember to take some clothes out of the basket before I go to sleep so there is space for me.' Rebellion in schools, on streets, against Apartheid education, against second-class housing, resources and sports facilities and in solidarity with adult struggles inspired and illuminated the country. But these same children were hearing the sounds of freedom coming ever closer. An exiled school student, twelve years old, in the Solomon Mahlangu Freedom College in Tanzania, wrote this poem, 'The Sound of Freedom':

> The sound of freedom
> Hear it
> It is coming
> It is coming slowly
> But it's surely on its way
>
> Hear it
> It is almost here
> Soon it will be here
> Soon we will be free
> We will be free
> We will love our freedom
>
> If we want freedom
> We must fight for it
> We must study for it
> We must work for it
> But we will get our freedom
> The freedom that we want.

And you can hear this freedom coming closer in 'Year of the Child' from *Angolian Cry*. Dyani begins, with Hart clashing his cymbals, then Tchicai on bass clarinet and Beckett's pure brass sound duet before Beckett rises to a solo of particular beauty and delicacy, offset by Tchicai's clarinet and Dyani's twanging bass notes. Tchicai's solo is worrisome, flickering with the unexpected, filled with childhood leaps into the unknown. A brilliantly realised and narrated piece of jazz is 'Year of the Child', as is 'Does Your Father Know?' – a question asked of many a South African child after arrest and during long and brutal interrogations. The sounds are fast, hard and relentless, the two horns in a frenetic colloquy, speaking of the pain and ordeals of children, and Dyani's buzzing, stinging bass offers no release.

By October 1986, Dyani had died in Berlin and he was only forty-one. The surviving Blue Notes – McGregor, Pukwana and Moholo cut a tribute album called *Blue Notes for Johnny* as, with Dyani too, they had recorded *Blue Notes for Mongezi*, after Feza's early death in 1975. The three survivors play with great love and skill, but the huge rhythmic and virtuoso hole left in the bottom of the music by Mbizo's departure is almost over-whelming. As John Stevens said of Dyani: 'The fact that Johnny isn't around any more means that you will never hear that sound again, other than through plastic, as he invented the way he played.'

But in 1987 Stevens and Pukwana played 'as a trio for two' in another album dedicated to Dyani, *Mbizo Radebe (They Shoot to Kill)*. This was a climactic year of mass agitation and resistance in South Africa, with consequential intense repression. One and a half million workers stayed away from work to commem-orate the Soweto rising and there were widely-supported strikes in the mines and public sector. You can hear all this emerging in this two-person amalgam of drums, alto, soprano, piano, vocals and mini-trumpet, but again, how Mbizo is missed. The sadness is that both Pukwana and McGregor died in 1990, the year of Mandela's release, the unbanning of the ANC and the final pathmaking to freedom from Apartheid, and their English comrade Stevens departed four years later.

Miles' Contribution

By the mid-eighties Miles Davis was the most luminous figure in jazz. His hugely-selling Columbia albums, world tours and sell-out concerts had rivalled Armstrong's most populist years, and his sudden switch of recording labels, to Warner Brothers, had given even more artistic and commercial impetus to the veteran hornman. Davis had also adopted his ex-sideman, bassman and multi-instrumentalist Marcus Miller, as new musical director, so the stage was set for a revival of his creative energy.

By early 1986 at sixty years old, he was recording his first album for the new label, intended to be called *Perfect Way*, after one of its chosen tunes. But when its producer, Tommy LiPuma, suggested that the album be named *Tutu*, after the Anglican Archbishop of Cape Town who had been awarded the Nobel Peace Prize in 1984, Davis – recognising the power of titles and the signal place of the Anti-Apartheid struggle in the imagination of young people – was more than amenable. Miller also contributed another composition as the album's finale, 'Full Nelson', which was dedicated to the leader of the African National Congress, still being held in prison. *Tutu* was very well received by critics, became a big seller and in 1987 won a prestigious 'Grammy' award, continuing the tradition of making jazz a prime agent and eminent publicist in solidarity with the struggle of the South African people.

Miller's part in the creation of *Tutu* was crucial. Instead of a horn partner for Davis, he employed synthesizers against the trumpeter's muted horn in the title tune and the other tracks. Miles plays with an inspired dynamism – his characteristic melancholy mixed with defiance, as if he is reaching beyond what is to what might be, against the sound pillars of solid chords and Miller's resounding electric bass. 'Full Nelson', however, has a much chirpier and optimistic sound, with Miller playing soprano saxophone, Miles squeezing his notes, and the mood more like that of a children's song, as if a new generation will benefit from their parents' sacrifices, and this coming era is not so far away.

In 1989, Davis' album *Amandla* was released (much of it had been recorded in 1987), the title bearing the battle cry of the African National Congress. '*Amandla*, that means freedom,' he told the British writer Charles Shaar Murray: 'That's all I can do, to say "freedom" for Africa, for South Africa. Tutu was to say, "we know what you people are goin' through," this is to say, we know what they got to do now.' Miles worked alongside the artist Jo Gelbard to create the album's iconic sleeve painting, with Davis' face and horn painted across Africa's continental form. The album was another collaboration with Marcus Miller and featured the young Detroit-born altoist Kenny Garrett, his horn ringing from the percussion and synthesiser mix on seven of the eight tracks, including the title tune where Davis plays with a striking melodic lyricism and duets with Garrett as the performance soars to its climax. Two years later Davis was dead and *Amandla* had been his final significant creation, presaging the release of Mandela and the final overthrowing of Apartheid.

Miles was only one of many American jazz musicians whose music became a sound of solidarity with the South African people. Through the years of Apartheid and the brave struggle to remove it, transatlantic African-American jazz messages reached out with a more intense fervour when exiled South African jazz talents like Ibrahim and Masekela joined their utterance. In 1977 Ibrahim cut an album with the veteran Texas tenor saxophonist and ex-Basie stalwart Buddy Tate. One of the tracks was Ibrahim's 'Goduka Mfundi' or 'Going Home', a statement of the pianist's creative optimism, played as a pianoless trio with the energy of the bass and drums of Cecil McBee and Roy Brooks with some vivacious tenor choruses from Tate. Ibrahim joins in for 'Heyt Mazurki', another of his originals – a portrait of 'the indestructible man of Soweto' a year after the massacre of its schoolchildren. McBee's cavernous vibrations are featured, Ibrahim has a Monkish solo and Tate's tenor provides the melody.

Another evocation of Soweto came in 1979, when the Los Angeles drummer and ex-confrere of Ornette Coleman, Billy Higgins, named a tune and an album after the giant Johannesburg township. In a quartet setting with tenorist Bob Berg, ex-Jazz Messenger pianist Cedar Walton and bassman Tony Dumas, Higgins plays what sounds like a one-stringed African guitar on the title track before Walton enters, playing solo piano, followed by Higgins again on traditional jazz drums, Dumas and a particularly boisterous Berg. Higgins pounds a solo, the theme returns and Soweto is crystallised again in jazz sounds.

As it is too in an album by another iconic drummer, Tony Williams, who played with Miles Davis between 1962 (when he was seventeen) and 1969. Williams' 1986 album, *Civilization*, includes a track called 'Soweto Nights' which opens with a thunderous drum roll, before an ensemble passage played by the two horns, Billy Pierce on soprano and trumpeter Wallace Roney. Williams steps up the pace as Pierce solos, pianist Mulgrew Miller comps behind him and the strong ensemble theme returns with Williams' tumultuous drumming in full fury.

In December 1989, the Art Ensemble of Chicago, for long the avant-garde of the avant-garde, shared a recording in a Brooklyn studio with the South African male chorus, Amabutho. As an expression of solidarity with the South African people they called their album *America – South Africa*, and for the occasion renamed themselves the 'Art Ensemble of Soweto'. Multiple reedman Joseph Jarman wrote the lyrics to the opener 'U.S. of A. – U. of S.A.' and drew the grim similarities between black life in both lands, under both governments:

> The law for the poor is just the same,
> U.S. of A. – U. of S.A,,
> Killing the people without a blame,
> America – South Africa
> South Africa – America,
> No education for all poor men
> All locked up in a cage of pain,
> U.S. of A. – U. of S.A.,
> That's the way it is.

The Ensemble's amalgam of free-bop and African rhythms, blistering half-valve breaks from trumpeter Lester Bowie, wails from Jarman and fellow reedman Roscoe Mitchell, whistles, vocalese outbreaks, scrapes, clangs and other percussive effects, the bass and belafon of Malachi Favors Maghostut and the huge drum sweep of Famadou Don Moye all accompany the calling of names of American and South African black resistance heroes in the pursuit of freedom: from Mandela to George Jackson, from Steve Biko to Rosa Parks, from Walter Sisulu to Martin Luther King, Malcolm X and Medgar Evers, from the warriors of Umkhonto we Siswe to Fannie Lou Hamer – shared struggle, shared pain and shared achievement.

Then, after Mandela's final release from Robben Island incarceration and the prospect of the beginning of the dismantling of Apartheid in 1991, Hugh Masekela and his flugelhorn joined the New York-based 29th Street Saxophone Quartet, of Bobby Watson and Ed Jackson on alto saxophones, Rich Rothenberg on tenor and Jim Hartog on baritone, on the *Underground* album for the track 'Free at Last (For Mandela)'. As Hartog's baritone provides the rhythmic undertow, Masekela's chirping horn blows his message of hope and freedom through the ensemble of tenor and alto reeds after more than four decades of struggle across continents and oceans from the Americas to Cape Town, from Brooklyn to the dream of a newly-forged South Africa.

Pioneers

Of the exiled pioneers of South African jazz, only Ibrahim, Masekela and Moholo have survived to live and work in its post-Apartheid society. Through the last decade of the anti-Apartheid struggle, Ibrahim released a string of albums, mostly on the Germany-based ENJA label. In 1983 he recorded the album *Zimbabwe*, celebrating the final independence of South Africa's neighbour, after fifteen years of the people's struggle against white minority rule, a harbinger of his own country's freedom from Apartheid. The title tune features the serene flute of Panama-born Carlos Ward singing the theme melody, which he then reprises on alto. Also on the album is Ibrahim's tribute to the migrant gold miners of South Africa, many coming to and from their work from far parts of the nation and also Mozambique on the train called 'Bombella'. This has the sound of an express, its boisterous theme and improvisational passages moving fast along Ibrahim's rumbustious keys, and you remember an earlier epoch when the pianist encountered his future in Switzerland in the person of Duke Ellington – the master of train tunes – 'Midnight Express', 'Happy Go-Lucky Local', 'The 'A' Train' – and the South African's life changed forever.

And this union between the jazz of America and the jazz of Africa, so personified by Ibrahim with his love of Monk, Fats and Duke, and Ellington with his early 'jungle' sound and later his mature appreciation of the continent in his *Togo Brava Suite, Liberia Suite* and other classic recordings, is given fuller expression in *Cape Town Revisited*, Ibrahim's album of 1997. It contains the extraordinary syncretism of a three-part suite, 'Cape Town to Congo Square', in which Ibrahim traces the fervent jazz spirit shared between the tip of Africa and New Orleans – all the sea and strife between District Six and Storyville. The entire album, recorded in Cape Town, is a celebration of South African freedom, but this suite is special, with a South African pianist and American drummer and bassist, George Gray and Marcus McLaurine. The first movement is a sound picture of an 'African Street Parade' and Ibrahim makes it redolent of both cities with its jive, its eternal stride and vibrancy, his own roots coming full circle with the roots of jazz. A moment too to remember all those who played with him, their days of estrangement and exile, and their lives without the final happiness of living in their liberated country.

Another great survivor, also a returnee to Cape Town, is Louis Moholo-Moholo. In 1993 he took his band, Viva La Black, to South Africa, and an album of its music, *Freedom Tour: Live in South Africa* was released, with Moholo carrying the huge emotional burden of being the only remaining Blue Note. There are some deeply affecting performances, in particular of Dyani's 'Ewe Radebe', a choric version of Kirk's 'Volunteered Slavery', a dream-filled, fragile playing of Armstrong's 'What a Wonderful World' followed directly by a free reading of Ellington's anthem 'Come Sunday' with some furious piano by Pule Pheto and a merged-in concertina solo by Sean Bergin. There's also a rampant 'Bird Lives' by Pukwana, with Moholo in a frenzy, and an emotive finale of Feza's 'You Ain't Gonna Know Me 'Cos You Think You Know Me', in which Moholo chants his love for his newly restored country.

But an even more highly charged session from 1995, *Bra Louis – Bra Tebs*, ('Bra-Tebs' being the abbreviation of Moholo-Moholo's African name, Tebugo) was released in 2006 as a double CD along with a reissue of his first album as leader (made in 1978), *Spirits Rejoice!* It is an exhilarating experience to listen to them chronologically, and one immediately after the other. The 1978 recording tells its own vibrant story of the huge effect that Moholo and his South African confreres had on the British musicians with whom they played. The two South African bassists, Johnny Dyani and Harry Miller, both play on this record, giving the rhythmic propulsion a heaving undertow, while Moholo's furious drumming simultaneously gives an exultant uplift. The effect they have on the playing of tenorist Evan Parker, the Toronto-born trumpeter Kenny Wheeler and pianist Keith Tippett is, to say the least, tempestuous. It was as if British jazz was Africanised, revolutionised by the effect of these three South Africans and their other Blue Note comrades. Listen to Parker and Tippett on Moholo's 'Khanya Apho Ukhona' (Shine Wherever You Are) for example, or Wheeler's dramatic solo on the part-hymnal, part-anthemic 'Amexesha Osizi' (Times of Sorrow), where the octet's sound has a direct similarity to that of the Liberation Music Orchestra. By the 1995 live session the 'times of sorrow' had changed. Apartheid had been defeated, and Moholo returns with a young band that carries with it not only the pride of internationalism (including the vocalist, Francine Luce, from Martinique and the young Anglo-Caribbean altoist, Jason Yarde) but other South African exiles returning, trumpeter Claude Deppa and pianist Pule Pheto. The boiling hot 'Unisone' gives the true message, with the furious duetting of Yarde and Deppa bringing exiles and estranged brothers together on African soil after four centuries, with Moholo's ancestral drum-pulse making the way and at last making the opportunity. And the session's final tune is the traditional 'Ntyilo-Ntyilo', beloved and often played and recorded by Dyani and Ibrahim. Its familiar melody is given a living new sound in Moholo's arrangement, becoming a song of greeting as Deppa, sounding more than a little like Rex Stewart on 'Menelik', comes home with some extraordinary vocalese horn with the two saxophones playing a lowdown riff behind him. Jazz never left Africa, but one of its great contenders returns, after years of agony and struggle.

In 1995 Moholo dedicated a reissue of the Blue Notes' 1964 *Live in South Africa* to his departed confreres: to Pukwana, Dyani, McGregor and Feza, but also to Moyake, Miller, Dumile Feni and John Stevens, adding that 'our song, Free Mandela, Free South Africa was not in vain.' And he declares:

> I cannot enjoy my country's freedom (South Africa) without thinking of you. I cannot imagine my country free without thinking of you, because freedom is you. We have walked this lonely road together with music in our hearts. I cannot think of you absent, because freedom is you.

Jim Crow and Apartheid challenged by jazz: in Birmingham, Alabama to Cape Town and Jo'burg, it was the music of freedom, for those who played, and for those who listened and acted.

8

sacred common ground

In 1965 Don Cherry, who was touring in Rome, met a young Argentinian saxophonist with a ferocious, incendiary sound called Leandro 'Gato' Barbieri. He brought him back to New York and recorded two landmark Blue Note albums with him, *Complete Communion* (1965) and *Symphony for Improvisers* (1966). Cherry also drew Barbieri into Charlie Haden's Liberation Music Orchestra, and his raucous tenor is at the centre of the Spanish Civil War tune 'Viva La Quince Brigada' on their first album, in all its power and defiance. Nobody, not even the roaring Pharoah Sanders, had made a sound on the saxophone quite like Gato before and, largely through his faraway Argentinian origins in the town of Rosario and his very distinctive sound, he began to emblematise a 'Third World' genre of jazz, a sound of the distant Americas that was not a USA jazz sound. In 1969, shortly after his experience with the LMO, Barbieri recorded an album called *The Third World*, attaching himself to a concept that was highly-charged and relevant, and within the nexus of radical thought around the ideas of Frantz Fanon in his *Wretched of the Earth*, which was first published in its English paperback edition in 1967. This album included Haden and trombonist Roswell Rudd from the LMO, the Africanist drummer Beaver Harris and the pianist Lonnie Liston Smith. A sleevenote for the album declared:

Gato Barbieri, born in Rosario, Argentina – also the birth-place of Che Guevara – considers himself a member of the Third World. And Gato's music, finally, after a long odyssey of self-discovery, is also of the Third World.

This change and growth in consciousness in Barbieri brings added dimension to the jazz experience, for it was through jazz that Barbieri began his journey – initially into other cultures and then back to his own roots. But first, the term itself, Third World. 'So far as I can recall,' says Barbieri, 'it was originally used by De Gaulle to represent an inde-pendent political force, a third force, between the Russian and American blocs. But after De Gaulle, Third World has come to mean the common interest of Asia, Africa and Latin America. As an Argentinian, I am a part of that Third World.'

It was a strong personal and political jazz declaration, and Gato roars through his chosen tunes – two from Brazil, includ-ing 'Bachianas Brasileiras'. In this version, the rhythm changes and the tune becomes an African song by Abdullah Ibrahim. His 'Tango' becomes a flute song played by shepherds in north-ern Argentina and his own film music from the Glauber Rocher film, *Antonio das Mortes*, tells the story of a man who kills rebels for the government but who, after a long reflection, realises these rebels are on the side of the poor, and becomes one himself. There is also 'Cancion del Llamero' – the song of the llama herdsman, containing a fiery solo, identifying Gato with the working people, the peasants and farmers of his continent. *The Third World* introduces the concept of the other people of the Americas as the makers, carriers and subjects of jazz, as their music, through Barbieri's furious horn, drifted and blasted up from the southern tip of the southern continent. As he conjectured in the sleevenotes of his 1973 album *Bolivia*:

You can bring revolution into your art, but you can't make a revolution with art. The revolution has to come by political means. But perhaps the music, if it is beautiful enough, can help people to change a little bit – begin to change in their consciousness so that they will be ready to move in other ways, political ways. Perhaps.

Gato had already set down his 'Third World' credentials through an unusual and crucially original recording with another unorthodox and non-North American jazz luminary Dollar Brand (Abdullah Ibrahim). In March 1968 they met in Milan, and recorded an album together entitled *Hamba Kale*, the name of one of Brand's two compositions on the album. It is an astonishing encounter of these two audacious musicians from the cones of two huge continents separated by a vast ocean. On side one, the duo plays Brand's 'The Aloe and the Rose' and 'Hamba Kale', and Barbieri enters the South African's music with a fusion of frenzied passion and empathy in the former, bringing his own searing Pampas sound to all Brand's Cape African intensity and sense of loss, sharing his consciousness and welding his rasp to the pianist's percussive power and his dark, bowed cello. 'Hamba Kale' is shorter, more a melody of greeting, and more formal and restrained. Barbieri's two tunes, drifting into one, and '81st Street' are on the flipside of the original album. 'To Elsa' begins with three minutes and more of solo Brand, who seems totally attuned to Gato's theme with his muscular, percussive notes, Monkish harmonies and his races up and down the keyboard. It is as if this is Brand's tune, so inside it is he. Barbieri's solo voice howls, squeals and blasts its faraway majesterial beauty through the beginning of '81st Street' for another four minutes while Brand sits out. When he finally enters he plays a long solo full of agonised notes and indignant phrases, while Brand provokes him with his own discordant keyboard patterns. It is an extraordinary sound made by two non-US jazzmen, both in exile from their continents of origin, and both adapting each other's music to their own stock of traditions and timbres. Certainly it could not have emerged from the USA jazz universe, and its power and drama signalled something not only new but also linked to the realities of the struggles of the people of two unlikely jazz-playing continents, but with an exemplary unity that defied land, sea and distance.

Another album, *El Pampero*, was recorded live at the Montreux Jazz Festival in 1971, and again profiled Gato as a personification of Third World culture and struggle. Robert Palmer, in the sleevenotes, exhorted his readers:

> Gato has a vision of a Third World music that speaks to, and for, the dispossessed peoples of the materially under-developed parts of the planet. The power of this Third World, like the power of Gato's music, is spiritual rather than economic; closer to nature than to technology, more akin to earth and sky than to the constructions that separate them. This world and this music is certain of the future, because the future belongs to it; the energy that once sent Western man out across the ocean and into the interior reaches of every hemisphere is now coming back at the West from lands that were only occupied, never won. The purpose, patience and faith that have helped Gato realise his vision are the same forces that sustain the peoples of the Third World against the vampires who are trying to turn their countries into interchangeable annexes of corporate-owned luxury hotels.

A credo of its time, doused in rhetoric, but also a signal of Gato's sound in *El Pampero* – the man of the pampas, with the weapon of his horn, but now playing with musicians normally accompanying the soul and funk of Aretha Franklin and King Curtis – Bernard 'Pretty' Purdie on drums and Chuck Rainer on electric bass. Gato winds up his huge sound while Sonny

Morgan's congas and Lonnie Liston Smith find their own vortices, and soon there is a true blast across the pampas, filling the whole of the Americas. It seems astonishing that Gato's almost superhuman titanic rasp can enfold a ballad with beauty and gentleness, but he does this with his volcanic vision of 'Mi Buenos Aires Querido'. Straight after comes Barbieri's 1971 version of the popular/nostalgic songbook ballad, 'Brazil', which, far from creaming the romantic centre of melody about this huge nation whose people at the time were enduring untold repression and brutality under the *cambao* (yoke) of the military government, is a raw gruelling sound experience, with Barbieri assaulting the listener's ears with his anger and passion. This was a country whose peasants had a life expectancy of twenty-seven years and who, since April 1964, had lived under a regime of 'Christian values and order' after the CIA-inspired military coup had begun a long period of authoritarian rule, where all popular movements were suppressed and progressive politicians were exiled, killed or jailed, with the banning of free political parties. When Gato's rasping sound plays the theme of 'Brazil', and you hear the silent lyrics of the ballad – 'return I will to old Brazil', the listener knows precisely what he means.

By the time that Barbieri recorded his *Chapter Three: Viva Emiliano Zapata* album in June 1974, military coups had shocked Brazil (1964) and Chile (1973) and a state of emergency was shortly to be declared in Argentina, which would give the armed forces a virtual free hand and lead inexorably to the eventual military government of 1976. 'My Beloved Buenos Aires' was rapidly becoming a centre of dictatorship, following the horrific repression in Chile under General Pinochet. One of Barbieri's tunes on the *Zapata* album is 'La Podrida' – Argentinian slang for 'something rotten happening', and there were *podridas* in progress throughout the southern continent. On this album Barbieri combined with the Cuban arranger Chico O'Farrill, renowned for his previous scores with luminaries like Machito (*Afro-Cuban Jazz Suite*) and Miguelito Valdes, as well as Dizzy Gillespie ('Manteca') and Stan Kenton, and although there are rhythms of tango, cha-cha-cha and mambo throughout the album, there is also a subliminal understanding of the grim realities of governance and repression across the continent. The opener, 'Milonga Triste', a habanera dance employing an Argentinian melody, has a mournful mood, almost dirge-like, the notes of sadness and defiance searing from Barbieri's horn. 'La Podrida' itself is faster, with the four Latin percussionists, Ray Armando, Luis Mangual, Ray Mantilla and Portinho taking particular prominence. Gato is agile, blowing hard against O'Farrill's brass ensemble, and screeching furiously as the track reaches its climax.

As for the title tune, Barbieri declared to sleevenote writer Nat Hentoff, 'it is so titled because at this particular moment in Latin America, there is nothing else to say.' The invocation of the Mexican peasant leader and the historical memory of his rebellion was, as Gato's wife Michelle told Hentoff, 'an exclamation – an exclamation of the need for hope that we feel'. The performance begins with some romping piano by Eddie Martinez and driving percussion, before the entire twenty-piece orchestral ensemble enters behind Gato's roaring tenor. 'Viva Emiliano Zapata' is as joyous and redolent of hope as anything that Barbieri ever recorded, supported as he is by O'Farrill's fullness of rhythm and sound. Coming as it did during one of the worst epochs in his continent's modern history, it equated jazz with the message of hope, democratic revival and the eventual power of ordinary people.

Hemphill and Chile

The tragedy of Chile in September 1973 was witnessed by the New York poet James Scully. As he wrote in the sleevenotes of the 1980 album *Chile New York*:

In 1973–74 I was living in Santiago de Chile, writing home about the terror there. The Chilean military, in a US-engineered coup, had overthrown the Popular Unity government, murdered President Allende, and was engaged in a bloody repression. Prisoners, including the singer Victor Jara, were tortured and murdered in the national soccer stadium, which had become a concentration camp. Starting from letters and poems I'd been sending, Jeff Schlanger translated all this into a monumental Wall of Faces, a project culminating in the 1980 collaboration with Julius Hemphill.

Hemphill, born in 1938 in Fort Worth, Texas, was a profoundly innovative saxophonist who became a founder member and principal arranger/composer of the World Saxophone Quartet in 1976. He was also a multi-media enthusiast who strove to unify jazz utterance with other artistic genres, and seized the opportunity to bring his music to an artistic project in solidarity with the Chilean people in May 1980, when he joined with the sculptor Jeff Schlanger, who had created 400 individually-formed, glazed and named stoneware faces, heads and figures as a tribute to those killed in the savage Chilean repression. In the *Chile New York* album, Hemphill, together with the Chicagoan percussionist Warren Smith – who had recorded with jazz figures like Mingus, Miles Davis, Rahsaan Roland Kirk, Count Basie and Elvin Jones – provided the sound accompaniment to Schlanger's sculptures as they were exhibited in a street-level walk-through under the CUNY building on 42nd Street. The death squads, torture chambers and murder camps of Chile – as well as those in many other Latin American contexts, were given grotesque salience by this fusion of sculpture and jazz. Hemphill's swooping, moaning and growling notes unified with Smith's sudden bursts of drums, vibes, whining whistles, vocal effects and scuttling street noises, along with the tormented visages of the ceramics must have pricked the imaginations of hearers and beholders as they walked through this most surprising of exhibitions of real life agony at the other end of their continent.

Managua

In 1989, the trumpeter Freddie Hubbard went on a US State Department tour of Mexico, Guatemala and El Salvador. This must have been counted as a considerable cultural coup for a government with an aggressively interventionist attitude towards the nations of Central America and Latin America as a whole. 1989 was also the year of the US invasion and occupation of Panama, and yet another year of counter-revolutionary support for the 'Contras' of Nicaragua.

As for its neighbour, in 1983 the Assistant Secretary of State Thomas Enders had declared: 'the battle for the Western hemisphere' was being waged in El Salvador. It had become a venue of political and cultural contest. 'The only piece of territory we are interested in winning here,' opined ex-Vietnam veteran Colonel John Waghelstein, 'is the four inches between the ears of the Salvadorean peasants'. Perhaps the State Department thought that the great jazz trumpeter would turn his back on the spirit that created 'Sing Me a Song of Songmy' and pacify the rebellious inclinations of the Mexicans, Guatemalans and Salvadoreans, but it seems that such an intention was far from his mission. His album *Bolivia* of 1991 was a boiling musical affair, far closer to the revolutionary than conservative instincts of jazz, begun in a fervent mood with Giovani Hidalgo's vivacious congas on 'Homegrown'. And Hubbard had a very strong band, with ex-Jazz Messengers pianist Cedar Walton, the British and Brixton-born tenorist Ralph Moore, David Williams, who came originally from Trinidad, on bass and the remarkable Los Angeles-born Billy Higgins, who had been a vital member of the early days of the Ornette Coleman Quartet, on drums. Hubbard signals the theme of his album with his own composition 'Third World', beginning with some emphatic Walton chords and Higgins' punctuating drums. The young altoist from Hopkinsville, New York, Vincent Herring, is on hand firstly for a brash solo on alto, then, immediately after, comes a lively and floating soprano chorus. Hubbard had been experiencing some trouble with his lip prior to this recording but he enters with his customary strength and drama, clipping his notes in a gruff fanfare. Walton is posed and inventive, chiming down on his notes before Higgins' drums give their message. This doesn't sound like a 'Third World' savouring foreign domination. And even less so through Walton's composition, 'Bolivia'. Bolivia was, of course, the place of Che's death in October 1967, and Walton's generation knew that on their pulses. His rolling piano leads the theme, introducing first Hubbard, searching for his summit, then a much more mellow Moore and a chirping Herring on alto. 'Managua' is named after the capital of Nicaragua, epicentre of the Sandinista Revolution throughout the eighties, from the overthrow of the dictator Somoza in 1979, and the ten-minute performance of Hubbard's tune is free-flowing and potent with narrative. His solo has much of his old glory, surprise and invention, and Moore, the Brixton boy, is full of power and the strength of story with a rhythm section that is irrepressible. 'Managua' may have been recorded the year after the Sandinistas' exit from power in the elections of February 1990, but it is full of their spirit of movement and change.

Perhaps it is ironic that a key track on *Bolivia* is Hubbard's version of Billie Holiday's 'God Bless the Child', the lyrics of which characterised the values and aspirations of those who really controlled America. Holiday knew them well and suffered greatly through them, but the neo-conservative and corporatist US forces which provoked such brutality and poverty in the rest of the Americas in the three decades from Allende's fall onwards, had their approach to life and the world economy superbly and starkly put to words in Holiday's grimly insightful lyrics:

Them that's got shall get
Them that's not shall lose
So the Bible says
And it still is news
Mama may have
Poppa may have
But God bless the child
that's got his own,
that's got his own.

It is a message that Hubbard delivers with power and brilliance accompanied by his confrere Walton's empathy and the
lyrics forged by Holiday in the thirties had never had so much
social prophecy and political meaning.

Puerto Rico and Panama

In 1990, in the twilight of his long jazz life, Dizzy Gillespie,
ever the internationalist, formed his United Nation Orchestra
composed of musicians from across the Americas. One of
these was the tenorist David Sanchez, born in 1968 in
Guaynabo, Puerto Rico. Sanchez moved to New York City
when he was twenty, having decided to become a professional
musician. He went to Rutgers University, where he studied
with three eminent jazzmen, Kenny Barron, Ted Dunbar and
John Purcell. Although he moved into the highest levels of the
jazz world playing with, amongst others, Slide Hampton,
Hilton Ruiz and Kenny Drew Jr, he has always remained
deeply rooted in the ways and sounds of traditional Puerto
Rican music and never stepped away from being a Caribbean
musician in essence. His early albums established his advanced
bop credentials, but his series of recordings with Columbia,
beginning with *Obsession* (1997–98) are strongly immersed in
his Puerto Rican heritage. This is particularly so in his album
of 2000, *Melaza* (Molasses), in which – through a series of

related compositions – most of them by Sanchez, he examines the history of his island and its relationship with sugar. The sleevenotes comment that:

> For centuries sugar cane was not only the economic mainstay for countries throughout the Caribbean, but it was also synonymous with the years of slavery and struggle of the African extension of the Caribbean. For those who labored those long hours in the sugar fields, it was an extremely hard and painful life.

And throughout the album, there is the certainty that it still is. Sanchez assembled a band of powerful young Caribbean musicians to give his sound a genuine authenticity and directness, dedicating his record 'to those who are being subjected to unjust conditions. In particular, this humble offering is for the African extension, the indigenous peoples of the Americas and the community of Vieques for its years of struggle for peace.'

The most powerful track on the album is 'Cancion Del Canaveral' (Song of the Sugar Cane Field), an atmospheric and scorching performance, where the aching drums of Antonio Sanchez and Edsel Gomez's rolling piano found the narrative horn of Sanchez, supported by the supplementary reeds of altoist Miguel Zenon and guest tenorist Branford Marsalis. It is a resonant sound panorama of the centuries of Caribbean sugar, with Sanchez playing with a powerful authority and patriotic drive. Also impressive is the track 'Against Our Will', in which Sanchez again plays the musical griot, with a theme carrying a mood of coercion and cruelty, emphasised by Hans Glawischnig's pounding bass and the colloquy of suffering suggested by the reed interchanges of Sanchez and Zenon.

These themes are continued into Sanchez' next album, *Travesia*, of 2001. Keeping the same inspired young musicians, Sanchez' message is carried with a particular power in the track 'Paz Pá Vieques (Seis Chorreao)'. Vieques island is off the eastern shores of Puerto Rico and is the US armed forces' chosen site for massive sea invasion rehearsals. The 1983 assault on the island of Grenada, for example, had its full dry run off Vieques the year before, and for many years its people have campaigned for such hostile activities to cease and for the island to be allowed to return to a peaceful existence. Sanchez' tune is an expression of that wish, which was echoed a thousand times by the Grenadian people during the first two years of the eighties – particularly in August 1981 when the naval exercise 'Amber and the Amberines' using 120 thousand troops and hundreds of planes and landing craft was launched off Vieques. Since the official name for the nation of Grenada is 'Grenada and the Grenadines', the assumed target of the eventual operation was all but obvious. 'Paz Pá Vieques' has Sanchez and Zenon blowing a duet, without accompaniment at first, before Edsel enters, then makes way for the two reeds again, the 'Puerto Rican rainforest effects' dropping on the notes while Sanchez and Zenon finally take it out. It is a powerful dialogue of peace, and under the list of musicians in the sleevenote is the following declaration:

> This song is dedicated to the brothers of Vieques. The time is now to put a stop to the miserable conditions there. The long-time struggle must culminate with the will of the people – peace. It is shameful that such a situation has been created and sustained.

Another member of Gillespie's United Nation Orchestra was the Panamanian pianist Danilo Perez. Born in 1966, he first worked with Brazilian trumpeter Claudio Roditi and the Cuban reedman Paquito D'Rivera after moving to Boston and studying at Berklee. After cutting two albums for Impulse Records in which he strove to fuse his Latin roots with bop energies and patterns (*Panamonk*, 1996 and *Central Avenue*, 1998), in 2000 he turned towards his own origins and made a fascinating recording, *Motherland*. He invited some high-profile American jazz virtuosi (violinist Regina Carter, tenorist Chris Potter and guitarist Kurt Rosenwinkel) to help him delve into his own Panamanian roots. Not only in Panamanian dances like the Punto but within the context of the African contribution of the blues, spirituals and Caribbean dances, Perez builds a portrait of the musical history of his nation. But the central and most powerfully thematic track is 'Panama Libre' which, according to the sleeve essay, was 'inspired by the events that took place in Panama in December 1989' – the date of the US invasion and occupation, which safeguarded the canal company, the US military bases, the US based fruit companies, the banks – even the currency itself, which is the US dollar. It also safeguarded the Panamanian elite in the luxurious Pantilla suburb of Panama City – filled with gated seaside condos, designer homes with indoor swimming pools and huge garages with lavish cars. These are not the Panamanians that Perez celebrated in 'Panama Libre', or any section of *Motherland*. 'Panama Libre' is played by a prestigious quartet, three of whom (at the present time, September 2008), Perez, bassist John Patitucci and drummer Brian Blade, are members of the Wayne Shorter Quartet. It is a dignified, poised piece, with polished contributions from Perez and Rosenwinkel, with Perez in particular giving the notes of pride and grace in the people he loves, and reflecting the lyrics of a previous track, 'Song to the Land' by Ana Lucia Vlieg:

> Land, you still are not ours
> strength of the rock, cunning of the weeds.
> Your untiring smile still escapes us,
> smile of clear skies
> and the courage of the blue and the salt
> that are your very blood.

The nexus of the 2008 album *Across the Crystal Sea*, which Perez made with the arranger Claus Ogerman, is Ogerman's orchestration of Jules Massenet's 'The Saga of Rita Joe'. Rita Joe, who died in 2007, was a poet and elder of the Mi'kmaq people of Nova Scotia. When she was five her mother died and she was taken to a succession of foster homes and eventually to the Indian Residential School of Shubenacadie, where she endured and resisted the brutal stripping of her Indian identity, the experience of many thousands of native American and native Canadian children. Her culture and language were stolen from her and she later wrote:

> I lost my talk
> The talk you took away.
> When I was a little girl
> At Shubenacadie School.

Rita Joe's story, so wrenchingly and brilliantly told in her poems, was the expression of her poetical mission: 'write what comes from the heart. Do not wait until tomorrow, do it now!' Perez' music has the same audacity. Herbie Hancock said of him that he is 'not afraid of anything', his piano echoing Rita Joe's artistic courage. At the start of the 'saga', Ogerman's orchestral strings sound sinister, the theme carries menace and when Perez enters with a flurry of notes, the anxiety of a chained childhood is set down in a stressed sonic essay, with Luis Quintero's nagging drums always present. But Perez perpetually sounds as if his choruses are tearing for release, as if his jazz language is his and only his, and like Rita Joe, defiantly, 'Again and again, I voice what is in my heart.'

Jim Pepper's Blues

An unjustly undersung and under-recorded genius of the tenor saxophone was the native American jazzman, Jim Pepper. His mother was a Creek psychologist, his father a Kaw baker and a champion war dancer in his youth in Oklahoma. They moved to Portland, Oregon when Pepper was a boy, but he would return to Oklahoma every summer and earn pocket money chanting in the Peyote language and war dancing. Then, he declares in the sleevenotes of the 1983 album *Comin' and Goin'*, 'I heard Sonny Rollins on the radio,' and his life was changed. He moved to New York in 1964 and worked with Larry Coryell and his jazz-rock group Free Spirits, then with Charlie Haden and the Liberation Music Orchestra. He struck up a friendship with Don Cherry, who was himself part-Choctaw, and made some powerful records in the mid-eighties with Paul Motian, Mal Waldron and the trombonist Marty Cook. Pepper died in 1992, largely unrecognised, generally under-appreciated with only very few recordings under his name, but two of his albums, *The Path* and *Dakota Song*, are particularly fine. In his 1983 album, *Comin' and Goin'*, he included a traditional Sioux departing and greeting song ('Lakota Song'), a Kaw Peyote chant ('Ya Na Ho'), his 'Witchi Tia To' which was a Commanche ceremony chant and became a hit record, and a Kaw war dance song: 'Custer Gets It'.

These recordings were unprecedented: not only was Pepper bringing traditional native American song and music into a jazz embrace, he was frequently using some unlikely and heterogeneous artistes to achieve it. Whereas in his 'Squaw Song', Don Cherry, the Ornette Coleman alumnus, contributed a lyrical solo, in 'Water', the sitarist Colin Walcott made a fruitful contribution. In 'Ya Na Ho' he plays the tabla, the drum of India. And in the astonishing 'Custer Gets It', Pepper duets with the renowned guitarist John Scofield after a war dance vocal sung in Peyote and a Coltrane-like free tenor chorus. This was an extraordinary syncretism of cultures, and Pepper was recognising jazz as truly his people's music, with his own very vocalese saxophone sound becoming an extension of his singing voice. In the Creek stomp dance, 'Goin' Down to Muskogee', the Brazilian percussionist Nana Vasconcelos shares a Creek vocal with Pepper while adding the sound of his shaker, and in the rhapsodic 'Lakota Song', the sound of

Denver-born electronic effects guitar virtuoso Bill Frisell can be discerned behind the anguished vocal. The listener can only marvel at the new musical shapes and traditions that Jim Pepper would have created had he lived longer.

His life in music corresponded with the uprise in resistance and organisation of native American peoples within the USA and across the entire Americas, culminating in the February 1973 occupation of the village of Wounded Knee by activists of the American Indian Movement (AIM). They were occupying the very place where their ancestors had been mown down by the US Cavalry. The event, called 'Wounded Knee Two', was a spectacular protest against the corruption and injustice of the Bureau of Indian Affairs and the Reservation System that had mismanaged, exploited and underdeveloped native American life for more than a century. It was also a direct indictment of the genocidal treatment apportioned to the Indian by the American Government over the previous two hundred years. Jim Pepper's saxophone blew the truth of that history and the era of native American resistance of which he was a part, but he more often enveloped it all in beautiful jazz musicianship.

In *Dakota Song* Pepper is supported by a strong rhythm section, all playing in an advanced bop genre: Kirk Lightsey on piano, drummer John Betsch and the Panamanian bassist, Santi Debriano. The album combines Pepper originals with standards like 'What's New?', 'It Could Happen to You' and 'Polka Dots and Moonbeams' and an Ornette Coleman original, 'Comme Il Faut', and the apex of the session is the title song, where Pepper's tenor is dubbed behind his own Peyote singing, before he delivers a heartwrought solo. *The Path* involves the same quartet, plus trumpeter Stanton Davis and the Armenian percussionist, Arto Tuncboyaci. Pepper is an accomplished straight jazzman – listen to him, for example, on Monk's 'Reflections' or Paul Motian's 'Lullaby', but his true genius emerges when challenged by cross-cultural genres. His composition 'Bamasso' has a Caribbean feel, with Debriano's bass particularly emphatic, while the astonishing sounds of his solo on Lightsey's 'Habi Ba' are unique to the vocalisms of his own saxophone voice. 'Witchi Tia To' is given a straight jazz reading in a duet with Lightsey although vertical was never an adjective that could be applied to Pepper's playing. He approaches the melody almost quiescently, but his sudden change to voice and dubbed saxophone is like two voices singing, in the same language too: the language of people in the real world of real sounds and real life, always singing together.

Reservation Blues

In 1991 Don Pullen, the pianist on some of Mingus' most significant final albums, made his first album with a new band, the African-Brazilian Connection, which he called *Kele Mou Bana*. This extraordinary amalgam of musicians included Pullen – whose provenances are African-American (with a maternal grandmother who was part-Cherokee) – from Roanoke, Virginia; percussionist Mor Thiam of Dakar, Senegal, and Guilherme Franco of Sao Paulo, Brazil; bassist Nilson Mitta also of Sao Paulo and Carlos Ward, saxophonist, of Panama. The jazz writer Howard Mandel introduced this band in this way, in the album's sleevenotes:

> The first sound of *Kele Mou Bana* is the deliberate clatter of a berimbau, the bow-like instrument originally from Angola which came with slaves centuries ago to Brazil. The final sound is the slap of hand drums, humankind's earliest noise-makers, which make audible the earth's heartbeat. Between these points, composer-pianist Don Pullen and his African-Brazilian Connection substantiate the belief that a musical heritage is shared throughout the far-flung outposts of the African diaspora.

A living, human syncretism is the 'African Brazilian Connection', soon at work in the album's first track, Franco's

'Capoeria' – based on the African-derived Brazilian dance-like martial art, in which Ward digs in hard, well-practised in Africanist licks after his years with Abdullah Ibrahim. Pullen steps in next with his torrential keyboard runs flooding the studio beside the freeborn drums of Africa and Brazil. Thiam has many a drum at his side throughout the album – djembe, tabula, rainsticks and wind chimes to name a few. These are at work throughout the title tune, meaning 'The struggle of our race is won', referring in particular to the end of Apartheid in South Africa, and the symbolic unity between black Americans and Africans in the band itself, its joyous, anthemic sound finding a special potency in Ward's defiant notes.

Pullen made his last album in 1995. He called it *Sacred Common Ground*, and I believe it to be one of the greatest triumphs of jazz, made with extreme risk, audacity and skill. Pullen's own ancestry demanded that he make this record, the result of a long project that he developed with his 'African-Brazilian Connection' and the native American communities of the Satish and Kootenai peoples that he grew to know and love in the early 1990s. By the date of the actual recordings, Pullen was very ill with lymphoma and involved in a course of chemotherapy but he had spent the previous two years with the band, listening to the music of the Indian peoples and playing his music with them. He joined with the Chief Cliff Singers, and worked on the musical collaboration while on residency sessions in the reservations of Northwest Montana. What he achieved no jazz musician has achieved before: to fuse jazz with the music of the USA's indigenous peoples, to find another expression for their defiance, protest and pride, to unite the cry of the black man with the cry of the red man in a nation which has scorned both.

The Chief Cliff singers open the album with their drums and voices in 'The Eagle Staff is First', then suddenly the jazzmen are with them sublimating their sound; Joseph Bowie with his trombone slides groaning beneath them, and Pullen

himself, flaying his keys under everything. The spare and beau-
tiful piano notes that follow the opening chant of 'Common
Ground' are pressed with a gentle sadness and sense of elegy.
J. T. Lewis' brushes softly enter as Pullen winds deeper and
deeper into the tenderness of his theme, its melody weeping
the present. Then suddenly the drums again, and the wailing
Kootenai chant, continuing and concluding Pullen's song. Mor
Thiam's African percussion fits as a sonic glove over the Indian
drums of 'River Song' as if the music of two continents is one.
Pullen's percussive piano sound is still drum, more drum. On
'Reservation Blues' it is the jazz spirit which floats through the
reservation; the 'rez' of Washington-made underdevelopment
and joblessness, of its crimes of alcoholism and foetal alcohol
syndrome, of HIV, of youth suicide – but of defiance and
protest too in Bowie's slides, in Ward's cadences, in Pullen's
rocking notes. 'Message in Smoke' is solo Pullen for the first
two and a half minutes, then the singers and their drums and
Debriano's pulsating bass beneath. The ensemble builds like a
fire, with the singers flying all sides, and it is an America which
few have heard before this. 'Resting on the Road' is simply a
pure and beautiful melody – a classic theme birthed by jazz in
the most unlikely of contexts. Ward plays it with the same lyricism that he played Ibrahim's 'The Wedding' for year upon
year and Pullen's solo, largely bereft of his cyclones of notes, is
as beautiful as he has ever waxed.

Strange to me to read, though, the opinions of *Sacred
Common Ground* in the jazz record guides. One, the *Penguin*,
describes it as 'a curious mish-mash of influences, with little
imaginative centre'. Another, the *Music Hound*, puts it in its
'what to avoid' section and adds it 'has the aura of a project not
fully realised' and 'the music rarely gels', and the *All Music
Guide* gives it two stars out of five. Perhaps it takes an unmusi-
cal man like me to love it, learn from it and in ways that I
cannot understand – understand it. For if jazz is anything
about the unity of the disparate, the one heart beating from

the many – and of course, 'the sound of surprise,' then Don
Pullen's last work was a work of some genius.

In October 1996 Pullen's achievement was hailed by one of
his ex-confreres, the tenor saxophone master David Murray, in
a tribute album made for the Japanese DIW label, *The Long
Goodbye*. Murray was accompanied by ex-Pullen confreres
Debriano and drummer J. T. Lewis, and on piano was Pullen's
young Afro-Chinese-Canadian protégé from Montreal,
D. D. Jackson, with whom Pullen had worked during his final
sickness. The quartet reprise two tracks from *Sacred Common
Ground*. The first is 'Resting on the Road', surely now a classic
jazz melody, played with a superb finesse and power by Murray,
exploring the extremes of his horn but always returning to
Pullen's melodic foundation, and giving Jackson a free scope
for his own keyboard pathways. The second is 'Common
Ground', begun by some springing Panamanian bass from
Debriano, beautifully realised and full of the jazz life. Murray
strikes into the heart of Pullen's bold and anthemic tune,
continued by Jackson's church-like piano, and the tenorist
returns, playing at his most inventive and full toned all over his
horn. Thus was Pullen's musical brilliance further memori-
alised, and much more significantly so than in a few lines of a
jazz CD compendium.

A Prevailing Theme

Throughout the recorded history of jazz, the single most
salient theme that has hounded, hurt, oppressed, despaired,
sought to undermine yet simultaneously pricked the resistance
and struggle of generations of jazz musicians, has been racism.
From Armstrong to Mingus, from Basie to Holiday to Roach,
from Shepp and Ibrahim and Moeketsi and Dyani back
to Ellington, the foremost enemy with its Jim Crow
and Apartheid audiences and hotels, its cruel street and club
realities, its false claims to be 'white' music with its shining

orchestral 'kings', its way of hiding and smothering black genius, its devious ways of dividing the world – it has been racism.

Even into the 1990s and the new millennium, jazz musicians bravely, and increasingly much more openly, condemn its continued deformities. In 1990, the Baltimore altoist Gary Bartz (born 1940), recorded a live club date at Birdland, New York City – with its ghosts and echoes of the heydays of jazz innovation. This performance was issued on an album with a dramatic title that reflected a common enough white view of new black residents in their locale: *There Goes the Neighbourhood!* Bartz has the pianist who played so long with Dizzy Gillespie in his 'middle' period, the Philadelphian Kenny Barron, with bass supremo Ray Drummond from Brookline, Massachusetts, and Ben Riley, ex-Monkman, on drums. The first track is nearly ten minutes of a rampaging performance of jazz saxophone: 'Racism (blues in Double Bb Minor)'. Bartz comes straight in on a charge, hurtling into the theme, with Barron's speedy comping and Drummond's throbbing bass urging him on to give his implacable evidence. Barron's testifying solo is no respite as he chases Bartz' ideas, leaping into his own too, with Riley stoking the engine of drums behind him, then pressing forward with his own solo flourishes before Bartz returns in a breathless finish.

The New York-born, classically trained clarinettist Don Byron has done much more than restore jazz glory to his instrument after decades of under-exposure; his music, use of allusion and employing of sharp lyrics have also raised the efficacy again of jazz as a music of specific protest. Byron cleverly invokes the 'power of titles'. From 1992 onwards his albums have provocatively used titles and references to focus his listeners' minds emphatically upon issues of racism and oppression. His 1995 album *Music for Six Musicians* featured a piece entitled 'The Press Made Rodney King (responsible for the LA Riots)', in which his winding solo clarinet opening, joined by

Graham Haynes' cornet chimes and Edsel Gomez' discordant piano, give their commentary on the blatant and horrific police savaging of King, while the short and acerbic 'White History Month' fancifully imagines the racist historian's revenge, through poet Sadiq's words

> Hold it, hold it, hold it!
> So what?
> You think it fair if there was a white
>   history month?

Or there is 'Bernhard Goetz, James Ramseur and Me' from the 1999 album *Romance with the Unseen*, where Byron, master-drummer Jack De Johnette, guitarist Bill Frisell and Drew Gress on bass give their sound-commentary on the man who committed vigilante gun violence against four black youths on the New York subway. The dialogue-interplay between the clarinet and drums is astonishing, but you refer to the title to interpret their message. The allusion is even more oblique on Byron's recording of 2000, *A Fine Line*. Here the message is a small section of a New York street map in a corner of the sleeve. It refers to the death of Amadou Diallo, an African immigrant who was shot forty-one times by crazed officers of the New York Police Department in the doorway of his Bronx apartment building, and simply marks two locations within a few blocks of each other – the street of the murder, and the street where Diallo's parents live. His 2001 album, *You are #6: More Music for Six Musicians* has the very brief but pointed track, 'Dub-Ya', in which President George W. Bush's sobriquet marks a musical lampoon, suggesting the man's dangerous buffoonery in the spirit of Mingus' 'Fables of Faubus', with vocal mutterings and ironic, saccharine clarinet leading the way.

But Byron's finest and most pertinent work was on his first album of 1990 and the title track of *Tuskegee Experiments* –

music devoted to an anatomisation of the issues of race and class in America, using the real history of past events. Byron himself introduces the composition in the album's sleevenotes:

> Long before I finished this recording, I knew I would call it Tuskegee Experiments. The word 'Tuskegee' itself represents many different aspects of the African-American experience. 'Tuskegee Strutter's Ball' refers to the class scorn middle-class black folks feel for people 'below' them, and the title 'Tuskegee Experiments' refers to two experiments conducted on Black American men at the Tuskegee Institute.
>
> In 1932, the US Public Health Service, with generous assistance from local black medical professionals, initiated the longest human medical experiment in American history. More than half of the four hundred men chosen had syphilis while the rest formed a non-syphilic control group. None were informed of their condition, and they were observed for over forty years, but not treated, just to document the physical effects of syphilis left unchecked. In the Tuskegee aviation experiment, over-qualified and under-compensated black men endured unnecessary indignities simply to 'prove' they could be trusted to fly military aircraft.
>
> To me, these two experiments are metaphors for African-American life. In one, we see once again that black life is cheap, and that a person of color can be enlisted to work against the best interests of his group, for nothing more than a brief 'vacation' from the pain of invisibility or the pressure of being seen as part of an 'inferior' group. The aviation experiment reflects the struggle black people constantly face: having to be smarter, better, more qualified simply to justify being given any opportunity.

Byron assembled an impressive cast of musicians for these dramas, two fine bassists, one Reggie Workman, a veteran Jazz Messenger, the other, Lonnie Plaxico, a considerable modernist; the thunderous drummer and Blakey disciple Ralph Peterson Jr., Gomez on piano; postbop drummer, Pheeroan akLaff; and guitarist Bill Frisell. The poet Sadiq offers the words again:

> bring them to autopsy
> with ulcerated limbs,
> with howling wives,
> bring them in, one coon corpse at a time

The music matches the indignation of the poetry. Byron's squawking clarinet accompanies them, before raising itself to behold akLaff's troubling drums and the haranguing piano of Joe Berkovitz. *Tuskegee Experiments* is jazz at its most explicit. All complexes of needing to disguise or merely imply are gone. The history and the present reality are clear and critical in every note.

Finally, to England, and the trumpeter of African-Caribbean heritage, Byron Wallen who played on John Stevens' last album, *New Cool* (1992), which included a lament to Dudu Pukwana, 'Dudu's Gone'. In the sleevenote of his album *Indigo*, he reveals the internationalist roots of the music that he plays: 'The inspiration for the music comes from the deepest parts of the Central African rainforest, the remotest parts of Papua New Guinea and Indonesia and the early music of Europe as well as the more obvious influences of jazz, funk, dance music and blues.'

Yet, as a black London jazzman, it is the real streets of London that are his closest world, and the world that he must respond to. The effect of these streets and the ideas which the people who live within them carry inside their heads are set down in the track 'Crazy Black' from his 1995 album, *Sound*

Advice. Wallen takes lyrics from the poet Lemn Sissay and puts his jazz to them.

> I've been walking down the street
> just around the corner from hell,
> and if I'm in my head I got to be
> A crazy black man.
> Don't believe the way they see you
> Don't believe the way they see you
> Or you may die in your own reflection!

Wallen's agonised trumpet punctuates the lines, with Orphy Robinson's pacifying vibes and Dennis Rollins' riffing trombone, and the sense of hostility and alienation is rife. Echoes resound of the beatings of Powell and Monk, of streets of fear and violence – a theme returned to in *Indigo*, particularly in the track 'Closed Circle'. This is 'a dedication to the spirit of Stephen Lawrence', a black youth who was murdered on the streets of south-east London on April 22 1993 by a gang of racist white youths, who until now have not been convicted. Stephen and Emmett: Wallen remembers them both and them all in 'Closed Circle', playing with the Ghana-born baritone and soprano saxophonist Tony Kofi, Larry Bartley on bass and drummer Tom Skinner. A soft sound of steel drums and the sound of the sea tell of Stephen's Caribbean family origins, and his Jamaican grave. Wallen and Kofi's baritone duet throughout the performance in brotherly sadness, yet with an elegiac beauty too. Kofi's African sound rumbles with an obstinate hope and Wallen's Caribbean notes hover above him in the sky of jazz tenacity. It is another story, much like many others that the music has told, and will never stop telling.

tailpiece –

the groove continues

Political Blues: World Saxophone Quartet

How have US jazz musicians responded to the politics of the Bush era during the war and occupation in Iraq and the tragedy of Hurricane Katrina in New Orleans? A part of the answer can be found within the sounds and messages of the new album of the World Saxophone Quartet, *Political Blues*, with its sleeve illustration of a defiant and brandished alto horn.

The quartet comprises at least three of the greatest living saxophonists: altoist Oliver Lake of Arizona, baritonist Hamiet Bluiett from Illinois and tenorist David Murray from Berkeley, California. Also playing on this record are alto and soprano man Bruce Williams, with guests including trombonist Craig Harris, trumpeter Jeremy Pelt, the prodigious young drummer Lee Pearson, bassist Jamaaladeen Tecuma and the Ornette Coleman-inspired guitarist James 'Blood' Ulmer.

The blast of Murray's title blues crashes across America, coast to coast:

> I've got the political blues
> The country's in another war,
> I've got the political blues
> The homeless is knocking at my front door.

The furious rhythm is the amplified heartbeat of American indignation. The passionate succession of solos by Harris, Pelt,

Murray and Bluiett are the voices of resistance of a people 'stuck with Bush, Cheney and Rice':

> Leave the brown countries alone,
> Keep your politics to yourself
> And leave the Third World alone!

Or there is 'Amazin' Disgrace' sung by Carolyn Amba Hawthorne, the parody of a hymn so essentially American:

> Amazin' disgrace
> When they brought us to
> This God-forsaken place.
> They raped our mothers
> Incarcerated our fathers
> And stole all the land . . . .

And then Murray's angry artistry in his searing chorus.

Political Blues becomes the political jazz album of its epoch. Between the expressive shouts and notes of anger there are periods of calm and intense beauty – as in Murray's tribute to fellow tenorist Hal 'Cornbread' Singer, 'Hal's Blues', or the extraordinary horn interaction of 'Bluocracy'. Ulmer's vocal on the classic Muddy Waters blues theme 'Mannish Boy' shows how the roots of the country blues are still watered by superbly creative jazz musicians fifty years later, and Harris' composition, simply called 'Harlem', recalls all the Ellington evocations of the great black village of the twenties and thirties – twenty-five blocks long and six blocks wide and a crucible of jazz, resistance and creative glory. Murray, Lake, Bluiett and Harris are all wondrous on this track.

The album's closer is 'Spy on Me Blues', by Lake, a commentary on 'Nawlins' and the effects of Katrina which killed 1500 New Orleans residents, the majority poor and black. This is the WSQ, unusually, with a springing rhythm section, and after Lake and Bluiett deliver their solos, Lake returns with a vocal – a succession of 'Oopses' in a commentary of government neglect, and almost a ghostly resonance of Bessie Smith's 'Backwater Blues':

> Oops! King George, your president is golfing on the
> Day after the catastrophe.
> Oops! King George does a flyover on the third day . . . .
> Could it be racial?
> I need a few seconds to think.

A jazz statement of naked musical power, humour, and meaning is *Political Blues*, redolent of its times and their crimes, its people's tragedies and their irrepressible human artistry.

Lawn Chair Society: Kenny Werner

Now the decline of empire can be described in many startling figurative ways. One morning the Brooklyn-born pianist Kenny Werner woke up in his upstate New York home after a strong overnight wind and noticed that a row of chairs on his back garden lawn had been blown over. He later wrote:

> I thought it was a metaphor. It was sad, like the end of an empire. The title *Lawn Chair Society* started to come to me. It's a comment on an American culture that is living in its own unreal world, yet completely unaware of the desolation and darkness that half the world is experiencing, It's about decadence and fantasy. 'Lawn chairs' connotes a vacation, a day at the beach, a society focused upon complete triviality treated as earth-shattering news.

Werner's thoughts have been set out intriguingly in this haunting album, in the company of some of contemporary jazz' finest practitioners. There are two strong horns in the persons of trumpeter Dave Douglas and Chris Potter on tenor. Scott Colley is the bassist and on drums is the marvellously versatile

Brian Blade. They combine to carry through Werner's vision as
if they too are working out an eschatological dream.

Potter's jerking bass clarinet begins the opener, 'Lo's
Garden' with Blade's hard strokes and Werner's rambling key-
boards beside him. 'New Amsterdam' is punctuated by the
pianist's grunting expostulations before the two horns enter in
ensemble over Colley's dancing bass figures. Douglas' solo res-
onates with dramatic sonic shapes, always climbing – before
Potter's tenor comes in, belching out phrases which seem to be
testimonies of agony. And as you look at the quizzical photograph within the sleevenotes of a crombie-coated Werner
beholding and peering at an overturned chair in front of a
green-lawned and blue-skied backdrop, it is as if the pianist's
vision is working its way into sound.

'The 13th Day' is an opportunity to take in Werner's keen-
edged piano fluency. His long solo becomes as a preface to
Douglas' discovering brass, full of metallic fire and Potter's
succeeding choruses, pellucid and breathing messages at every
turn. A superb, revelatory track, this, but how to describe the
beauty of the performance of 'Uncovered Heart'? Werner's
bare, entirely vulnerable piano begins, blues-tinged yet replete
with melody, before the entry of the horns and bass. Colley's
notes, deep and tearfully joyous, anchor Werner's sadness
while never tethering the patterned artistry of his sound.

'Lawn Chairs (and Other Foreign Policy)' is the crux of the
album, and how would you expect a ten-minute jazz essay on
Bush's external wars, mayhem, divisiveness and foreign cruelty
to sound? Werner brings in Lenny Picket on wooden flute for
another sonic dimension, and each musician has the chance to
express his own commentary on Werner's dream as well as
combine for a formidable alloy of sound. Werner's own choruses turn corners of outraged surprise at every juncture, Potter's
tenor resonating with a sense of frustrated confinement, sow-
ing the mind-seeds of nights in Abu Ghraib or Guantanamo,
and when the pianist turns to organist he brings echoes of fear,

while Douglas blows cries of terror and ravishment. Every ear, of course, will hear something different – so listen, listener, and consider Bush's America in the world.

From the Plantation to the Penitentiary: Wynton Marsalis

The rimshot hammer blows of drummer Al Jackson Jr. that begin Wynton Marsalis' album, *From the Plantation to the Penitentiary*, have the stir of history about them – a history born of oppression and resistance five centuries old. For New Orleans-born Marsalis has been combining his jazz with the telling of history for many a year, right back from his early albums like *Black Codes from the Underground* and the *Soul Gestures in Southern Blue* trilogy to his *Blood on the Fields* oratorio of slavery and his present day performances with the Lincoln Center Jazz Orchestra, where he celebrates the great jazz innovators of the past, from Ellington to Blakey, from the New Orleans pioneers to the Kansas City swing merchants.

For many critics, Marsalis has substituted jazz's true commission of discovery, surprise and discomfiture with neoclassicism, historicism and nostalgia, but the music needs its brilliant griots and historians to bring contemporary life to the beauty and innovation of the past, and Marsalis does that both consciously and creatively, often with stirring political effect. Does he succeed in *From the Plantation to the Penitentiary*, heralded as it is with its resonating title, akin perhaps to the Archie Shepp Impulse albums of the sixties and seventies, redolent with their sonic images of lockdown America, incarcerated hero-martyrs like George Jackson and full-scale prison revolts like that in Attica, New York state?

Marsalis declared while launching his new album that the USA was built upon a system 'when that dollar becomes so important that anything else around it becomes nothing' and, commenting upon his track 'Supercapitalism', he added: 'We are a people very poorly led. We are led by the urge to make money – our leadership plays on the ignorance of people.' As for Marsalis, his trumpet notes burst from his belief 'in the creativity of the people. I believe in we, not y'all, but we.' And such belief cries out from the grooves of this album, and are put into voice by Jennifer Sanon in Marsalis' lyrics in the title track:

> From the 'no book' rules
> To the raggly public schools,
> From the coon and shine
> To the unemployment line,
> In the land of freedom . . . in chains
> In the land of freedom . . . insane.

In the sleevenotes, Marsalis' long-time explicator, Stanley Crouch, writes of the realities which inspired the music. 'Some of it,' he says, 'is horrible but it is taken on by the beautiful,' and such words are indeed profound when applied to the jazz life. Listen to Marsalis' free-blown trumpet surge in 'Find Me', the insistent bass of Carlos Henriquez in 'Doin' (Y)our Thing' or Walter Blanding's soaring soprano saxophone chorus on the title track. On 'Love and Broken Hearts' Marsalis plays with a painful yet burnished lyricism, a lament for a seemingly lost black culture of love, pride and mutual respect assaulted by a cash-driven musical self-hate which the song's lyrics challenge and reject:

> I aint your bitch, I aint your ho
> And public niggerin' has got to go . . .

'Supercapitalism' is the album's pivotal track. Not only are the powerful sentiments rapturously expressed by Blanding's earthy blues tenor, Dan Nimmer's enigmatic piano and Al Jackson's thrashing drums, all offered – as the sleevenotes proclaim – in a mode that is 'fast swing, Charleston, Cha-cha and slow shuffle'. In the stark repetitive lyrics of relentless acquisition ('Let me see that, I got to have it all for me'), Marsalis shows how endemic social criticism and political commentary are and have always been within the head and heart of jazz. And the penultimate track, 'Where Y'all At?', asks a passing generation

> All you sixties' radicals and world beaters,
> Righteous revolutionaries and Camus readers,
> Liberal students and equal rights pleaders,
> What's goin' on now that y'all are the leaders?

Marsalis' keening horn gives no answers, only a sublime emphasis and assertion of his question, as Bush's America is 'runnin' all over the world with a blunderbuss'. The riposte must come from from those who listen to the music.

A Life in the Day of B19: Tales of the Tower Block:
Soweto Kinch

And what about England, a borrowed land of jazz? Listen to altoist Soweto Kinch, born in 1978, and remember where his name came from.

As his first album, *Conversations with the Unseen*, amply showed, the Birmingham (England)-raised Kinch is a rare jazz talent indeed, and one who has challengingly and successfully contrived to bring jazz together with its more recent urban comrade, hip-hop – while also blowing through his roots with his performances with the Jazz Jamaica All Stars.

His second major recording is expressively called *A Life in the Day of B19: Tales of the Tower Block*, and according to its sleevenotes, it is inspired 'by the network of concrete estates in Birmingham 19, rowdy kids at the back of the bus, regular working people trying to clear their debts, jazz musicians practising the changes in their council flats . . . . train delays, the hunger and ambition of young underground artists, shadowy rodents in the background and B19-ers linked by tower block-scale aspirations . . . pursuing the secret of true happiness.'

In short, stories in sound of a real urban world that remind the listener of Duke Ellington's Harlem sound-stories, Abdullah Ibrahim's musical reflections of Cape Town or Malachi Thompson's free-bop essays of Chicago's 47th Street. Birmingham 19 is not so far away from all these locations and Kinch is its musical chronicler.

The familiar voice of black newsreader and jazzlover Moira Stewart gives the narration to Kinch's Birmingham tales, yet it is his own witty and critical lyrics which detail the realism of the young jazzman's days, for his 'quest to excel is a solitary one', surrounded by sterile blocks, the sounds and panoramas of the high council estates forming 'the tapestry of stresses and personal crises' of the people that he knows and loves living there. As the saxophonist's notes rise out of the midland wasteland, deserted except for him, the jobless, the single mothers and their infants and the truants and those excluded from school, Kinch and his confreres make their evocative music. In 'The Mission', tingling solos from alto and the springing guitar of Femi Temowo contrast with the dark and muffling episode in the form-filling hell of 'The Job Centre' that follows, as the musician is told, 'you just gonna have to take the first job that comes up on the screen.' This is followed by the haunting theme of 'Adrian's Ballad', where Kinch's horn and Abraham White's lyrical trumpet tell their friend's cautionary story upon the buoyant wave of uplift achieved by Troy Miller's drums and Michael Olatuja's levitating bass. The amalgam of blues-sound and poetical word-painting of a whole urban world has its only precedent in the tracks made by poet Langston Hughes and a group of Mingus men nearly half a century earlier in a New York studio.

The Birmingham day continues: broken-down lifts, hellish shafts, 'neo-nazi tenants who hate their Somali neighbours', the thirteenth-floor desert of the unemployed and weeping young mothers, the youths like Marcus with their cable TV channels, seduced by illusions of rap celebrity and riches. And the tune 'Marcus' Crisis' which follows is full of surging alto runs, more springing bop guitar by Temowo and a cutting trumpet solo by White, all billowing with the inner city landscape. And there is Adrian, a thirty-four-year-old bus driver 'oppressed by his growing powerlessness and his forlorn thoughts of a far-away infant son in America', coming even more alive as he walks home from the bus garage after a shift. His dreams are played out through the electric visions of 'Out There', followed by a jumping rendition of 'A Friendly Game of Basketball' where the rival youths assail each other with flinging musical phrases, with White's scorching horn and Kinch's super-rapid alto suggesting lightning moves all over the court.

The album ends with Adrian building a new house in the most desolated site of the neighbourhood and 'The House that Love Built' signs off the first volume of this sound-chronicle, with more life-telling reedplay from Kinch and tenorist Denys Baptiste. And as the man called Soweto writes in his sleeve-message: 'I hope this story elevates, inspires and brings clarity to people told they're least likely to succeed. Part Two draws nearer.' And the listener will wait for it urgently, for such music manifests the spirit and a century's history of jazz. For here is jazz where jazz should be, absolutely and unequivocally – in the real world and real lives of real and struggling people in Birmingham and everywhere.

books cited

Louis Armstrong: *Satchmo: My Life In New Orleans*, Jazz Book Club, London, 1957

Danny Barker and Jack V Buerkle: *Bourbon Street Black: The New Orleans Black Jazzman*, Oxford University Press, Oxford, 1973

Laurence Bergreen: *Louis Armstrong: An Extravagant Life*, Harper Collins, London, 1997

Taylor Branch: *Parting the Waters: America in the King Years*, 1954–63, Simon & Schuster, New York, 1988

Ian Carr: *Miles Davis: The Definitive Biography*, Harper Collins, London, 1988

John Chilton: *Roy Eldridge: Little Jazz Giant*, Continuum, London, 2002

Buck Clayton: *Buck Clayton's Jazz World*, Oxford University Press, Oxford, 1986

Bill Cole: *John Coltrane*, Schirmer Books, New York, 1976

Richard Cook: *The Biography of Blue Note Records*, Secker and Warburg, London, 2001

David B Coplan: *In Township Tonight: South Africa's Black City Music and Theatre*, Longman, London, 1985

Angela Y. Davis: *Blues Legacies and Black Feminism*, Vintage Books, New York, 1999

Michael Denning: *The Cultural Front*, Verso, London, 1996

Scott DeVeaux: *The Birth of Bebop*. University of California Press, Berkeley, 1997

Duke Ellington: *Music is My Mistress*, W.H. Allen, New York, 1974

Sidney Finkelstein: *Jazz: A People's Music*, Citadel Press, New York, 1948

David J Garrow: *Bearing the Cross: Martin Luther King and the Southern Christian Leadership Conference*, Vintage, London, 1993

Leslie Gourse: *Art Blakey, Jazz Messenger*, Schirmer Books, New York, 2002

Leslie Gourse: *Straight, No Chaser: The Life and Genius of Thelonious Monk*, Schirmer Books, New York, 1997

John Edward Hasse: *Beyond Category: The Life and Genius of Duke Ellington*, Omnibus, London, 1993

Geoffrey Haydon: *Quintet of the Year*, Aurum Press, London, 2002

E. J. Hobsbawm ('Francis Newton'): *The Jazz Scene*, McGibbon and Kee, London, 1959

Langston Hughes: *The Panther and the Lash*, Alfred A Knopf, New York, 1967

George Jackson: *Soledad Brother: The Prison Letters of George Jackson*, Jonathan Cape, London, 1971

George Jackson: *Blood In My Eye*, Jonathan Cape, London, 1972

Derek Jewell: *Duke: A Portrait of Duke Ellington*, Elm Tree Books, London, 1977

Max Jones and John Chilton: *Louis: The Louis Armstrong Story 1900–1971*, London, Mayflower, 1975

Frank Kofsky: *John Coltrane and the Jazz Revolution of the 1960s*, Pathfinder, New York, 1970

George McKay: *Circular Breathing: The Cultural Politics of Jazz in Britain*, Duke University Press, Durham and London, 2005

Kenny Mathieson: *Cookin': Hard Bop and Soul Jazz 1954–65*, Canongate, Edinburgh, 2002

Albert Murray: *Good Morning Blues: The Autobiography of Count Basie*, Random House, New York, 1985

Stuart Nicholson: *A Portrait of Duke Ellington*, Sidgwick and Jackson, London, 1999

Alan Robertson: *Joe Harriott: Fire in His Soul*, Northway, London, 2004

Paul Robeson: *Paul Robeson Speaks: Writings, Speeches, Interviews 1918–1974*, (Ed. Philip S. Foner), Quartet, London, 1978

Gene Santoro: *Myself When I Am Real: The Life and Music of Charles Mingus*, Oxford University Press, Oxford, 2000

Alyn Shipton: *Groovin' High: The Life of Dizzy Gillespie*, Oxford University Press, Oxford, 1999

Vladimir Simosko and Barry Tepperman: *Eric Dolphy: A Musical Biography and Discography*, Da Capo Press, Washington DC, 1974

Martin Smith: *John Coltrane: Jazz, Racism and Resistance*, Redwords, London, 2001

Jay Allison Stuart: *Call Him George*, Jazz Book Club, London, 1963

Rob van der Blick (ed): *The Thelonious Monk Reader*, Oxford University Press, Oxford, 2001

quotation credits

'I Got It Bad and That Ain't Good'
Words by Paul Webster, music by Edward Ellington.

'Dream Deferred'
from Langston Hughes: *The Panther and the Lash*, Alfred A Knopf, New York, 1967, courtesy of David Higham Associates.

index